Reading Matters 4

SECOND EDITION

Reading Matters ❹

An Interactive Approach to Reading

Mary Lee Wholey

Continuing Education Language Institute
Concordia University

Nadia Henein

Continuing Education Language Institute
Concordia University

▶ For teaching notes, answer key, and other related instructor material, as well as for additional student activities related to this book, go to *college.hmco.com/pic/wholeyfour2e*.

▶ To obtain access to the Houghton Mifflin ESL instructor sites, call 1-800-733-1717.

Houghton Mifflin Company

Boston   New York

Publisher: Patricia A. Coryell
Editor in Chief: Suzanne Phelps Weir
Sponsoring Editor: Joann Kozyrev
Senior Development Editor: Kathleen Sands Boehmer
Editorial Assistant: Evangeline Bermas
Senior Project Editor: Margaret Park Bridges
Associate Manufacturing Buyer: Brian Pieragostini
Executive Marketing Manager: Annamarie Rice
Marketing Associate: Andrew Whitacre

Printed in the U.S.A.

Library of Congress Control Number: 2005934056

Student Text
  ISBN-10: 0-618-47515-X
  ISBN-13: 978-0-618-47515-5

Instructor's Examination Copy
  ISBN-10: 0-618-73259-4
  ISBN-13: 978-0-618-73259-3

123456789-CRS-10 09 08 07 06

Contents

Introduction to the Second Edition

The *Reading Matters* series is a four-level reading program comprising texts at the high-beginning/low-intermediate, intermediate, high-intermediate, and advanced levels. It fosters the development of active readers through a multifaceted approach to interaction: interaction with the text, with other readers, and with readings from sources beyond the classroom. This new edition includes new and updated readings as well as additional readings in the "Expanding Your Language" section of each chapter. The *Reading Matters* series features stimulating extensive reading combined with intensive practice provided by well designed tasks that develop both fluency and accuracy at each level. The series incorporates the latest approaches to teaching productive strategies—from understanding the purpose and nature of different texts to guessing meaning from context, learning vocabulary for academic and professional success, and learning how to access information in the media and over the Internet.

In brief the series provides for:

- The development of active readers through interaction with a variety of texts, with other readers through reading-retell tasks, and with authentic reading outside of the classroom.

- Thematic units featuring high-interest, level-appropriate, informative topics that include texts about culture, science, the environment, business, innovation, sports, and entertainment.

- A wide variety of reading types, such as articles, interviews, essays, charts, and graphs.

- A skills and strategies overview of the comprehensive reading skills and strategies in each chapter that feature the development of critical thinking and information processing.

- Opportunities for personal reading, writing, and speaking activities.

- An index of key vocabulary aimed at both academic and professional needs (provided at *college.hmco.com/pic/wholeyfour2e*).

- Access to the *Reading Matters* Online Study Center website, which includes individualized learning and testing materials, at *college.hmco.com/pic/wholeyfour2e*.

Extensive Reading

To develop fluency in reading, students need significant exposure to text—that is, extensive reading. Extensive reading provides the opportunity to develop automatic text-processing skills. *Reading Matters* offers high-interest reading selections of sufficient length so that readers get the chance to increase the amount of time spent in silent reading. Variety in text styles is an important component of extensive reading. The series features a variety of styles and genres including articles, interviews, graphs, and charts, so that readers develop an awareness of the scope of reading as well as the various purposes for which texts are written. Authentic texts or adapted authentic texts are used at appropriate levels.

Intensive Reading

Reading Matters features thematically-related units on topics of interest and relevancy today. These topics range from social issues, scientific advances, the environment, and the business world to the fields of leisure, entertainment, and culture. The activities in each unit help students develop fluency and accuracy in reading by activating two complementary text processing methods: top-down and bottom-up.

The Process of Reading

Top-Down

Reading Matters enhances the approaches readers use to understand reading globally. In this series, the readers' background knowledge of the topic and critical thinking skills are engaged and readers are encouraged to make predictions about what they expect to find in a text. The reader reads to confirm or modify these predictions and begins to build a mental framework of the information in the reading selection. Awareness of rhetorical patterns, such as chronological ordering, cause and effect relationships, and other discourse features aids in the comprehension of information from the reading. In addition, *Reading Matters* helps the reader develop an awareness of the range of reading strategies, such as skimming, scanning, or previewing, that readers have at their disposal. The ability to apply these strategies appropriately is an important component of reading competency.

Bottom-Up

Knowledge of grammar and vocabulary has an effect on reading ability. Although readers can predict content from their knowledge of text structure or their background knowledge, a certain level of vocabulary recognition is required for processing text. *Reading Matters* introduces and develops vocabulary-building skills through such activities as guessing from context, recognizing meaning, grouping words, and identifying the use of special terms. Well-designed tasks help the reader learn new vocabulary and key words in the text. In the context of thematic units, the reader's vocabulary develops naturally through exposure to a range of texts. Students engage in a gradual process of acquiring key vocabulary by building from a basic level of vocabulary to a wider net of related terms. Students build their understanding through repeated use of language that contains key concepts and information.

In addition to a solid vocabulary, fluent readers have a good knowledge of syntactic structure.

Actively examining the important grammatical features of a text provides a meaningful context for this kind of learning. To build reading competency, the amount of exposure to reading as well as the identification and practice of learning strategies for both vocabulary and grammar are tremendously important. *Reading Matters* provides direction to readers through activities in the "Vocabulary Building," "Expanding Your Language," and "Read On" sections.

Skills Integration and Interaction

Reading is an active process. Interaction between and among students helps to facilitate this process. In exchanging ideas about the information in a text, readers confirm what they have understood. This confirmation process helps to develop accuracy in reading. It also provides a motivation as well as a clear purpose for reading. Interaction with other students can be best accomplished when speaking tasks are an integral part of a reading activity or the activity leads to the undertaking of writing tasks.

The interrelationship of skills integration and interaction requires a holistic approach to task design. The activities in *Reading Matters* are sequenced, and the recycling of tasks in various combinations allows the progressive development of reading competency in ways that are fresh and effective. The tasks are structured so that the learner builds skills and strategies progressively but in ways that offers challenge as well as variety. In *Reading Matters*, the reader uses and reuses the language of the selection both implicitly—to bolster an answer—and explicitly, as in the exchange of information from paired reading selections that provide complementary or contrasting information on a topic. Readers orally explain the information from their reading selection to readers who chose a different selection. Then, together, they apply that information to carry out a new activity.

Text Organization

Reading Matters 4 contains six thematic units with two chapters in each unit. In the second edition, each chapter features three to six reading selections. Many readings have been updated and new readings have been introduced. The unit themes feature topics of high interest to both academically-oriented and general audiences. Most importantly, the selections are of sufficient length for students to progressively develop fluency in reading. Through the chapter readings, students are able to build a rich semantic network without sacrificing variety so that interest in the topic is not exhausted. Within each unit, reading selections are structured so that the information from one selection can be compared with another.

You can choose among the chapters of a unit selectively to suit the needs of various program types and teaching approaches. Complexity in both text type and length, and difficulty in task type are structured to build gradually from chapter to chapter and unit to unit. Some overlap in level of language and task is built into each of the texts in the *Reading Matters* series so that you can accommodate the various levels of students within a class.

Unit Organization

Each unit in *Reading Matters 4* features the following components:

▶ Introducing the Topic: This introductory section identifies the theme. It features the unit opener photo and quote, which are designed to stimulate the readers' curiosity about and prior experience with the theme, or its personal relevance. The tasks are interactive and draw on a variety of media: text, photos, and graphics.

▶ Chapters: The two chapters in each unit present various topics loosely related to the theme.

Chapter Organization

For each of the reading selections the following tasks are presented:

▶ **Chapter Openers** include pre-reading reflection and discussion questions, graphs, questionnaires, surveys, or illustrations. The purpose of this section is to stimulate discussion of key ideas and concepts presented in the reading and to introduce key vocabulary. Encourage students to explain their ideas as completely as possible. Teach students strategies for maximizing their interaction, such as turn taking, eliciting responses from all group members, and naming a group leader and reporter. Whenever possible, re-form groups to give students a chance to talk more until they feel comfortable with the topic. Elicit key ideas and language from the students.

▶ **Exploring and Understanding Reading** contains content questions of varying levels of complexity. These questions guide students in the development of their reading strategies for improving general comprehension, developing an awareness of text structure, and evaluating the content of a text in detail. Emphasize the purpose of the activity and how it is tied to the development of a particular strategy. Point out the ways in which students can apply their skills to reading assignments. Help students build their tolerance for uncertainty. Point out that the purpose of comparing and checking their answers with the information in the reading is to verify as well as to become familiar with the information in the reading. Act as a resource to help students find the accurate information. An answer key that the instructor can use as needed is provided on the *Reading Matters* website at *college.hmco.com/pic/wholeyfour2e*.

▶ **Paired Readings** include interactive Recapping, Retelling, Reacting to the Reading, and Discussing the Story activities that involve oral presentation of information from the readings, oral exchanges of information, and discussion that involves critical evaluation of ideas, including comparison/contrast and debate. At this level, talking about the reading they do is crucial for improving students' language use. Emphasize the importance of explaining the information in as natural and conversational a style as possible. Help students to develop their skill at extracting important information from a text by pointing out the purpose of note taking, highlighting, and underlining key information. Emphasize the importance of practicing at home for in-class presentations.

▶ **Vocabulary Building** comprises tasks that introduce vocabulary-building strategies such as the understanding of key terms, the interrelationship of grammatical structure and meaning, using context cues, and developing other aids to the fluent processing of reading selections. This edition adds exercises in each chapter that focus on learning the meaning of verbs and working with word form and function to foster the understanding of academic and general vocabulary.

▶ **Expanding Your Language** presents activities that offer students additional opportunities to use the material and strategies in the chapter. This section often includes additional extended readings. Encourage students to use these activities to further their own comprehension of the readings. Through these activities, students can improve their speaking and writing fluency.

▶ **Read On: Taking It Further** presents opportunities for personal reading and related activities, including suggestions for further reading as well as reading and writing journal entries, keeping a vocabulary log, and word play. Although most of this work will be done outside of class, time can be found in the class schedule to report on some of the activities. This gives students a purpose for the work and practice in developing their reading skills and strategies.

Reading Matters Online Study Center Website

Students gain confidence in their reading abilities as they discover how to access information more easily from the press, over the Internet, and in their professions or fields of study. The Internet activities give students a chance to consolidate and extend their reading skills. Using the *Reading Matters* website offers students the opportunity for productive work on an individual basis at any time of day or night that's convenient for them. Students are directed to the Online Study Center website at the end of each chapter.

Reading Matters Online Teaching Center Website

As with all Houghton Mifflin textbooks, there is a specific website devoted to necessary teaching tools that come in handy while using the text. Instructors using *Reading Matters* can access useful chapter notes and the answer key at the site. In addition, there are downloadable chapter tests that instructors can administer to students. These tests focus on comprehension skills and important vocabulary. Finally, a sample syllabus is included for instructors who need some guidelines about how to use the text effectively throughout the semester. To access the Online Teaching Center, go to *college.hmco.com/pic/wholeyfour2e.*

Acknowledgments

We are grateful to Susan Maguire, who first suggested the idea for the series. A special thanks goes to Kathy Sands Boehmer, who has been an invaluable help throughout the lengthy process of bringing this manuscript into its present form. Thanks also to Margaret Bridges and the rest of the production and editorial staff at Houghton Mifflin.

Our gratitude to the people who read the manuscript and offered useful suggestions and critical comments: Gaye Childress, *University of North Texas,* Denton, Stefka Choumanova, *College of Lake County,* David Dahnke, *North Harris College,* Sally Gearhart, *Santa Rosa Junior College,* Marte Mirman, *Baltimore City Community College,* and Pam Sherman, *Ulster County Community College.*

We would like to acknowledge the support and inspiring work of colleagues and students at the Continuing Education Language Institute (CELI) of Concordia University in Montreal. A special thanks goes to Adrianne Sklar for her advice and suggestions after reading drafts of the material. The continuing support of Lili Ullmann and Phyllis Vogel has been invaluable to us. Thank you also to Louise Kyrtatis, who helped in the preparation of the answer key. We are also grateful to Ioana Nicolae for her work on material for the student and instructor websites.

Finally, thanks to our families—Jerry, Jonah, and Yael and Sherif, Ghada, and Dina.

Mary Lee Wholey and Nadia Henein

Reading Matters 4: Overview

Unit	Skills	Activities	Vocabulary	Expansion
UNIT 1 **Creativity**	• skimming (1, 2) • highlighting (1, 2) • surveying (1, 2) • chunking (1) • scanning (1) • previewing (1, 2) • recognizing imagery (2) • note taking for presenting arguments (2)	• agree or disagree (1) • information from the news (1) • giving your opinion (1) • analyzing expressions (1) • discussion questions (2) • recapping and retelling information (2) • paraphrasing (2) • summarizing a text (2)	• word form (1, 2) • suffixes (1, 2) • synonyms (1, 2) • language of research (1) • determining the referent (2) • jigsaw sentences (2)	• technical reading (1) • oral presentation (1, 2) • topic writing (1) • reading questionnaire (2) • keeping a vocabulary log (2) • keeping a reading journal (2) • personal dictionary (2) • studying online (1, 2)
UNIT 2 **Body Science:** **Moving in New** **Directions**	• previewing (3, 4) • surveying (3, 4) • scanning (3, 4) • chunking (3, 4) • following an argument (3) • predicting (4) • analyzing an introduction (4) • skimming (4) • reporting on studies (4)	• giving opinion (3, 4) • analyzing statistics (3) • using charts/graphs (4) • reacting to information (3, 4) • recapping and retelling (4) • comparing information (4)	• defining terms (3) • word form (3, 4) • cohesive devices (3) • determining the referent (3) • vocabulary in context (4) • using quotes (4)	• oral presentation (3) • reaction writing (3, 4) • debating (4) • report writing (4) • studying online (3, 4)
UNIT 3 **The Environment**	• predicting (5, 6) • analyzing an introduction (5) • chunking (5) • idea trees (5) • skimming (5, 6) • note taking (5) • previewing (6) • tellback (6) • scanning for details (6) • identifying main ideas (6)	• using quotes (5) • questionnaire (5) • defining terms (5) • applying information (5) • ranking (6) • using charts and graphs (6) • recapping, reacting to, and retelling information (6)	• word form (5, 6) • inferring meaning (5) • using examples (6)	• speaking from experience (5) • summary writing (5) • giving opinion (6) • debating (6) • reaction writing (6) • position writing (6) • reading journal (6) • studying online (5, 6)

Unit	Skills	Activities	Vocabulary	Expansion
UNIT 4 **The Age of Communications**	• predicting (7) • previewing (7, 8) • analyzing an introduction (7) • chunking (7) • note taking (7, 8) • highlighting (7, 8) • answering questions from notes (7) • skimming (7, 8) • tellback (7) • scanning (7, 8) • understanding studies (8) • surveying (8)	• questionnaire (7) • giving opinion (7, 8) • agree or disagree (7) • using quotes (7) • making a timeline (7) • reacting to a story (7) • discussing ethical issues (7) • problems and solutions (7) • inferring opinion (8) • applying information (8)	• word forms (7, 8) • expressions in context (7, 8) • word choice (7) • vocabulary in context (8)	• two-minute taped talk (7) • debating (7) • reaction writing (7, 8) • topic writing (7, 8) • giving advice (8) • role playing (8) • interviewing (8) • oral presentation (8) • studying online (7, 8)
UNIT 5 **Economics**	• surveying (9) • skimming (9) • scanning (9, 10) • skimming (9) • arguing a point of view (9, 10) • previewing (10) • note taking for retelling (10)	• personalizing (9, 10) • reacting to the news (9) • discussion (9, 10) • giving an opinion (9) • applying information (9) • recapping, retelling, and reacting to information (9, 10) • debating (9) • reacting to arguments (10)	• word form (9, 10) • antonyms (9, 10) • expressions (9) • vocabulary in context (9) • adverbs (10) • jigsaw sentences with *if, while, then* clauses (10)	• oral presentation (9, 10) • topic writing (9, 10) • debating (10) • reaction writing (10) • short story (10) • reading for pleasure (10) • studying online (9, 10)
UNIT 6 **The World of Man and Animals**	• examining charts and tables (11) • skimming (11, 12) • scanning for the development of an argument (11) • previewing (12) • surveying (12) • analyzing an introduction (12) • scanning (12) • note taking (12) • analyzing a conclusion (12)	• giving explanations (11) • analyzing quotes (11) • getting information from the news (11, 12) • free writing (11, 12) • recapping, reteling, and reacting to information (11) • essay writing (11) • tabulating information (12) • making a time line (12)	• word form (11, 12) • verb phrases (11) • understanding language of research (11) • descriptive language (11) • suffixes (12) • synonyms (12) • analyzing quotes and paraphrases (12)	• debating (11) • topic writing (11) • analyzing quotes (12) • summary writing (12) • personal narrative (5) • reaction writing (12) • reviewing vocabulary log (12) • reviewing reading journal (12) • studying online (11, 12)

Creativity

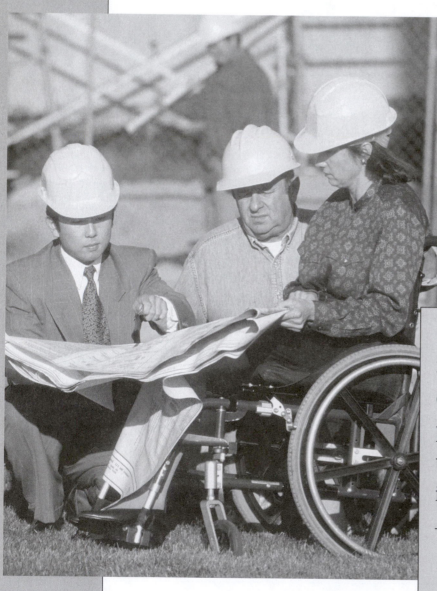

Creativity involves breaking out of established patterns in order to look at things in a different way.

—*Edward de Bono*

Introducing the Topic

Are people naturally creative? The word *creative* has the power to both frighten and excite people. At first glance, creativity seems elusive and mysterious. In the chapters of this unit we will discover some of the processes of creativity and the way the mind operates when we work creatively. Chapter 1 looks at laughter and explores questions about the role it plays in our lives. We examine jokes to find out what makes them work and what's funny around the world. Chapter 2 explores creativity and problem solving. What are some of the processes that we can use to boost our creativity?

Points of Interest

What's Your Opinion?

Exploring Different Points of View Circle *A* if you agree or *D* if you disagree with the following statements.

1. A D   All human beings are capable of being creative; it is part of our nature.

2. A D   True creativity is the work of genius.

3. A D   A creative person is a happy individual.

4. A D   Good work takes one percent inspiration and ninety-nine percent perspiration.

5. A D   People who like to laugh live long lives.

6. A D   One of the best mottoes for life is "Don't worry, be happy."

7. A D   When skies are gray, just let a smile be your umbrella.

Work with a partner or in a small group. Explain the reasons for your opinions.

1 Laughter: The Creative Force

⬤ Chapter Openers

Discussion Questions

⬤ Think about these questions. Share your ideas with a partner or in a small group.

1. What kinds of jokes, films, books, or other entertainment make you laugh?
2. Who do you think laughs more, men or women?
3. Do you think that a sense of humor helps in life? Explain how this could be.
4. Do you think you have a good sense of humor?

⬤ Check (✔) the areas in our lives where you think humor can affect us in an important way.

_____ Good health	_____ Friendships
_____ Problem solving	_____ Academic success
_____ Job promotions	_____ Family relationships
_____ Job satisfaction	_____ Financial success

Information from the News

Jokes are not easy to tell and it's hard to know if or why people find a joke funny. The news report that follows is about the efforts of some researchers who take a "scientific" approach to an unscientific topic.

> **Reading Tip**

Skimming is **reading** an article **quickly** to **get a general idea** of what it is about. It's especially useful for short news articles. Skimming helps you focus on what you can understand in the reading and makes rereading easier and more productive. ■

⬤ **Skimming** Quickly skim the article and answer the following questions.

1. What is Laughlab and what is its purpose?

   _____

2. What joke was rated the world's best?

   _____

The Science of Jokes

❶   Laughlab advertises itself as the world's largest experiment into the psychology of humor, with more than 100,000 people from seventy countries rating more than 10,000 jokes.

❷   Led by University of Hertfordshire psychologist Dr. Richard Wiseman and conducted in conjunction with the British Association for the Advancement of Science, the Laughlab study gets visitors to the Internet to rate jokes on a five-point "smileometer" scale. Of eleven ranked nationalities, Americans gave a very funny rating to only 27 percent of jokes, just ahead of Canadians at 26 percent. Most easy to amuse were Germans, who offered the highest rating to 35 percent of the jokes.

❸   After three months of collecting ratings from people around the world, it was revealed Wednesday that the world's best joke was submitted by Geoff Anandappa of Blackpool, England. Garnering a top rating from 47 percent of participants, it's about the famous fictional detective Sherlock Holmes on a camping trip with his assistant, Dr. Watson.

The pair pitch a tent, but in the middle of the night, Holmes wakes up, nudges his companion and says, "Watson, look up at the stars and tell me what you deduce."

Watson replies, "I see millions of stars, and if there are millions of stars, and if even a few of those have planets, it is quite likely there are some planets like Earth, and if there are a few planets like Earth out there, there might also be life."

To which Holmes says, "Watson, you idiot! Somebody stole our tent."

❹   The following joke, the top rated by American participants, was a close second in the worldwide rankings.

A couple of New Jersey hunters are out in the woods when one of them falls to the ground. He doesn't seem to be breathing; his eyes are rolled back in his head. The other guy whips out his cell phone and calls emergency services. He gasps to the operator, "My friend is dead! What can I do?"

The operator, in a calm soothing voice says, "Just take it easy. First, let's make sure he's dead." There's silence, then a shot is heard. The guy's voice comes back on the line. He says, "Okay, now what?"

❺   Wiseman pointed out that these are only preliminary results. "While we have some interesting findings, the data collection period will continue until the end of the year, when we move to the second phase of the experiment," he said in a release on the Laughlab website. "In the meantime, we challenge people to submit a funnier joke than the top-rated one so far."

❻   The two jokes receiving the poorest ratings both involve chickens—the one about the chicken crossing the road to get to the other side and the other asking the question, why do chickens make good workers? Because they work around the cluck. Each one of those for-the-birds stabs at humor earned the worst possible rank from 74 percent of participants.

❼   The study also found differences in the humor rankings of men and women. This joke was loved by all men, and disliked by all women: "This guy runs home and bursts in yelling, 'Pack your bags sweetheart, I've just won the lottery, all six numbers!' She says, 'Oh wonderful! Should I pack for the beach or the mountains?' He replies, 'I don't care ... just pack and shove off!'" This next joke got high ratings from women, but not from men: "A man had a dog called Minton. One day Minton ate two shuttlecocks. When the owner found out he said, 'Bad Minton!'"

❽   "These findings reflect fundamental differences in the ways in which males and females use humor," Wiseman said. "Males use humor to appear superior to others, while women are more linguistically skilled and prefer word-puns." Herbert Lefcourt, a psychology professor at Ontario's University of Waterloo, has also studied and written about the human sense of humor. He agreed with the finding that men and women have their funny bones tickled in different ways. "There's a tendency for men to use humor in an aggressive way, putting others down, whereas women get others to laugh with them at their experience," he said.

❾ However, Lefcourt, a New York native, said with a laugh that he didn't know if he agreed that Canadians were the hardest to make laugh. He also questioned the way the study was carried out, saying a series of jokes told in a row is the worst way to find out if people find something funny. "Pick up any book of jokes and by the end, you'll find you are bored." Lefcourt said. "You feel after a while that you are being endlessly manipulated. Part of a good joke is a surprise, and if there is a whole mess of jokes, they feel contrived, because you are expecting a twist. It's when the twist takes you by surprise—that's what makes it funny."

Top Jokes By Country

Germany (tie)

- Why is television called a medium? It is neither rare nor well-done.
- To tell the weather:

    Go to your back door and look for the dog. If the dog is at the door and he is wet, it's probably raining. But if the dog is standing there really soaking wet, it is probably raining really hard. If the dog's fur looks like it's been rubbed the wrong way, it's probably windy. If the dog has snow on his back, it's probably snowing. Of course, to be able to tell the weather like this, you have to leave the dog outside all the time, especially if you expect bad weather.

    Sincerely, The Cat

France

    "You're a high-priced lawyer! If I give you $500, will you answer two questions for me?"

    "Absolutely! What's the second question?"

Belgium

    Well, you see, there are basically three kinds of people in the world. Those who can count and those who can't.

Australia

    A man left for a vacation to Jamaica. His wife was on a business trip and was planning to meet him there the next day. When he reached his hotel, he decided to send his wife a quick e-mail. Unable to find the scrap of paper on which he had written her e-mail address, he did his best to type it in from memory. Unfortunately, he missed one letter, and his note was directed instead to an elderly preacher's wife whose husband had passed away only the day before. When the grieving widow checked her e-mail, she took one look at the monitor, let out a piercing scream, and fell to the floor dead. At the sound, her family rushed into the room and saw this note on the screen: Dearest Wife, Just got checked in. Everything prepared for your arrival tomorrow. Your Loving Husband. P.S. Sure is hot down here.

Sweden

A guy phones the local hospital and yells "You've gotta send help! My wife's in labor!" The nurse says, "Calm down. Is this her first child?" He replies, "No! This is her husband!"

New Zealand

A priest conducts a service in a church. "The person who puts the most in the church collection box can choose three hymns," he says. The collection box comes back to him after being filled up and he finds that someone has donated a thousand pounds. "Who has donated a thousand pounds?" he asks. A woman raises her hand. The priest invites her to the front and tells her to choose three hymns. Pointing at the three most handsome men in the church she says, "I'll have him, him, and him."

Adapted from Jeremy Sandler, *The Vancouver Sun*

Highlighting

Highlighting is a useful strategy for **finding** and **remembering important facts** and ideas that you read. To highlight, use a colored highlighting pen to mark information. Be careful to mark only the words and phrases that you want to stand out—not the whole sentence. The highlighted words will help you to explain ideas in your own way. ■

▶ **A** Reread the article and highlight the facts that relate to these important ideas:

1. Response to jokes in different countries
2. The world's funniest joke
3. The top-rated American joke
4. Differences between how men and women approach jokes
5. What makes a joke funny
6. A joke rated most funny by three different countries

▶ **B** Working with a partner, compare what you highlighted. Discuss whether you highlighted too much or too little. Complete any additional highlighting needed.

▶ **C** Using *only* what you highlighted, take turns telling each other the important information in the article. Make sure you explain the information as completely as possible.

Reacting to the Information

▶ **A** Discuss these questions with your partner or others in a small group.

1. Which joke do you think is the funniest?
2. Do you agree that men and women react differently to jokes?
3. Do you think that some jokes are universally funny?

▶ **B** Find a joke that you find funny and practice telling it. Write the joke and submit it to your teacher. In groups, tell your jokes to each other. Discuss why it's hard to "get" jokes in your second language.

Exploring and Understanding Reading

What's Your Opinion?

▶ Circle *A* if you agree or *D* if you disagree with the following statements.

1. A   D   Laughter is contagious.

2. A   D   It's easy for people to make themselves laugh on purpose.

3. A   D   Men laugh more than women do.

4. A   D   There are more male than female comedians.

5. A   D   Women rate having a good sense of humor as a very important criterion when they are looking for a man to date.

6. A   D   People are more likely to laugh at a joke than at an ordinary remark such as, how're you doing?

7. A   D   People with a good sense of humor live longer.

8. A   D   Laughter can help reduce feelings of physical pain.

9. A   D   The primary benefit of laughter is that it unites people.

▶ Work with a partner or in a small group. Explain the reasons for your opinions. After the discussion, work with your group to scan the reading and look for information that supports or disproves each statement.

Surveying

Surveying is a **useful** reading strategy to use with **longer readings**. It helps you to get a sense of the important ideas in a text without getting bogged down in details. ▪

▶ Read the first two paragraphs (introduction) of the next reading and the beginning of every paragraph after that. Notice the key words and write the main idea of each paragraph in the margin.

Chunking

Chunking means **grouping paragraphs** that **develop** the **same major idea**. It helps you see the general outline of a reading and makes comprehension much easier. ▪

▶ Analyze which paragraphs develop each general idea. List the paragraphs that develop the idea and write it in the following table. The first is done for you as an example.

Paragraphs	Main Idea
1, 2	Introduction—the importance of laughter
	Observations from research done on laughter
17	Conclusion—the need for further research

▶ Share your ideas with a partner or in a small group.

The Science of Laughter

Far from mere reactions to jokes, hoots and hollers are serious business: They're innate—and important—social tools.

❶ Whether overheard in a crowded restaurant, punctuating the enthusiastic chatter of friends, or as the noisy guffaws on a TV laugh track, laughter is a fundamental part of everyday life. It is so common that we forget how strange—and important—it is. Indeed, laughter is a "speaking in tongues" in which we're moved not by religious passion but by an unconscious response to social and linguistic cues. Stripped of its variation and nuance, laughter is a regular series of short vowel-like syllables usually transcribed as "ha-ha," "ho-ho," or "hee-hee." These syllables are part of the universal human vocabulary, produced and recognized by people of all cultures.

❷ Given the universality of the sound, our ignorance about the purpose and meaning of laughter is remarkable. We somehow laugh at just the right times, without consciously knowing why we do it. Most people think of laughter as a simple response to comedy, or a cathartic mood-lifter. Instead, after ten years of research on this little-studied topic, I concluded that laughter is primarily a social vocalization that binds people together. It is a hidden language that we all speak. It is not a learned group reaction but an instinctive behavior programmed by our genes. Laughter bonds us through humor and play.

Nothing to Joke About

❸   Despite its prominence in daily life, there is little research on how and why we laugh. I thought it was time that we actually observed laughing people and described when they did it and what it meant. Research on laughter has led me out of my windowless laboratories into a more exciting social world of laughing gas, religious revivals, acting classes, tickle wars, baby chimpanzees, and a search for the most ancient joke.

❹   As a starting point, three undergraduate students and I observed 1,200 people laughing spontaneously in their natural environments, from the student union to city sidewalks. Whenever we heard laughter, we noted the gender of the speaker (the person talking immediately before laughter occurred) and the audience (those listening to the speaker), whether the speaker or the audience laughed, and what the speaker said immediately before the laughter.

❺   Although we usually think of laughter as coming from an audience after a wisecrack from a single speaker, contrary to expectation, the speakers we observed laughed almost 50 percent more than their audiences. The study also showed that banal comments like, "Where have you been?" or "It was nice meeting you, too," are far more likely to precede laughter than jokes. Only 10 to 20 percent of the laughter episodes we witnessed followed anything joke-like. Even the most humorous of the 1,200 comments that preceded laughter weren't necessarily that funny: "You don't have to drink, just buy us drinks!" and "Was that before or after I took my clothes off?" being two of my favorites. This suggests that the critical stimulus for laughter is another person, not a joke.

❻   Students in my classes confirmed the social nature of laughter by recording the circumstances of their laughter in diaries. After excluding the social effects of media (television, radio, books, etc.), its social nature was striking: Laughter was thirty times more frequent in social than solitary situations. The students were much more likely to talk to themselves or even smile when alone than to laugh. However happy we may feel, laughter is a signal we send to others and it virtually disappears when we lack an audience.

❼   Laughter is also extremely difficult to control consciously. Try asking a friend to laugh, for example. Most will announce, "I can't laugh on command," or some similar statement. Your friends' observations are accurate—their efforts to laugh on command will be forced or futile. It will take them many seconds to produce a laugh, if they can do it at all. This suggests that we cannot deliberately activate the brain's mechanisms for affective expression. Playfulness, being in a group, and positive emotional tone mark the social settings of most laughs.

Giggly-Girls, Explained

8   Linguist Deborah Tannen described gender differences in speech in her best-selling book, *You Just Don't Understand* (Ballantine, 1991). The gender differences in laughter may be even greater. In our 1,200 case studies, my fellow researchers and I found that while both sexes laugh a lot, females laugh more. In cross-gender conversations, females laughed 126 percent more than their male counterparts, meaning that women tend to do the most laughing while males tend to do the most laugh-getting. Men seem to be the main instigators of humor across cultures, which begins in early childhood. Think back to your high school class clown—most likely, he was a male. The gender pattern of everyday laughter also suggests why there are more male than female comedians. (Rodney Dangerfield likely got more respect than he claimed.)

9   Given the differences in male and female laugh patterns, is laughter a factor in meeting, matching, and mating? I sought an answer in the human marketplace of newspaper personal ads. In 3,745 ads placed on April 28, 1996, in eight papers from the *Baltimore Sun* to the *San Diego Union-Tribune*, females were 62 percent more likely to mention laughter in their ads, and women were more likely to seek out a "sense of humor" while men were more likely to offer it. Clearly, women seek men who make them laugh, and men are eager to comply with this request. When Karl Grammar and Irenaus Eibl-Eibesfeldt studied spontaneous conversations between mixed-sex pairs of young German adults meeting for the first time, they noted that the more a woman laughed aloud during these encounters, the greater her self-reported interest in the man she was talking to. In the same vein, men were more interested in women who laughed heartily in their presence. The personal ads and the German study complement an observation from my field studies: The laughter of the female, not the male, is the critical index of a healthy relationship. Guys can laugh or not, but what matters is that women laugh.

10   In many societies worldwide—ranging from the Tamil of Southern India to the Tzeltal of Mexico—laughter is self-effacing behavior, and the women in my study may have used it as an unconscious vocal display of compliance or solidarity with a more socially dominant group member. I suspect, however, that the gender patterns of laughter are fluid and shift subconsciously with social circumstance. For example, the workplace giggles of a young female executive will probably diminish as she ascends the corporate ladder, but she will remain a barrel of laughs when meeting up with old friends. Consider your own workplace. Have you ever encountered a strong leader with a giggle? Someone who laughs a lot, and unconditionally, may be a good team player, but they'll seldom be a president.

The Laughter Virus

⑪   As anyone who has ever laughed at the sight of someone doubled over can attest, laughter is contagious. Because our laughter is under minimal conscious control, it is spontaneous and relatively uncensored. Contagious laughter is a compelling display of *Homo sapiens*, a social mammal. It strips away our outer layer of culture and challenges the hypothesis that we are in full control of our behavior. From these synchronized vocal outbursts come insights into the neurological roots of human social behavior and speech.

⑫   Consider the extraordinary 1962 outbreak of contagious laughter in a girls' boarding school in Tanzania. The first symptoms appeared on January 30, when three girls got the giggles and couldn't stop laughing. The symptoms quickly spread to 95 students, forcing the school to close on March 18. The girls sent home from the school were vectors for the further spread of the epidemic. Related outbreaks occurred in other schools in Central Africa and spread like wildfire, ceasing two-and-a-half years later and afflicting nearly 1,000 people. Before dismissing the African outbreak as an anomaly, consider our own technologically-triggered mini-epidemics produced by television laugh tracks. Laugh tracks have accompanied most television sit-coms since September 9, 1950. At 7:00 that evening, "The Hank McCune Show" used the first laugh track to compensate for being filmed without a live audience. The rest is history. Canned laughter may sound artificial, but it makes TV viewers laugh as if they were part of a live theater audience.

⑬   The irresistibility of others' laughter has its roots in the neurological mechanism of laugh detection. The fact that laughter is contagious raises the intriguing possibility that humans have an auditory laugh detector—a neural circuit in the brain that responds exclusively to laughter. (Contagious yawning may involve a similar process in the visual domain.) Once triggered, the laugh detector activates a laugh generator, a neural circuit that causes us in turn to produce laughter. Furthermore, laughter is not randomly scattered through speech. A speaker may say "You are going where? … ha-ha," but rarely, "You are going … ha-ha … where?" This is evidence of "the punctuation effect," the tendency to laugh almost exclusively at phrase breaks in speech. This pattern requires that speech has priority over laughter. The occurrence of speaker laughter at the end of phrases suggests that a neurologically-based process governs the placement of laughter in speech, and that different brain regions are involved in the expression of cognitively-oriented speech and the more emotion-laden vocalization of laughter. During conversation, speech inhibits laughter.

Laughter: Mediocre Medicine

⑭   Authorities from the Bible to Reader's Digest remind us that "laughter is the best medicine." Print and broadcast reporters produce upbeat, often bubbly stories like, "A Laugh a Day Keeps the Doctor Away." A best-selling Norman Cousins book and a popular film *Patch Adams* amplified this message. But left unsaid in such reports is a disturbing truth: Laughter did not evolve to make us feel good or improve our health. Certainly, laughter unites people, and social support has been shown in studies to improve mental and physical health. Indeed, the presumed health benefits of laughter may be chance consequences of its primary goal: bringing people together.

⑮   Laughter is an energetic activity that raises our heart rate and blood pressure, but these physiological effects are incompletely documented and their medicinal benefits are even less certain. Lennart Levi, of the Karolinska Institute in Stockholm, reported that comedy activates the body's "fight or flight" system, increasing hormone levels in urine, a measure of activation and stress. Lee Berk, DHSc, of the Loma Linda School of Medicine, countered with a widely cited study that reported that laughter reduced hormone levels. This reduction in stress and associated hormones is the mechanism through which laughter is presumed to enhance immune function. Unfortunately, Berk's studies show at best a biological response to comedy. His reports included only five experimental subjects, never stated whether those subjects actually laughed, and were presented in only three brief abstracts.

⑯   Does a sense of humor or a lighthearted personality add years to your life? Not necessarily. A large-scale study by Howard Friedman, Ph.D., professor of psychology at the University of California at Riverside, found that, contrary to expectation, optimism and a sense of humor in childhood were inversely related to longevity. This may be because people with high optimism indulge in risk-taking, thinking, "I'll be okay." Pain reduction is one of laughter's promising applications. Rosemary Cogan, Ph.D., a professor of psychology at Texas Tech University, found that subjects who laughed at a funny video or underwent a relaxation procedure tolerated more discomfort than other subjects. Humor may help soften intense pain. James Rotton, Ph.D., of Florida International University, reported that orthopedic surgery patients who watched comedic videos requested fewer aspirin and tranquilizers than the group that viewed dramas. Humor may also help us cope with stress. In a study by Michelle Newman, Ph.D., an assistant professor of psychology at Pennsylvania State University, subjects viewed a film about three grisly accidents and had to narrate it either in a humorous or serious style. Those who used the humorous tone had the lowest negative affect and tension. However, a problem with these studies is that none of them separate the effects of laughter from those of humor. None allow for the possibility that presumed effects of laughter or humor may come from the playful settings associated with these behaviors. And none evaluate the uniqueness of laughter by contrasting it with other vocalizations such as shouting.

⓱   Rigorous proof that we can reduce stress and pain through laughter remains an unrealized but reasonable prospect. While we wait for definitive evidence, it can't hurt—and it's certainly enjoyable—to laugh.

Reprinted with permission from "The Science of Laughter," by Robert R. Provine, *Psychology Today Magazine,* November/December 2000. Copyright © 2000 Sussex Publishers, Inc.

Scanning

◗ **Explanations of the Issues** Scan for the answers to these questions. Mark the question number in the margin of the reading. Write your answers in note form.

1. Why did the author think it was important to research laughter?

    _____

2. What surprising facts about the circumstances in which people laugh did the study reveal?

    _____

3. What might explain why there are more male than female comedians?

    _____

4. What evidence would suggest that humor is important to women?

    _____

5. What examples suggest that laughter is contagious?

    _____

6. What evidence is given that laughter may be neurologically triggered?

    _____

7. What evidence is given that Berk's conclusion that laughter reduces stress is not well proven?

    _____

8. a. What have studies shown about laughter and pain reduction?

_____

   b. What further studies are needed?

_____

▶ Work with a partner to ask and answer the questions. Use the information you marked in the margin to support your answers.

Applying the Information

▶ **Analyzing Expressions** Discuss the meaning of the following expressions. Use information in the reading as well as your own ideas to decide if you agree or disagree with each.

1. Laughter is the best medicine.
2. Act happy. Genuine joy will follow.
3. Laugh and the world laughs with you. Cry and you cry alone.
4. Happy are those who can laugh at themselves, for they shall never stop being amused.
5. Laughter is the shortest point between two people.
6. The human race has only one really effective weapon and that is laughter.
7. Humor is not a gift of the mind, but of the heart.
8. He laughs best who laughs last.
9. If you don't learn to laugh at your troubles, you won't have anything to laugh at when you grow old.

▶ What sayings about laughter in your first language do you know of? Think of one to share with others.

▶Vocabulary Building

Word Form   ▷ **A** Study these five words and their forms. Then choose the correct form for each part of speech in the chart below. These words are commonly found in general and academic texts.

conclude (v.)	exclude (v.)	precede (v.)	react (v.)	respond (v.)
conclusion (n.)	exclusionary	precedent	reaction	responsively
concluding (adj.)	excluded	preceded	reacting	respondent
conclusive (adj.)	exclusion	preceding	reactively	responding
conclusively (adv.)	exclusive	precedence	reactive	responsive
	exclusively		reactor	response

Verb	Noun	Adjective	Adverb
exclude	1.	1.	1.
		2.	
		3.	
precede	1.	1.	
	2.	2.	
react	1.	1.	1.
	2.	2.	
respond	1.	1.	1.
	2.	2.	

▷ Compare lists with a partner.

▷ **B** Write three sentences using words from the list.

▷ **C** In English, the form of the word can change when it is used as a different part of speech. For example, a suffix (ending) can be added to change the adjective *good* to the noun *goodness*. Some common noun suffixes are *-ence, -ness, -tion, -ment, -or, -y,- ism*, and *-ity*.

▶ Read each sentence and circle the correct word to use in the sentence. Write *N* if the word is a noun or *ADJ* if the word is an adjective.

1. _____ Despite its **prominent / prominence** in daily life, there is little research on how we laugh.

2. _____ Contrary to **expectation / expected**, the speakers we observed laughed 50 percent more frequently.

3. _____ Men seem to be the main **instigated / instigators** of humor across cultures.

4. _____ Because laughter is under **minimal / minimum** conscious control, it is spontaneous.

5. _____ **Contagious / Contagion** laughter is a compelling display of human nature.

6. _____ The **irresistibility / irresistible** of other's laughter has its root in the brain.

7. _____ Pain **reduced / reduction** is one of the benefits of laughter.

8. _____ Dr. Friedman found that **optimism / optimistic** and a sense of humor are essential.

9. _____ This could be a very **reason / reasonable** project.

10. _____ This allows for the **possibility / possible** of studying the effects of laughter.

Vocabulary in Context

▶ **Reading Tip**

When you are writing about a certain topic, some ideas or concepts may come up repeatedly. It is boring to use the same words over and over again. That is why **synonyms** are very important. ■

▶ **Synonyms** Refer to "The Science of Laughter" to find the words below in context. Match the words in Column A with words that have the same meaning in Column B.

Column A

_____ 1. instinctive

_____ 2. spontaneous

_____ 3. enthusiastic

_____ 4. banal

_____ 5. solitary

_____ 6. futile

_____ 7. affective

_____ 8. contagious

Column B

a. common

b. ineffective

c. spreading

d. unaccompanied

e. inborn

f. emotional

g. spirited

h. impulsive

Language of Research

Researchers often use certain words to explain their work. Some of the most common verbs include the following: *state, report, find, raise, consider, show, study, suggest, witness, observe*, and *describe*. To avoid using the same verb again and again, writers can choose to use a different verb with a similar meaning. In choosing, it is important that the verb convey the statement's meaning accurately. For example, the words *state, express*, and *explain* can all be used to convey the same or similar meanings in research.

▶ Circle the verb that best completes each of the following sentences.

1. The study **showed / witnessed** that banal comments were more likely to precede laughter than jokes.

2. I **suspect / describe** that the general patterns of laughter are fluid and shift subconsciously.

3. The gender pattern of everyday laughter also **suggests / studies** why there are more male than female comedians.

4. I **concluded / described** that laughter is primarily a social vocalization that binds people together.

5. I **observed / suspected** 1,200 people laughing spontaneously in their natural environments.

6. These physiological effects are incompletely **documented / concluded** and their medicinal benefits are even less certain.

▶ Find the sentences in the text to check your answers. Highlight other verbs used in reporting research in "The Science of Laughter." After highlighting, discuss which verbs can be substituted for each other.

❰Expanding Your Language

Reading

 Reading Tip

Technical Terms In some texts, the authors use **boldface** for **technical terms** that are specific to the topic. Use the information in parentheses and terms you understand in the reading to help you guess at their meaning. ■

▶ The following is a short excerpt from a longer article. It contains some technical terms that are specific to the topic. Read the excerpt to find information related to the following questions: What is laughter? What happens to us when we laugh?

How Laughter Works

Laughter is not the same as humor. **Laughter** is the physiological response to humor. Laughter consists of two parts—a set of **gestures** and the **production of a sound**. When we laugh, the **brain** pressures us to conduct both of these activities simultaneously. When we laugh heartily, changes occur in many parts of the body, even the arm, leg, and trunk muscles.

If you want to get specific about it, it works like this: Under certain conditions, our bodies perform what the *Encyclopedia Britannica* describes as "rhythmic, vocalized, expiratory, and involuntary actions"—better known as laughter. Fifteen facial muscles contract and stimulation of the **zygomatic major muscle** (the main lifting mechanism of your upper lip) occurs. Meanwhile, the **respiratory system** (the set of organs involved in breathing) is upset by the **epiglottis** half-closing the **larynx** (parts of the throat), so that air intake occurs irregularly, making you gasp. In extreme circumstances, the **tear ducts** are activated, so that while the mouth is opening and closing and the struggle for oxygen intake continues, the face becomes moist and often red (or purple). The noises that usually accompany this bizarre behavior range from sedate giggles to boisterous guffaws.

Behavioral neurobiologist and pioneering laughter researcher Robert Provine jokes that he has encountered one major problem in his study of laughter. The problem is that laughter disappears just when he is ready to observe it—especially in the laboratory. One of his studies looked at the **sonic structure**, or sounds, of laughter. He discovered that all human laughter consists of variations on a basic form that consists of short, vowel-like notes repeated every 210 milliseconds. Laughter can be of the "ha-ha-ha" variety or the "ho-ho-ho" type but not a mixture of both, he says. Provine also suggests that humans have a "detector" that responds to laughter by triggering other neural circuits in the brain, which, in turn, generates more laughter. This explains why laughter is contagious.

Humor researcher Peter Derks describes laughter response as "a really quick, automatic type of behavior." "In fact, how quickly our brain recognizes the incongruity that lies at the heart of most humor and attaches an abstract meaning to it determines whether we laugh," he says.

Punctuation Effect

One of the key features of natural laughter is its **placement in speech**, linguists say. Laughter almost always occurs during pauses at the end of phrases. Experts say this suggests that an orderly process (probably neurologically based) governs the placement of laughter in speech and gives speech priority access to the single vocalization channel. This strong relationship between laughter and speech is much like punctuation in written communication—that's why it's called the **punctuation effect**.

Speaking

 **Three-Minute Taped Talk** Refer to the readings in this chapter. Choose several compelling ideas about what we know today about laughter, how it works, and the crucial role that laughter plays in our lives. Find supporting information to explain these ideas and make a short outline of the ideas you plan to explain. Make notes of your presentation. Use the notes you prepared and practice your talk a few times before you record it. Record your talk and give your audio CD or audiotape to your teacher for feedback.

Writing

▶ **Topic Writing** Using the information you prepared for your taped talk on laughter, write a draft outline of this topic. Do this work in your journal notebook. A sample draft outline is provided below.

Understanding the Complexities of Laughter and Jokes

Paragraph 1.   The physical processes of laughter (neurological control, sound, etc.)
Paragraph 2.   The characteristics of laughter (social nature of laughter, contagiousness of laughter, etc.)
Paragraph 3.   The gender and cultural differences (male and female reactions to jokes, laughter, jokes in different countries)

▶ Reread and, if possible, show your draft to a partner for peer review. Make any suggested changes in the essay, such as reorganizing or adding information, editing for grammar, and correcting spelling. Then rewrite your draft and give the final essay to your teacher for feedback.

Online Study Center   For additional activities, go to the *Reading Matters* Online Study Center at *college.hmco.com/pic/wholeyfour2e.*

2 Our Creative Brain

⬤ Chapter Openers

Exploring Emotions

▶ Check (✔) the emotions that you might experience when you begin to work on a new project.

I might feel

_____ 1. joyful.

_____ 2. fearful.

_____ 3. indifferent.

_____ 4. overwhelmed.

_____ 5. liberated.

_____ 6. excited.

_____ 7. traumatized.

_____ 8. powerful.

_____ 9. powerless.

Problem Solving

▶ Read the short excerpt from *Bird by Bird* and answer the following questions:

1. What problems do people have at the beginning of a writing project?
2. What lessons about how to begin working did she learn and from whom?

▶ Discuss your ideas with a partner or in a small group.

From *Bird by Bird*

By Anne Lamott

E. L. Doctorow once said "writing a novel is like driving a car at night. You can see only as far as your headlights, but you can make the whole trip that way." You don't have to see where you're going, you don't have to see your destination or everything you will pass along the way. You just have to see two or three feet ahead of you. This is right up there with the best advice about writing, or life, I have ever heard.

So after I've completely exhausted myself thinking about the people I most resent in the world, and my more arresting financial problems, I remember to pick up the one-inch picture frame and to figure out a one-inch piece of my story to tell, one small scene, one memory, one exchange. I also remember a story that I know I've told elsewhere but that over and over helps me to get a grip: thirty years ago my older brother, who was ten years old at the time, was trying to get a report on birds written that he'd had three months to write, which was due the next day. We were out at our family cabin in Bolinas, and he was at the kitchen table close to tears, surrounded by binder paper and pencils and unopened books on birds, immobilized by the hugeness of the task ahead. Then my father sat down beside him, put his arm around my brother's shoulder, and said, "Bird by bird, buddy. Just take it bird by bird."

❶Exploring and Understanding Reading

Discussion Questions

❯ Think about the following questions before reading. Share your ideas with a partner or in a small group.

1. What is creativity?
2. What are some creative things that you have done?
3. What is the source of an individual's creativity?
4. What kind of process or processes do people go through in producing creative work?
5. At what stages of life is creativity more (or less) difficult?

Previewing

 ❯ Reading Tip

Remember that **previewing** is a critical reading strategy that helps you **predict** what **information** the reading will contain. ▪

❯ Quickly read the title and quotes contained in this selection. Based on your preview, make a list of four (or more) important ideas that you expect will be explained in the reading.

1. _____
2. _____
3. _____
4. _____

❯ Compare your answers with a partner. Highlight the information on which you based your predictions. Return to these predictions after you have finished reading and verify your answers.

Skimming

❯ Read paragraphs 1–14 of the selection quickly and answer the following question:

Why is it difficult for many people to feel comfortable with the idea that they might be creative?

❯ List three possible reasons.

• _____

• _____

• _____

The Creative Brain

By Ned Herrmann

❶   Prevailing mythology has it that creativity is the exclusive domain of artists, scientists, and inventors—a giftedness not available to ordinary people going about the business of daily life. Partly as a result, *ordinary* people often hold the *creative* person in awe, finding little gradation in genius. It's either the Sistine Chapel ceiling or nothing.

Creative? Who, Me?

❷   Our awe of creativity is like a dragon that blocks the gate to our personal creativity, and that we must slay before we can enter our own creative realm. For many of us, the dragon is a balloon, one of our own making, like a fugitive from the Macy's Thanksgiving Day parade. It is a fear inflated by our minds into a monster before which we shrink, trembling. We've created this dragon to protect ourselves from something worse: the possibility that we might really go for it, do the very utmost we can do—and find people out there who still don't think it's good enough and reject not only what we've done, but *us* as individuals.

❸   What we need to understand is that by refusing to risk being creative at less than genius levels, we are already rejecting ourselves, passing judgment without evidence. While that judgment mechanism may have served to protect us from censure as children, we as adults no longer need to feel as vulnerable as we did when we were young. What we need to do instead is assume full responsibility for ourselves: for

> "Our creativity is limited only by our beliefs."
>
> —Willis Harmon

encouraging our own inner child, for applauding our courage to try something, for praising our own spontaneity, for admiring our own willingness to start again when something comes out differently from the way we expect, and for delighting in our small and humble expressions of creativity, of which there are many every day.

❹ In fact, most individual creativity is pretty humble—no Sistine Chapel ceiling, no Beethoven's Ninth Symphony, no Thomas Edison invention, just a solution to such a mundane problem as getting the microwave merry-go-round to work by turning it over and using it upside down, or finding a new way home, or writing a silly verse to a friend, or arranging and decorating a living room. One man got a faulty thermometer to shake down by attaching it to the blades of a fan and running it for a minute; he thinks that's "just technical," but it's fully creative. It's creative to design a house, develop a new business, paint a picture, lay out a garden, solve a new problem, find a way to feed the cat when you're away for three days. All of these are valid examples of creative behaviors, because the doing of them includes an element of newness, novelty, and difference.

Exposing Myths about Creativity

❺ If we understand creativity in this sense, three things are clear:

1. All human beings are capable of being creative—it is part of our birthright.

2. It is not necessary to be a genius to be creative.

3. No matter how severely our creativity may have been repressed in the past, it can be reaccessed, stimulated, and developed through life experiences and specialized programs.

❻ I would expect that less than one percent of the total population could rank in the genius category, yet of the thousands of people I've worked with (who by and large didn't consider themselves creative), a good seventy to eighty percent have been able to demonstrate to their own satisfaction that: (1) they do have creative abilities, and (2) exercising those abilities can bring them a great deal of joy and profit.

❼ This is good news not only for the creatively uninformed or uninitiated. The same techniques that can open the creative world to a novice can set off a creative explosion in the adept. One GE inventor—with thirty-four patents to his credit—took our ACT I Workshop and said, "If I had known all this twenty-five years ago, I would now have a hundred patents!"

> "Discipline and focused awareness contribute to the act of creation."
>
> —John Poppy

Obtaining Keys to Your Creativity

❽ What made the difference for this inventor and for thousands of others who've moved into creative functioning? The keys are:

1. An understanding of the creative process and its component stages, and how the four modes of knowing come into play at each stage.

2. An understanding of what hinders each mode at each stage.

3. A commitment to heightening one's own creative awareness and functioning.

❾   This chapter, the first of four devoted to helping people who want to heighten their creativity, elaborates on each of these areas of understanding.

What Is Creativity, Anyway?

❿   I resist defining creativity; each person's experience of it is so unique and individual that no one can formulate a definition that fits everyone else. However, you need to know what I'm talking about, so in this section I will be defining the word. Add to this extended definition in any way that works for you.

⓫   Many people think of creativity purely in terms of inventiveness, and that is surely part of it. "Hot" ideas are great and we revel in them when they hit. But if the process stops there, the "flash" evaporates. The world goes on, unchanged. The idea is usually lost. What's more—and this is the point—ideas in and of themselves, if they begin and end in our heads, produce neither growth nor full satisfaction because there's no basis for feedback to encourage more ideas. The reinforcement loop doesn't close.

⓬   My own thinking is that *creativity in its fullest sense involves both generating an idea and manifesting it— making something happen as a result*. To strengthen creative ability, you need to apply the idea in some form that enables both the experience itself and your own reaction and others' to reinforce your performance. As you and others applaud your creative endeavors, you are likely to become more creative.

> "Also, creativity can be learned. Once you have become convinced and aware that you can bring new things into being, then it is simply a matter of choosing a particular way to create."
>
> —Unknown

⓭   Defining creativity to include application throws the whole subject into a different light, because:

1. Although *ideas* can come in seconds, *application* can take days, years, or even a lifetime to realize.

2. Although *ideas* can come out of only one quadrant of the brain, *application* ultimately calls on specialized mental capabilities in all four quadrants.

3. Although *ideas* can arrive in a single flash, *application* necessarily involves a process consisting of several distinct phases.

⓮   Defining creativity to include application also makes creativity totally applicable in the world of business, where it tends to go under the label of *problem solving*.

The Source and Process of Creativity

⓯   *Creativity's source is the brain—not just one part of the brain, but all of it*. Today, this theme song is well established and accepted, but when I first proclaimed it in 1975, it was a new idea and some of my associates in the training field thought I was nuts. Why? Because none of the well-known literature on creativity mentioned the brain once! It simply wasn't part of the prevailing frame of reference regarding creativity. I made the connection when others hadn't simply because: (1) I had specifically been asking about where creativity comes from at the moment of stumbling across the split-brain research, and (2) my awareness of duality had been strong since childhood. Others, whose frame of reference and background differed from mine, simply couldn't relate to what I was saying. Knowing that creativity arises in the brain makes an enormous contribution to our ability to access, stimulate, develop, and apply the process, because it tells us: (1) what process we need to follow, and (2) how that process calls on the brain's specialized capabilities at each stage.

❶❻   Researcher Graham Wallas, many years ago, set down a description of what happens as people approach problems with the objective of coming up with creative solutions. He described his four-stage process as follows:

1. In the *preparation* stage, we define the problem, need, or desire, gather any information the solution or response needs to account for, and set up criteria for verifying the solution's acceptability.

2. In the *incubation* stage, we step back from the problem and let our minds contemplate and work it through. Like preparation, incubation can last minutes, weeks, even years.

3. In the *illumination* stage, ideas arise from the mind to provide the basis of a creative response. These ideas can be pieces of the whole or the whole itself, i.e., seeing the entire concept or entity all at once. Unlike the other stages, illumination is often very brief, involving a tremendous rush of insights within a few minutes or hours.

4. In *verification*, the final stage, one carries out activities to demonstrate whether or

not what emerged in illumination satisfies the need and the criteria defined in the preparation stage.

This four-stage description has helped me define what happens in my own creative endeavors.

The Key to Creative Living: Reclaiming Our Passion

❶❼   A major key—perhaps *the* key—to living creatively is passion. By passion I mean a highly compelling, energetic attention to something. Turned-on people of all kinds are passionate. So are people who've just fallen in love. So are collectors, sports nuts, and horse-crazy kids, boys who've just discovered baseball cards or video games, and computer hackers.

❶❽   Little children are passionate about almost everything they see. In fact, they are passionate about seeing itself—and feeling, and smelling, and hearing, and tasting, too. Their passion embraces life itself with all its experiences. Even timid children, once they've been reassured, have enormous enthusiasm. They reach out for everything they can —spiders, flowers, butterflies, blocks, hands, eyes, cats, food, wind, water, worms, you, music— everything. They are natural experimenters, dedicated explorers, fascinated examiners of you-name-it. As time goes on, they begin to make connections between things: One child, seeing oil in a puddle of water, exclaimed, "Oh look! A dead rainbow!" So extraordinary and novel are their perceptions that Art Linkletter made his reputation by interviewing children. Apart from

> "The weakest among us has a gift, however seemingly trivial, which is peculiar to him and which, worthily used, will be a gift also to his race."
>
> —Ruskin

committing the indiscretions that horrified their parents and delighted the audience, they resensitized us repeatedly to the wonder of the world around us.

19 The natural passion for life in all its unexpectedness that characterizes children also features strongly in the personalities of people who have chosen to retain or reclaim their own creativity. They are constantly exercising their curiosity, trying new things, and delighting in the experiment for its own sake—even if the results themselves don't please. They are open to the moment for whatever it may bring. They approach life with expectancy, enthusiasm, and energy.

"Once we are destined to live out our lives in the prison of our mind, our one duty is to furnish it well."
—Peter Ustinov

20 How do we reclaim our passion if it has been allowed to dim in our lives? What if we are one of those many people whose zest for life has grown faint or even faded? If we despair of having an original thought all our own? One way—an important way—is to increase the amount of genuine pleasure we allow into our lives. There are many things that make life more pleasurable—but in the next section I want to focus on one thing: what we can learn—or re-learn—from children.

Tellback

> ➤ **Reading Tip**

Using this technique of **retelling** helps you both to **paraphrase** the **ideas** in what you read more effectively and to speak more easily. ■

▶ **A** Working with a partner, read a section (one or more paragraphs), and then take turns explaining from memory what you read in paragraphs 1–14. Use the following sequence of steps.

▶ **1.** Read the first section.

2. Close the book and tell as much of the information as you remember. Explain in your own words, if necessary.

3. Ask your partner to add any information you may have forgotten.

4. Repeat Steps 1–3 for the remaining sections, taking turns telling the information.

▶ **B** Choose three important ideas that are interesting or new to you. Explain why these are important with a partner.

Paraphrasing

 Reading Tip

Paraphrasing is the process of **putting the writer's ideas into your own words.** To paraphrase, you change the wording and the order of ideas you read. Be careful not to lose or change any of the ideas you paraphrase. ▪

▶ Paraphrase the writer's suggestions to answer the following questions. To do this, highlight the information and then restate the ideas in your own words.

1. What does the writer believe are the three keys to creativity?

   a. _____

   b. _____

   c. _____

2. What has to happen for a creative idea to be fully realized?

   _____

3. Why is the understanding that creativity arises in the brain an important idea?

   _____

4. What characterizes creative people and why is this quality important?

   _____

▶ Work with a partner to compare your answers. Your wording will be different but the ideas should be the same. Check to see if you have highlighted the same information. Share your answers with others in the class.

Imagery and Example

 Reading Tip

Imagery is the use of vivid or descriptive language to **represent ideas.** Think of it as using words to paint or draw ideas. One famous example is "My love is like a red, red rose." ▪

▶ In "The Creative Brain," the writer makes use of imagery and example to describe people's attitudes toward creativity. Scan the reading and underline the images and examples that the writer uses to describe:

a. What people think about being creative.

b. What prevents people from being creative.

c. How children make connections between things.

▶ Work with a partner or in a small group and compare your answers. Discuss how effective these images and examples are in conveying the writer's ideas.

▶Paired Readings

▶ These two readings are about different observations concerning how adults can learn about creativity from the ways children act. Choose one of these short readings and prepare to explain your ideas to a partner who read a different reading.

❶Children Are Our Best Teachers, Part A

Highlighting ▶ Read the following and highlight the key words in the reading that will help you prepare notes on the selection.

Special Talents, Part A

❶   Children have a lot of special talents to offer. Their pursuit of novelty and wonder is both a cause and an effect—a gift of the life fully lived and one of the things that makes life worth living. Anyone who knows children can tell you that they do the following:

> "Play teaches children to master the world."
> —Jean Piaget

❷   *Children follow their interests.* If a kid is bored, you know it. None of this polite interest stuff the rest of us get stuck in. What they like, they do, and this teaches them that following what they like makes them happy—so they do it some more.

❸   *Children seek out and risk experimenting with new things.* If kids are confronted with something unfamiliar, they will take a chance and try it out. They prod and poke it, smell it, look at it from all angles, try using it in different ways, look to see what you think about it—maybe even give it to you to see what you do with it. We adults, by contrast, slap a label on it, say, "I know what that is," and dismiss it. What we're really saying is, "I know what I already know about that, and there's nothing more worth knowing," which is almost never true of anything or anyone.

❹   *Children pay attention to their own rhythms.* We grownups tend to drive ourselves until something's done, or until a certain hour strikes, but children do things when they feel like it. Naturally, since someone else tends to their necessities, they may have more time and freedom to do that, but we would do well to follow their lead where we have the choice. When we work during our most productive times and rest during our other times, we make the most of our energies. That means if we do our best work between 4 P.M. and 2 A.M., then we should strive to arrange our day to make use of those hours. We become more trustworthy to ourselves and others.

Note Taking

▶ **Main and Supporting Ideas** Using the information you highlighted, prepare notes to explain the ideas to someone who read a different selection. Write the main ideas for each point and the related details using a divided page outline on separate pages of your own.

Main Ideas	Supporting Points/Details

▶ Use your notes to discuss the selection with a partner who read a different one. Explain as much as possible.

❷ Children Are Our Best Teachers, Part B

Highlighting   ▶ Read the following and highlight the key words in the reading that will help you prepare notes on the selection.

Special Talents, Part B

❶   Children have a lot of special talents to offer. Their pursuit of novelty and wonder is both a cause and an effect—a gift of the life fully lived and one of the things that makes life worth living. Anyone who knows children can tell you that they do the following:

❷   *Children honor dreams and daydreams.* Children pay attention to, talk about, and follow up on their dreams and fantasies. They may draw pictures they saw in their dreams, conduct conversations with dream characters, and try to recreate something experienced in dreams and daydreams. These are all creative acts. Moreover, they are important: Mankind has learned that dreams are a language the subconscious uses to communicate to the conscious. Many people say they don't remember their dreams, but I know of no serious

> "Play teaches children to master the world."
>
> —Jean Piaget

effort to connect with one's dream life that hasn't succeeded. Those who succeed often report an experience of waking and sleeping that is like living two lives, each one feeding and nourishing the other.

❸   *Children consider mistakes as information, rather than as something unsuccessful.* "That's a way it doesn't work. I wonder how else it doesn't work?" For children, the process of figuring something out is in itself a win. We, however, are hung up on outcomes, so we lay judgments on our mistakes—"We did it wrong" and what is worse, we take it further— therefore, "People won't love us," "We're never good enough," and "We'll be all alone." No wonder mistakes frighten some of us so deeply. Patterns like that aren't learned overnight, and changing them may take more than a few tries, but they can be changed.

❹   *Children play.* Kids make a game out of everything. Their essential business is play, so to speak. They delight in spoofing each other, parents, and personalities. They love to mimic, pretend, wrestle, hide and seek, surprise, and play practical jokes. They love to laugh, tell secrets, devise stories of goblins and fairies and giants and monsters and heroes. They're not hung up on accuracy. When in doubt, they know they can always make

> it up. Many adults, however, have withdrawn permission from themselves to be silly, to expose the part of themselves that feels young.

Note Taking

▶ **Main and Supporting Ideas** Using the information you highlighted, prepare notes to explain the ideas to someone who read a different selection. Write the main ideas for each point and the related details using a divided page outline.

Main Ideas	Supporting Points/Details

▶ Use your notes to discuss the selection with a partner who read a different one. Explain as much as possible.

Comparing the Readings

Reacting to the Information

▶ Based on the information you explained and heard, discuss the following questions.

1. Which of these special talents exhibited by children do you think are the most important for adults to remember and maintain throughout their lives?

2. If it is true that adults have lost these child-like abilities, why and how does this happen?

Writing

Reading Tip

Summarizing is a strategy that helps you to **identify** and **explain** the **writer's purpose** for conveying information in a reading. It is a technique that helps us identify what is important from what is secondary. ■

▶ **A** **Summarizing Information from a Text** A summary is a brief piece of writing that explains the author's purpose in a larger work by identifying the main ideas and important details expressed therein. Summaries are useful for work in both academic and professional spheres.

Use the information from "Paraphrasing" on page 29 to make an outline that includes the following:

• The author's purpose in writing "The Creative Brain"
• The important ideas he expresses
• Important details or examples critical to the understanding of these ideas

▶ **B** Use your outline to write a short summary of about 150–200 words on separate pages of your own. Give your summary to a partner. As you read each other's writing, do the following:

  • Highlight the ideas from the reading that are included in the summary.
  • Ask yourself whether or not all the important ideas are included.
  • Ask yourself if these ideas are paraphrased.
  • Are any ideas left out?
  • Are any unnecessary details included?
  • How would you rate this summary? Use a scale where 5 = excellent, 4 = very good, 3 = good, 2 = incomplete, and 1 = very incomplete.

▶ Use the feedback from your partner to rewrite your summary. Give the summary to your teacher for feedback.

Applying the Information

◐ **Analyzing a Situation** Read the following short article that presents some techniques for increasing creativity. Referring to the four-step process explained in the preceding reading, identify the following:

1. What steps in the process are described here?
2. What steps in the process are not included?
3. What further steps would you suggest to complete the process?

◐ Discuss your ideas with a partner or in a small group.

Mental Breakout

"Mind mapping" tries to tap the creative problem-solving potential of employees.

By Tawn Nhan

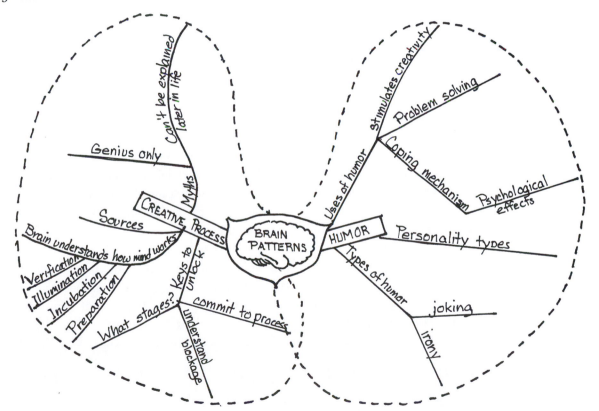

Charlotte, N.C.—About a dozen IBM executives, engineers, and computer programmers walked into a meeting and almost immediately began breaking the rules of corporate etiquette.

Like children, each ripped open a pack of brightly colored pens and began doodling. Instead of taking notes, they drew large circles, arrows, and stars.

They were mind mapping, an alternative note-taking technique that doubles as a creative thinking tool. It's a popular training tool on the corporate circuit, with companies such as IBM hoping to get an edge on competitors by improving the thinking skills of their workers.

Mind mapping was introduced years ago by Tony Buzan, an English creativity consultant who explained the concept in his book, *Using Both Sides of Your Brain*. Unlike conventional note taking, mind mapping maximizes the strengths of both sides of the human brain because it uses words as well as images, according to Anne Durrum Robinson, a mind-mapping consultant training IBM workers.

Mind mapping allows you to personalize your notes.

Instead of using the conventional Roman numerals and letters, you use pictures and color. You start by jotting down a main idea or creating an image in the middle of the page. Then you add ideas by drawing branches from the main idea. Icons, sketches, and color are used to highlight priorities. The words are generated from the left brain. The shapes and images come from the right side.

But mind mapping is more than just a way to take notes. Robinson said it's really a way to develop the right side of the brain, which few people fully tap.

"It's a wonderful way to explore mental diversity," Robinson said. "Mind mapping gets people to tap into their whole mind, and we use so little of the marvelous minds we have."

Robinson should know. The eighty-one-year-old owner of Creativity, Communication and Common Sense, a workplace consulting firm in Austin, Texas, began using mind maps in the early 1970s to improve her efficiency as a writer.

Today, Robinson said she writes entire articles using a mind map. While waiting for a flight this week, Robinson said she wrote the bulk of a journal article using a mind map.

"It worked for me, and I decided that it had so much value that it would be helpful to others," Robinson said.

Executives use it to write speeches, and workers use it to plan and execute projects and solve problems, Robinson said.

Boeing, 3M, British Petroleum, and Fluor Daniel are among the companies that use mind mapping, said Robinson, who leads ten to twelve mind-mapping seminars a year.

James Donahue, an IBM project executive, said the mind-mapping exercise made him aware of how little he uses his right brain.

"My brain is very left-brained. I have a lot of 'to do' lists. … I keep a lot of checklists," he said. "I don't tap into the right side of my mind enough. That's why I'm here.

"If you spend more than twenty years in a company, you begin to think in a rigid way," Donahue said. "My view of this is that it's a good investment of my time to find out new ways to think and do things differently."

Vocabulary Building

Word Form

▶ **A** Study these five words and their forms. Then choose the correct form for each part of speech in the chart below. These words are commonly found in general and academic texts.

diversify (v.)	maximize (v.)	reinforce (v.)	retain (v.)	specify (v.)
diversity (n.)	maximizing	reinforced	retentive	specific
diverse (adj.)	maximum	reinforcement	retainer	specification
	maximal	reinforcing	retaining	specified
	maximally		retention	specifically

Verb	Noun	Adjective	Adverb
maximize	1.	1.	1.
		2.	
reinforce	1.	1.	
		2.	
retain	1.	1.	
	2.	2.	
specify	1.	1.	1.
		2.	

▶ Compare lists with a partner.

▶ **B** Write three sentences using words from the list.

▶ **C** In English, the form of the word can change when it is used as a different part of speech. For example, a suffix (ending) can be added to change the adjective *good* to the noun *goodness*. Some common noun suffixes are *-ence, -ness, -tion, -ment, -ity, -or,* and *-y.*

Read each sentence and circle the correct word to use in the sentence. Write *N* if the word is a noun or *ADJ* if the word is an adjective.

1. _____ What made the **different / difference** for this inventor and for thousands of others who've moved into creative functioning?

2. _____ There's no **basis / basic** for feedback to encourage more ideas.

3. _____ Defining **creativity / creative** to include application throws the whole subject into a **different / difference** light.

4. _____ Little children are **passion / passionate** about almost everything they see.

5. _____ Their **passion / passionate** embraces life itself with all its experiences.

6. _____ The **natural / nature** passion for life in all its **unexpected / unexpectedness** that characterizes children also features strongly in creative people.

7. _____ We need to understand that by refusing to risk being **creative / created**, we are passing judgment on ourselves.

8. _____ We need to assume full **responsibility / responsible** for ourselves.

9. _____ Add to this **definition / defined** in any way that works for you.

10. _____ Many people think of creativity purely in terms of **inventive / inventiveness**.

11. _____ This was not part of the prevailing frame of **referred / reference** regarding creativity.

12. _____ They are not hung up on **accurate / accuracy**.

Vocabulary in Context

▶ **A Synonyms** Refer to "The Creative Brain" to find the words in context. Match the words in Column A with words that have the same meaning in Column B.

Column A	Column B
_____ 1. uninitiated	a. subliminal
_____ 2. evaporated	b. improper behavior
_____ 3. endeavors	c. area
_____ 4. quadrant	d. skill
_____ 5. capability	e. new
_____ 6. indiscretion	f. attempts
_____ 7. subconscious	g. disapproval
_____ 8. censure	h. dried up

◯ **B Determining the Referent** In a complex English sentence, pronouns are often used to refer to ideas given in a preceding sentence or in an earlier part of the sentence. In the following sentences taken from "The Creative Brain," decide what idea the pronoun in boldface refers to. Look at the reading to help you decide.

1. (Paragraph 2) Our awe of creativity is like a dragon **that** blocks the gate to our personal creativity.

   _____

2. (Paragraph 4) One man got a faulty thermometer to shake down by attaching **it** to the blades of a fan and running **it** for a minute; he thinks that's "just technical," but it's fully creative.

   a. _____

   b. _____

3. (Paragraph 7) **This** is good news not only for the creatively uninformed or uninitiated.

   _____

4. (Paragraph 11) Many people think of creativity purely in terms of inventiveness, and **that** is surely part of **it**.

   a. _____

   b. _____

5. (Paragraph 12) My own thinking is that creativity in its fullest sense involves both generating an idea and manifesting **it**—making something happen as a result.

   _____

6. (Paragraph 13) Defining creativity to include application also makes creativity totally applicable in the world of business, where **it** tends to go under the label of problem solving.

   _____

◯ Check your answers with a partner.

▶ **C Jigsaw Sentences** Match the beginning of each sentence in Column A with the ending that fits best in Column B.

Column A

_____ 1. If we understand creativity in this sense,

_____ 2. If kids are confronted with something unfamiliar,

_____ 3. If I had known this twenty-five years ago,

_____ 4. If the process stops there,

Column B

a. they will take a chance and try it out.

b. the flash evaporates.

c. three things are clear.

d. I would now have a hundred patents.

▶ Check your answers with a partner. Take turns reading the completed sentences.

▶ Expanding Your Language

Speaking

▶ Think of a creative person you are interested in. You may want to focus on a well-known musician, an artist, or a dancer. You may decide to focus on someone who is not well known but whose creative work you admire or who meets the criteria for creativity in everyday life that Hermann sets out in "The Creative Brain."

Prepare to talk about your subject by researching the following:

- Background or general information about your subject
- Type of work or area of study undertaken
- Important moments in your subject's life
- Difficulties faced
- Reason(s) you admire this person

▶ Using these points, prepare notes for a five-minute presentation. Practice your presentation and then give your talk to others in a small group. Prepare three questions for your audience to focus discussion after your presentation.

Writing

▶ Choose a topic related to the discussions in the chapter readings or any other topic that interests you. Try to write about the topic every day for a week. Use the mind-mapping technique to help you develop and expand on your ideas. You can choose a topic in the news or choose to write about the creative person you researched for your oral presentation.

❮Read On: Taking It Further

**Reading
Questionnaire**

▶ Researchers have found that the more you read, the more your vocabulary will increase and the more you will understand. A good knowledge of vocabulary will help you to do well in school and in business. To find out more about making reading a habit for yourself, answer the following questionnaire.

▶ Rank the activities that you think help you to increase the language you understand. Mark 1 beside the one that helps you the most to learn new language. Mark 2 beside the second most helpful activity, continuing with 3, 4, and so on. Mark the same number if you find two activities that help you equally.

_____ Memorizing word lists

_____ Reading texts that are assigned for class

_____ Reading texts that I choose for myself

_____ Talking about the texts that we read for class

_____ Talking about the texts that I choose for myself

_____ Learning how to guess the meaning of words that are new

_____ Doing vocabulary exercises for readings that we study in class

_____ Doing extra vocabulary exercises for homework

_____ Studying the dictionary to find out the parts of words

_____ Using the dictionary to look up new words I don't understand

▶ Discuss your questionnaire with a partner. Do not change your answers. Give reasons for your ranking and explain your experiences with reading. Are there other activities that help you to increase your vocabulary? Explain what these are and how they help you. Discuss the reading strategies that you use and when you use them.

A Reading Journal

> Tip

Keep a notebook to write your reading journal and vocabulary log entries.

▶ An important way to improve your reading skills and increase your vocabulary is to find material that you choose to read. This activity is called "Reading for Pleasure." Here are some ideas to start you out.

▶ **A Reading** Find some readings on the topics in this unit that you are interested in and that are at your level. Your teacher can help you prepare a list of books, stories, or magazine articles to read for your pleasure. For example, you could choose a short story by a comic writer such as Steve Martin or S.J. Perlman. Another source of reading material is your bookstore or library's magazine and newspaper section. Discuss what you would like to read with others in a small group. Your group members could recommend something good for you to read. Try to work with a reading partner. Select a reading that your partner or partners will read as well. Make a schedule for the times when you plan to do your personal reading and a time when you would like to finish.

▶ **B Speaking** Be ready to talk about what you read with a partner or with others in a small group. You can use your reading journal to help you remember what is important for the others to know.

▶ **C Reading Journal Report** Include the following information in your journal entry.

Title of the reading: _____

Author: _____

The type of reading:

_____

_____

_____

What is the subject of the reading (the theme or topic)?

1. _____

2. _____

3. _____

4. _____

5. _____

What are some of the important ideas?

1. _____

2. _____

3. _____

4. _____

5. _____

Recommendation

This selection is (is not) worth reading because:

1. _____

2. _____

3. _____

4. _____

5. _____

Vocabulary Log ▷ **A** Choose ten important words that you learned from this unit. Write the words and a definition in your notebook. Check your definition with the teacher.

Chapter 1

Word	Definition
1. longevity	the duration of an individual life
2. …	

▷ On a separate page, write several sentences using one of the words you chose in each sentence.

▷ **B Personal Dictionary** A personal dictionary is a good way to record the new words you learn as you read. To create your dictionary, divide a notebook into sections for each letter of the alphabet. Then, write the word and the definition on the appropriate page. You can also write the way to use the word in a sentence (as a verb, as a noun, as an adjective, as an adverb, or in more than one way). Look for the word in the reading or write the word in a sentence of your own. You can also find synonyms (words that mean the same) or antonyms (words that have an opposite meaning) and write them in your dictionary.

 **Online Study Center** For additional activities, go to the *Reading Matters* Online Study Center at *college.hmco.com/pic/wholeyfour2e.*

Body Science: Moving in New Directions

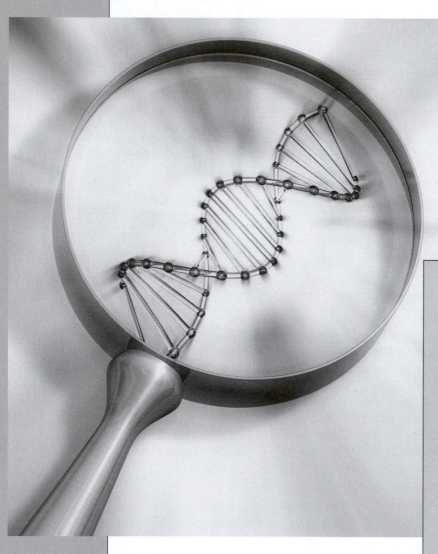

If anything is
sacred, the
human body
is sacred.

—*Walt Whitman*

Introducing the Topic

Recent research in the biological sciences is allowing us to better understand how our body functions. Using this knowledge we can potentially do many things. We can modify, improve, or even change what we don't like. But, as with so many other advances in science, there are pros and cons. This unit explores some of these advances and looks at some of the questions they raise. Chapter 3 addresses the issue of delaying the aging process. How can it be done and what are some of the consequences? Chapter 4 examines the ever-increasing problem of being overweight and the measures being taken to combat it.

▶ Points of Interest

What's Your Opinion?

▶ The following list identifies some of the areas that scientists/researchers are working on these days. Read the list and answer the questions that follow.

- Improve memory
- Increase strength
- Extend life
- Reduce appetite
- Alter body shape

1. What do all of these areas have in common?
2. In which of these areas have scientists been successful and how?
3. What are some of the advantages and disadvantages of each?
4. Do you agree that scientists should be working in these areas? Why or why not?

3 Aging

▶**Chapter Openers**

Defining the Terms

▶ **A** Some of the terms that will appear frequently in this chapter are listed below. Match each term with its definition.

Term

1. _____ life span

2. _____ life expectancy

3. _____ mortality rate

4. _____ genome

5. _____ enzyme

6. _____ longevity

7. _____ senility

Definition

a. a protein made by living cells that speeds up biochemical reactions

b. mental or physical deterioration of old age

c. the statistically determined number of years that a person may be expected to live

d. long duration of life

e. the frequency of deaths in a given period

f. the length of time for which a person lives

g. the genetic material of an organism

▶ **B** Think about the following:

• The age at which you consider someone to be old

• The difference between an old person and a young person

• The signs of old age

• The message behind the following Greek myth:

Eos, the Goddess of morning, fell in love with young Tithonus, son of Troy, whom she carried away in a golden chariot. Thereupon, she went to Zeus, the King of the Gods, and begged him to grant Tithonus immortality. He agreed. But she forgot to ask for perpetual youth. Tithonus became daily older, grayer, and more shrunken. His voice grew shrill, and, when Eos grew tired of caring for him, she locked him up in her bedroom, where he turned into an insect.

▶ Discuss your thoughts with a partner or in a small group.

Exploring and Understanding Reading

Analyzing Statistics

◐ Use the short text and the graph below to discuss these questions.

1. What has been happening to the average human life span over the last 100 years?
2. What are some possible reasons for this?
3. What percentage of the world population was (will be) made up of people sixty years and older in the year 1900? 2000? 2050?

Challenges of Longevity

About a hundred years ago, as improved health care, sanitation, and nutrition became more available, we began to make dramatic steps in fighting the forces that had traditionally shortened human existence. In 1900, some 10 million to 17 million people were aged sixty or older, and they made up less than one percent of the world's population. Survival rates began to climb for infants, children, and women of childbearing age, gradually lifting humanity's average life span. By 2000, 606 million were aged sixty or older, and they made up almost ten percent of the world's population. According to the United Nations report *World Population Prospects*, by 2050 that group could swell to 1.9 billion and constitute one-fifth of the world's projected population. The fastest-growing segment is the so-called oldest old, those aged eighty and above. In 2000, 69 million people were in that category, and in 2050, their number could reach 377 million.

Mariette DiChristina, *Scientific American*

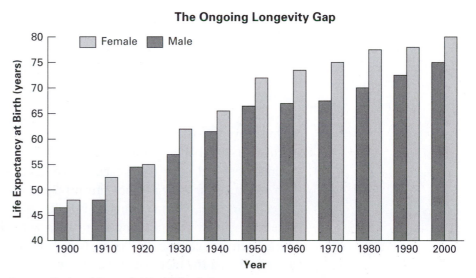

The Ongoing Longevity Gap

Source: *National Center for Health Statistics*

◐ Discuss your answers with a partner or in a small group.

Previewing   ◖ The following article is about some of the work scientists are doing in the field of aging. Read the title and the subtitle and predict what the article will focus on.

_____

Surveying   ◖ **Verifying Your Prediction** Read paragraphs 1–2 (introduction). Read the first sentence of paragraphs 3–9 and all of paragraph 10 (conclusion). Verify the preview prediction you made above. If necessary, change or modify your prediction.

Reversing Human Aging

Already, scientists have extended the maximum life span in two species: to twice normal in the fruit fly (Drosophila) *and six times normal in the nematode worm* (C. elegans). *Extending the human life span appears almost within reach.*

❶   Imagine your grandmother looking like a teenager, playing soccer, and partying at the clubs all night. Or imagine your grandfather teaching you the latest high-tech computer software while listening to loud heavy-metal music. Such a scenario is hard to envision because we are taught to accept aging and the resulting suffering and death as an unavoidable fact of life. We cannot picture our grandparents in better physical shape than we are, yet the day may soon come when they will be white-water rafting with our grandchildren.

❷   To date, the more than fifty percent increase in longevity of the past century has been due mainly to advancements made in the war on infectious diseases, not in a war against aging itself. Current anti-aging treatments do not slow aging and do not extend life span more than quitting smoking, exercising, eating vegetables, or following ordinary medical advice do. The only way to achieve a further increase in human longevity is to find ways to slow down the aging process itself. Several promising approaches to changing the boundaries of aging—ranging from the administration of drugs to the manipulation of genes—are now being explored.

❸   In recent years, many advances in anti-aging science have been made at the cellular level. Normal human cells have a built-in program that prevents them from replicating more than a predetermined number of times. Each cell contains sticky areas called telomeres. These telomeres control cell life; the more often the cells divide, the shorter the telomeres get. Eventually, the telomeres are so short that the cells are unable to divide, and they die. The telomeres appear to serve as the biological clock that determines our maximum physiological life span.

❹   Recent discoveries suggest that this does not have to happen. Cancer cells, for example, continually make copies of their telomeres, hence resetting their clocks and allowing them to divide—and live—forever. Using that principle, researchers at the University of Texas are now building telomere "caps" that would essentially force any normal cell to always copy its telomeres—meaning that they would never shorten and the cell (and the person possessing it) would cease aging. But we could also try for more than stopping the clock—we could reverse it. Adding the enzyme telomerase prevents telomere shortening, so cells stay young and keep dividing, potentially indefinitely. It may be possible one day to produce a drug that will get to each of our 100 trillion cells and treat its ninety-two telomeres. The fantasy is that, at appropriate intervals during our adult lives, we will drink a telomerase drug cocktail, which will miraculously go to all our cells, keep them young—and we will live for an incredibly long time.

❺   Active research programs for telomerase inducer drugs are being conducted by the University of Texas's Southwestern University Medical Center and by Cold Spring Harbor Laboratory on Long Island, New York, as well as by biotech and drug firms. We have no way of knowing what the maximum healthy life span will become when we re-extend human telomeres. But we suspect that by using telomerase inducers, we can probably extend the human life span well beyond 120 years and that telomere manipulation should allow us to prevent most of the diseases we associate with aging: cancer (by the reverse process of inhibiting telomerase), atherosclerosis (and so most heart disease and strokes), osteoarthritis, Alzheimer's, and most other diseases of aging.

❻   But telomerase alone does not solve the aging problem. A decade ago, researchers reached the conclusion that aging was a very complex phenomenon because it involved multiple genes interacting with each other. This meant that it would be unlikely to find a single controlling gene that could be manipulated. That idea has changed dramatically. Werner syndrome for example—a condition in which a young person suffers all the signs of aging, such as very early hair loss, cataracts, blood vessel calcification, coronary heart disease, diabetes, and cancers, and which leads to death at an average age of forty-seven years—appears to be the result of only a single gene mutation. On the other hand, naturally occurring mutations of other single genes called age-1 and daf-2 result in an extraordinary prolongation of life span in earthworms.

❼   A variety of other single genes that may control critical pathways or may be the controlling factor in a series of events that define the aging process are now being investigated. If single genes can be found that play a controlling or dominant role in the aging process, their chemical makeup can be determined and, with our advanced pharmaceutical knowledge, drugs can be created that either mimic the ones considered desirable or interfere with the ones considered undesirable.

❽   Several research groups in the United States are conducting genetic research aimed at retarding aging. If the breakthroughs of recent years are anything to go by, it is likely that we will see several-fold longevity increases in mice within the next decade or so. Already such genetic manipulation has increased by almost fifty percent the life span of flies. Results are also promising in mammals; scientists have extended longevity in mice by fifty percent through genetic interventions. Achieving similar results in humans will be harder. Scientists have already identified genes that appear to accelerate human aging, but they have yet to find genes with the opposite effect. But with the sequencing of the human genome, we are now in a better position to find out more about aging in humans as well as animals.

❾   For those who cannot wait, there is one method available today that might delay human aging: caloric restriction. This means simply a diet with fewer calories. Experiments have shown longevity increases of more than fifty percent in certain mammals that follow such diets. Most people, however, feel that the secondary effects of this outweigh the benefits. After all, what is the point of living longer if you cannot enjoy life? If science is to extend human longevity, it will have to do so by extending the healthy life span while preserving youth and vitality, not by prolonging the duration of human life in age-related disability. The extra years of life must allow future grandparents to enjoy life, not just live.

❿   Although some scientists argue that aging will never be cured and our grandparents will continue to fit our stereotypes, many others remain confident that we will soon learn how to modulate the human aging process. "I believe our generation is the first to be able to map a possible route to individual immortality," says William Haseltine, CEO of Human Genome Sciences Inc. in Rockville, Maryland. If a therapy could slow human aging by fifty percent, for instance, we would have thirty or forty more years of life. In that time, new discoveries could be made that would allow us to live even longer, and the cycle could continue until a cure for aging is discovered. "It's possible that some people alive now may still be alive 400 years from now," claims gerontologist S. Michal Jazwinski of Louisiana State University Health Sciences Center. But what would be the consequences of extending human longevity or finding a real cure for aging?

Adapted from *The Futurist*

Scanning

▶ **Scanning for Specific Information** Read through paragraphs 3–9 and find the answers to the following questions. Underline or highlight the relevant information and note the number of the question in the margin for future reference. Write the answer in your own words and in note form.

1. What do normal human cells have?

   _____

2. What is the function of telomeres and how do they operate?

   _____

3. What principle is a telomere "cap" based on and what does the cap do?

   _____

4. What alternative is there to "stopping the clock?"

   _____

5. What do scientists hope to do be able to do in the future?

   _____

6. Explain how knowledge about Werner syndrome changed scientists' understanding of aging.

   _____

7. What could be done if a gene that controls the aging process is found?

   _____

8. a. What have scientists been able to achieve already in their experiments with animals?

      _____

   b. What is preventing them from achieving similar results with humans?

      _____

9. a. What method for delaying aging is already available today?

      _____

   b. What is the disadvantage of this method?

      _____

▶ Check your answers with a partner. Refer to the reading if you do not agree.

Chunking

▶ Using your answers to help you, identify the three ways scientists are working to delay the aging process and bracket the corresponding sections in the article. Take turns telling each other what you know about each way.

Understanding the Conclusion

▶ Read paragraph 10 again and answer the following questions.

1. Does the author seem to believe that aging can be delayed?
2. When does he think this could happen?
3. What question does he leave the readers with?

▶ Compare your answers in a small group.

Reacting to the Information

▶ Discuss the following questions with a partner or in a small group.

1. Do you agree that the aging process can be delayed indefinitely?
2. Would you like to live to be 150 years old? Why or why not?
3. Would you be willing to drink a "telomerase drug cocktail" every few years in order to stay young?
4. If you could live to be 150 years old, at what age do you think you would stop working?
5. What effect would our extended life span have on the younger generation?

Predicting

▶ **Using Author Credentials** The following article is one writer's reaction to the idea of extending life span. Use the background information given about the writer to predict what his opinion will be.

Previewing

▶ Read the title, subtitle, and section headings. Underline key words that help you identify the author's position. State what you think his position is in your own words.

_____

▶ Discuss what you wrote with a partner. Does it match the prediction you made?

Second Thoughts on Extending Life Spans

Researchers are making great strides in extending the boundaries of human aging. But the world may not be ready for an end-of-life population explosion.

By Donald B. Louria, MD, chairman emeritus of the Department of Preventive Medicine and Community Health, University of Medicine and Dentistry of New Jersey—New Jersey Medical School

❶   We are in the midst of an age of fantastic discoveries. The human life span at the beginning of the twentieth century was about 49 years. At the start of the twenty-first century, in countries like the United States, it is approaching 80 years. What if, by the end of this century, we could more than double the average life span to between 160 and 180 years?

❷   A concerted scientific attack on the aging process is already well under way. The world population is now more than six billion people. At the dawn of the next century, or the one after that, if these scientific endeavors are successful, there could be four or five people on this planet for every one we have now. More than one half of the population then could be over 65 or even 80 years old.

❸   Given that possibility, these are the issues that should be thoroughly discussed and debated: At some point, the number of people may become so large that it exceeds the carrying capacity of the planet, making life miserable for the vast majority of humans (and impossible for many other species), even sowing the seeds for our own destruction. The quality of life for very old people may be severely diminished if changing the boundaries of aging is not accompanied by reasonably good health. Certain tissues and organs may deteriorate even as life span is markedly prolonged, so people may live 140 years with ever-worsening sight, hearing, mental function, and musculoskeletal function.

❹   Meanwhile, we might be expected to work, support ourselves, and pay taxes until age 80, 90, 110, or older. Some of us will outlive our resources and spend our extended years living in poverty. This would likely create intense adversarial relations between younger and older persons as they compete for limited jobs and resources. Thus, the overriding question is, where is the research on aging going, where do we want it to go, and what limitations, if any, do we want to impose on it?

How Many More People?

❺   If we are able to delay death markedly by creating average life spans of 120, 140, 160, or 180 years, there will inevitably be a lot more people living on planet Earth at any given time, but, surprisingly, demographers have thus far virtually ignored the possibility of profound extensions of life spans. I have been unable to find any relevant published projections that focus on this issue. The population experts all use maximum average life spans of less than 100 years. That could be misleading. I asked Robbert Associates Ltd. of Ottawa, Canada, a future-oriented company, to use their "what if" software program to provide information on world population in the year 2100 if life expectancy increased to an average of 90 years by the year 2040 (a two-decade increase in life expectancy). Their model projects a 2.5-billion-person increase for every 10-year increase in life expectancy. Using different assumptions for ultimate world population projections, an expert demographer at the International Program Center of the U.S. Census Bureau estimated a 1.3-billion person increase in eventual world population for every decade increase in average life expectancy from 90 to 120 years. Using those two projections, the following would be the anticipated world population as life expectancy increases beyond 80 years:

Average Life Expectancy at Birth	Eventual World Population
100 years	12.6–15 billion
120 years	15–20 billion
140 years	17.6–25 billion
180 years	23–35 billion

❻   Obviously, catastrophic events could modify these projections, such as the deaths of hundreds of millions of people from emerging disease epidemics, bioterrorism, nuclear war, or other overwhelming events. The calculations are also based on equal longevity increases around the world. That, of course, would not happen initially. The life span prolongation will first take place in the developed world (Europe, North America), where the technologies are likely to be available earlier. Asia and Latin America would be expected to follow in a matter of decades. In Africa, where the aging of the population is occurring much more slowly, the emphasis will continue to be largely on reducing infant mortality; technologies to markedly prolong life spans will probably be utilized much later.

❼   Whatever the sequence of adoption of life-extending technologies, whatever calculations and assumptions are used, marked extension of life span would have a profound effect on world population. At some point, population growth and population size are likely to have substantial adverse effects on the planet and its inhabitants. The potential negative effects of population growth are magnified by global warming. Indeed, population growth and warming are inextricably interconnected: The greater the number of people on the planet, the more severe the global warming will be, because at least some portion of global warming is man made. Global warming, in turn, exacerbates many of the problems created by excessive population growth. For example, there are currently about 40 million people who are either refugees outside their own countries or internally displaced. In a world hotter by several degrees centigrade and with a population of 10 billion or more, the devastating effects of floods, drought, and wars could create hundreds of millions of refugees and internally displaced persons. That would most likely create a situation beyond our coping capacity.

❽   Common sense would suggest that excessive population growth could have some very unpleasant consequences, so ensuring the health and prosperity of humankind (as well as other creatures that share the planet with us) is likely to require us to stabilize population at some reasonable level (e.g., 10–12 billion people). If that notion is accepted, then it follows that the greatest threat to achieving population stability at reasonable levels will not be a failure to control birthrates but rather the extension of adult life span. That, in turn, invites the conclusion that the greatest threat to planetary stability is within the scientific community.

Guiding Science

❾   Some 40 years ago, author Archibald MacLeish argued that the loyalty of science is not to humanity, but to its own truth, and that the law of science is not the law of the good but the law of the possible. We are now more than ever in an era of scientific domination—a period of unfettered technology that has and will produce many stunning discoveries that will benefit humankind, but also some that are likely to harm our global society. As philosopher-scientist Rene Dubos put it, "We must not ask where science and technology are taking us, but rather how we can manage science and technology so they can help us get where we want to go." Today, there is no evidence that we are following Dubos's warning and first figuring out where we want to go, rather than reacting sometime in the future to the consequences of scientific discoveries that lengthen life spans profoundly.

❿   For starters, we need biologists, ethicists, philosophers, demographers, theologians, historians, and others to become a lot more interested in the potential consequences of our astounding and accelerating technological achievements in the area of aging. I would submit that we need to create thoughtful guidelines. We need to initiate thorough discussions both inside and outside the scientific community. We need vigorous debate and analysis to define our goals, and we need to establish sensible regulations and laws consistent with those goals. If we do not do this, the consequences of the technological and scientific achievements that markedly lengthen adult life spans will be imposed upon us. That could be a very unpleasant scenario.

⑪   I suggest that we concentrate on conquering diseases and slowing the aging process so people can live out their maximum physiological life span. That will benefit individuals. It will also challenge the global society, as average life expectancy increases by 20 or 30 years, but we can cope with those changes with a reasonable amount of thought and planning.

⑫   On the other hand, we should approach changing the boundaries of aging with great caution, insisting on debate and requiring that any attempt to change the boundaries in human beings be kept experimental. Such attempts should be accompanied by rigorous long-term assessment that includes evaluating the quality of life of these very old persons.

⑬   In sum, my view is: Maximizing physiological life span—full speed ahead. Changing the boundaries of human aging—go slow, with extreme caution. The research into aging is spectacular, but the implications and potential consequences are so profound that we cannot afford to leave it solely in the hands of the scientific community. We had better figure out where we are going or we may find some unpleasant surprises when we get there. Let the debate begin.

Excerpted from *The Futurist*

Following an Argument

▶ The author does have a very definite position and recommendation with regard to extending life span. However he does not state it at the beginning of the article. Answer the following questions about each section in order to understand the article and to see how he develops his argument.

Introduction (Paragraphs 1–4)

1. What information is given about the lengthening of the human life span?

   a. Beginning of the 20th century: _____

   b. Beginning of the 21st century: _____

   c. Possible by the end of the 21st century: _____

2. What possible effect could this have on world population at the beginning of the next century?

   _____

3. What two issues need to be discussed in light of that possibility?

   a. _____

   b. _____

Body: Part One (Paragraphs 5–8)

4. What life span have demographers been using in projecting future world population?

   _____

5. Where does the author get information on what the world population would be if life span were to exceed that?

   _____

6. a. According to these projections, what is the best-case scenario if life span is extended to 120 years?

   _____

   b. How does this compare to the current world population (see paragraph 2)?

   _____

7. What do these projections not take into account?

   _____

8. In what way are population growth and global warming connected?

   _____

9. a. What does the author consider to be a reasonable stable world population?

   _____

   b. For that to happen, is it more important to control birthrate or the extension of life span?

   _____

   c. What does the author imply is the greatest threat to reaching this stable population?

   _____

Body: Part Two (Paragraphs 9–12)

10. What two approaches to science are presented in paragraph 9?

    a. _____

    b. _____

11. Which one is being followed today?

_____

12. Besides scientists, who does the author feel needs to be involved in the discussion on aging? Why?

_____

13. What does the author believe we should concentrate on?

_____

14. What needs to happen before changing the boundaries of aging?

_____

Conclusion (Paragraph 13)

15. What two recommendations does the author make?

    a. _____

    b. _____

16. Who should not be solely in charge of research into aging?

_____

Analyzing the Information

▶ Refer to your answers above as you discuss the following questions about the development of the author's argument.

1. Paragraphs 1–2 contain a lot of numbers. What effect do these numbers have on the reader?
2. How does the author make the reader feel that increased life span is a negative thing?
3. Which issue does he expand on in the first part of his argument?
4. Why do you think he is careful to say that the population projections could be on the high side?
5. What does the author focus on in the second part of his argument?
6. How does he make the reader feel about science and scientists?
7. In your own words, state the author's position.

_____

▶ Compare what you wrote to the prediction you made in "Previewing" (page 52).

◗ Vocabulary Building

Word Form

◗ **A** Study these five words and their forms. Then choose the correct form for each part of speech in the chart below. These words are commonly found in general and academic texts.

assess (v.)	assume (v.)	conceptualize (v.)	constitute (v.)	theorize (v.)
assessment (n.)	assuming	conceptual	constitution	theoretical
assessor (n.)	assumption	conception	constituent	theory
assessable (adj.)	assumable	concept		theoretically
		conceptually		

Verb	Noun	Adjective	Adverb
assume	1.	1.	
		2.	
conceptualize	1.	1.	1.
	2.		
constitute	1.		
	2.		
theorize	1.	1.	1.

◗ Compare your lists with a partner.

◗ **B** Write three sentences using words from the list. Use different parts of speech.

Cohesive Devices

◗ **A** **Repetition and Synonyms** One successful way to help the reader keep ideas and concepts together is to repeat key words or to use synonyms. Synonyms can be single words or groups of words.

Example: In "Second Thoughts on Extending Life Spans", the term *extending life span* is found in the title and it is referred to as *double average life span* (paragraph 1), *very old people* (paragraph 3), and *changing the boundaries of aging* (paragraph 3).

◗ Find at least two other terms similar in meaning to *extending life span* and note which paragraph you found them in.

1. _____

2. _____

▶ Find synonyms or similar terms for the following words:

1. fantastic (paragraph 1)   _____   _____

2. diminish (paragraph 3)   _____   _____

3. profound (paragraph 7)   _____   _____

▶ **B Reference Words** Another linking device that "glues" ideas together is the use of reference words. These can be pronouns or demonstrative adjectives.

> *Example (paragraph 2, page 00): They (pronoun) in **They** range from the administration of pharmacological agents, to the manipulation of genes that are responsible for either aging or prolonged survival refers to Several promising approaches to changing the boundaries of aging … in the previous sentence.*

▶ In the following examples, find what the referent is referring to. They are all taken from "Reversing Human Aging" on page 48.

1. Recent discoveries suggest that **this** does not have to happen. (paragraph 4)

   _____

2. … which would mean **they** would never shorten. (paragraph 4)

   _____

3. **That** idea has changed dramatically. (paragraph 6)

   _____

4. Already **such** genetic manipulation has increased by almost fifty percent the life span of flies. (paragraph 8)

   _____

5. **This** means simply a diet with fewer calories. (paragraph 9)

   _____

6. In **that** time, new discoveries could be made that would allow us to live even longer … (paragraph 10)

   _____

▶ Check your answers with a partner.

Expanding Your Language

Reading

▶ **A** Think about the following questions.

1. What role do older people such as grandparents, uncles, aunts, etc. play in society?
2. What role did they play in the past?
3. How involved should grandparents be in the upbringing of their grandchildren?

▶ Discuss your ideas with a partner or in small group.

▶ **B** Read the following article and highlight any information you find interesting.

▶ Use what you highlighted as well as your own experience to discuss the following:

1. What impact did the two grandmothers have on the author?
2. Do you agree that grandmothers can be more important than fathers? Why or why not?

Science Values Grandmothers

If you ask me, the very best thing about my great-grandmother was how much of the day she spent sitting in one place.

I realize this flies in the face of everything we now know about longevity and healthy lifestyles, but at the time all that concerned me was that Nanny's lap remain pretty much constantly open for business. The only problem was getting there before my sister or brother or cousins did. I own a snapshot of my young self and my cousin Patty, glaring at each other across the bow of my great-grandmother's lap, and I vividly remember the struggle captured in the photo. But most of my detailed memories of Nanny include nobody but her and me—me in sole possession of the expansive lap, her telling stories from her girlhood that later turned out not to have been strictly true but nevertheless were instrumental in teaching me how to live.

Nanny and Sissy—her daughter, my grandmother—shared a big, beautiful house where they ate formal lunches every weekday in the dining room, took things fairly easy in the afternoons, and had supper on TV trays in the living room, wearing their robes and slippers. Was that ever the life! If they were feeling especially energetic, we all piled in the car and went shopping for clothing or antiques.

By contrast Mama Ree, my other grandmother across town, was the picture of industry. Her tiny house was filled with things she had cooked and made, which she was always giving away to people we didn't even know. She started her mornings when it was still dark outside, after a quick breakfast of Coca-Cola on the porch swing, and she was always in the middle of some ambitious project for the hospital or her church, something that somebody else had messed up and that she was going to have to get straightened out. She always had plenty of time to talk to me, and sing me odd country songs that I wish I had written down, but she was usually managing two other tasks at the same time. I thought her life was pretty marvelous too.

Not that I planned to grow up to be like any of my grandmothers. I was going to be somebody.

By the time that arrogant dream came true, things had changed more for women in America than my grandmothers could have ever imagined. A new generation of women suddenly had a choice about whether they were going to spend the whole last third of their lives sitting around with a bunch of little kids. A lot of them decided they had better things to do and it seemed as if grandmothering as I had known it was becoming a thing of the past.

Recently however, scientists have turned their tools of inquiry toward the question of whether there is anything better for society than all those unappreciated hours spent minding the grandchildren. What they are finding is that grandmothers are more than hugs, cookies, and free baby-sitting. Indeed, according to some of the latest research, the presence of hands-on grandmothers might be an even more critical component than fathers when it comes to child survival and family stability.

The emerging theory is that women live to a ripe old age to make sure their grandchildren eat. Without children of their own to feed, they have time to provision grandchildren. By feeding the third generation, grandmothers ensure their grandchildren's survival and improve the chances that their own genes are passed on. Once again "altruism" and the bonds of kinship appear to provide human beings with a selective advantage.

Of course, because this is academia, controversies are already springing up over whether maternal grandmothers hold more sway than paternal ones, and why that might be. But I'm just heartened that society appears to be rediscovering the usefulness of spending long, idle afternoons, talking about nothing with the little ones. Maybe that means I'll get my turn to give back. I can't wait.

Adapted from Barbara Peters Smith, *Sarasota Herald Tribune,* and Sydney Callahan, *Commonweal*

Speaking

▶ **Oral Presentation** Prepare a five-minute talk about a grandparent or any older person that has had a strong impact on your life. Include information on the following:

- Description of the person
- Type of relationship you have/had with this person
- What you have learned from this person

▶ Present your information to a group of three or four others.

Writing

▶ **Reaction Writing** Write about your reaction to the idea of gene manipulation or taking drugs in order to extend life. How do you feel about having your genes modified to resemble cancer cells so that they keep multiplying forever? Would you be able to drink a "telomerase" cocktail every few years?

 *Online Study Center* For additional activities, go to the *Reading Matters* Online Study Center at *college.hmco.com/pic/wholeyfour2e.*

4 Body Shape

Chapter Openers

What's Your Opinion?

▶ Circle *A* if you agree or *D* if you disagree with the following statements. Be prepared to give reasons for your opinion.

1. A D   Being overweight is mainly a North American problem.

2. A D   Being overweight is a bigger problem among the poor than the rich.

3. A D   Being overweight is more of a problem for women than men.

4. A D   The main reason behind being overweight is a lack of self-control.

5. A D   The main reason behind being overweight is modernization.

6. A D   The main reason behind being overweight is food companies.

7. A D   The main reason behind being overweight is genetic makeup.

Gathering Background Information

▶ Use the short excerpts, charts, and graphs below as you answer these questions.

1. In which parts of the world is obesity a problem?
2. What seems to be the relationship between development and obesity?
3. What types of food lead to obesity?
4. What factors are involved other than food?
5. What types of solutions are people trying?

> **Reading Tip**

Information in **charts** and **graphs** is very helpful in terms of getting an **overall understanding** of a topic. ■

How We Became So Sedentary

☐ Walk to Work

▨ Take Public Transportation to Work

■ Drive to Work

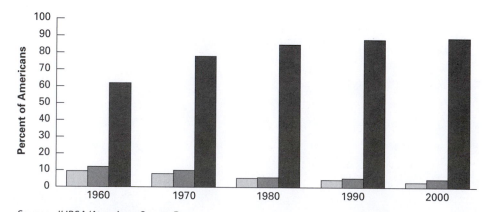

Source: IHRSA/American Sports Data

Overweight: A Widening Problem

North America States with the highest obesity rates—Mississippi and Alabama—are in the South. The more affluent and outdoorsy western states of Colorado and Utah have the lowest rates.

South America As Latin America becomes more developed, supermarkets stocked with processed foods have become the norm, rising from twenty percent of food retail during the 1980s to sixty percent in 2000.

Africa In some parts of Africa, obesity afflicts more children than malnutrition. In Tunisia, the urban population is shifting from traditional, healthy, whole-grain breads to white bread.

Asia In Shanghai, roads once filled with pedestrians and cyclists are now congested with cars. Kentucky Fried Chicken opened a drive-through restaurant in Beijing with more to come.

Europe Candy, fast food, and sweetened cereals account for more than half the food ads in ten European Union nations. In the United Kingdom, snack food consumption rose nearly twenty-five percent in five years.

Oceania Pacific islanders have always valued big physiques. Now their shift away from local foods to a high-fat, Western diet has made them among the world's fattest people.

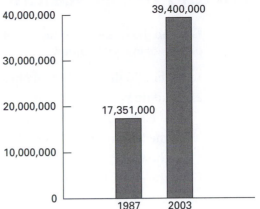

U.S. Health Club Membership

Source: IHRSA/American Sports Data

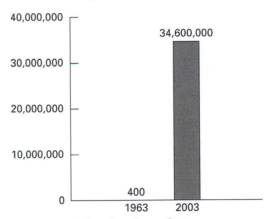

Weight Watchers Annual U.S. Attendance

Source: IHRSA/American Sports Data

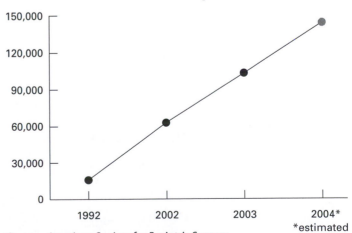

Estimated Number of Bariatric Surgeries in the United States

*estimated

Source: American Society for Bariatric Surgery

❰Exploring and Understanding Reading

Predicting

▶ Read the title and the subtitle of the next reading and discuss the following with a partner or in a small group.

1. When did the problem of obesity begin?
2. What do you know about:
   a. the kind of life our early ancestors led?
   b. the kind of food they ate?
   c. the way they obtained their food?
   d. the effect farming might have had on their way of life and eating habits?

Using the Introduction

 Reading Tip

Identifying the features of the introduction is an important critical reading skill. ■

An **effective introduction** has the following elements:

- **An attention grabber**—interesting information in the form of examples, statistics, surprising facts, etc., to make the reader want to continue reading
- **General information**—information that provides the reader with background about the topic
- Some of the **major ideas** to be discussed in the body of the article
- A **thesis statement**—one or two sentences (usually at the end of the introduction) that express the focus of the article as a whole

▶ **A** Read paragraphs 1–6 and identify each of these elements. Underline or bracket the section that contains each element and make a note in the margin. Use what you underlined or bracketed to complete the following.

1. Signs that Americans are overweight

   _____

   _____

2. Statistics on obesity

Who	Percent/Proportion
Overweight adults	2/3 of population
Overweight kids 6–19	_____
Almost overweight kids	_____
Overweight pets	_____

3. Cost of obesity

   Health: _____, _____, _____, _____, _____

   Financial: _____

4. What has been done to try to solve the problem?

_____

_____

▶ **B** Analyze the introduction by discussing the following with a partner.

1. Are the examples and statistics in paragraphs 1–4 interesting and relevant? In what way?
2. What point is the author making with this information?
3. What other kind of background information is given?
4. What point is the author making with this background information?
5. What are some of the major ideas that will be discussed?
6. Using the thesis statement and the major ideas, can you orally summarize what the article will be about?
7. Is this an effective introduction? Why or why not?

How We Grew So Big

Diet and lack of exercise are immediate causes—but our problem began in the Paleolithic era

❶   It's hardly news anymore that Americans are just too fat. If the endless parade of articles, TV specials, and fad diet books weren't proof enough or you missed the ominous warnings from the National Institutes of Health, the Centers for Disease Control and Prevention, and the American Heart Association, a quick look around the mall, the beach, or the crowd at any baseball game will leave no room for doubt: our individual weight problems have become a national crisis.

❷   Even so, the actual numbers are shocking. Fully two-thirds of U.S. adults are officially overweight, and about half of those have graduated to full-blown obesity. The rates for African Americans and Latinos are even higher. Among kids between six and nineteen years old, 15 percent, or one in six, are overweight, and another 15 percent are headed that way. Even our pets are pudgy: a depressing 25 percent of dogs and cats are heavier than they should be.

❸ And things haven't been moving in a promising direction. Just two decades ago, the incidence of overweight in adults was well under 50 percent, while the rate for kids was only a third what it is today. From 1996 to 2001, two million teenagers and young adults joined the ranks of the obese. People are clearly worried. A TIME/ABC News poll released in June 2004 shows that 58 percent of Americans would like to lose weight, nearly twice the percentage who felt that way in 1951. But only 27 percent say they are trying to slim down—and two-thirds of those aren't following any specific plan to do so.

❹ It wouldn't be such a big deal if the problem were simply aesthetic. But excess poundage takes a terrible toll on the human body, significantly increasing the risk of heart disease, high blood pressure, stroke, diabetes, infertility, gall-bladder disease, osteoarthritis, and many forms of cancer. The total medical tab for illnesses related to obesity is $117 billion a year—and climbing—according to the Surgeon General, and the *Journal of the American Medical Association* reported in March 2004 that poor diet and physical inactivity could soon overtake tobacco as the leading cause of preventable death in the United States. And again, Americans recognize the problem. In the TIME/ABC poll, they rated obesity alongside heart disease, cancer, AIDS, and drug abuse as among the nation's most pressing public health problems.

❺ So why is it happening? The obvious, almost trivial answer is that we eat too much high-calorie food and don't burn it off with enough exercise. If only we could change those habits, the problem would go away. But clearly it isn't that easy. Americans pour scores of billions of dollars every year into weight-loss products, health-club memberships, and liposuction and gastric bypass operations—100,000 of the latter in 2003 alone. Food and drug companies spend even more trying to find a magic food or drug that will melt the pounds away. Yet the nation's collective waistline just keeps growing.

❻ It's natural to try to find something to blame—fast food joints or food manufacturers or even ourselves for having too little willpower. But the ultimate reason for obesity may be rooted deep within our genes. Obedient to the firm laws of evolution, the human race adapted over millions of years to living in a world of scarcity, where it was beneficial to eat every good-tasting thing in sight when you could find it. While our physiology has stayed pretty much the same for the past 50,000 years or so, we humans have utterly transformed our environment.

❼ Over the past century especially, technology has almost completely removed physical exercise from the day-to-day lives of most Americans. At the same time, it has filled supermarket shelves with cheap, mass-produced, good-tasting food that is packed with calories. And finally, technology has allowed advertisers to deliver constant, virtually irresistible messages that say "Eat this now" to everyone old enough to watch TV. This artificial environment is most pervasive in the United States and other industrialized countries, and that's exactly where the fat crisis is most acute. When people move to the United States from poorer nations, their collective weight begins to rise. As developing areas like, for example, Southeast Asia and Latin America, catch up economically and the inhabitants adopt Western lifestyles, their problems with obesity catch up as well. By contrast, among people who still live in conditions most like those of our distant Stone Age ancestors—such as the Maku or the Yanomami of Brazil—there is virtually no obesity at all.

❽   And that's almost certainly the way it was during 99.9 percent of human evolution. For most of the seven million years or so since we parted ways with chimps, life has been very harsh. The average life expectancy was probably well under thirty. But that was mainly due to accidents, infections, traumatic childbirth, and unfortunate encounters with saber-toothed cats and other such predators. If a Cro-Magnon, say, could have gotten past these formidable obstacles, he might conceivably have lived into his sixties or even longer, with none of the obesity-related illnesses that plague modern Americans.

❾   Our earliest ancestors' diet was vegetarian. They probably ate much as their cousins the apes did, foraging for fruits, shoots, nuts, tubers, and whatever else grew in the forests and savannas of Africa. Because most wild plants are relatively low in calories, it took constant work just to stay alive. Fruits, full of natural sugars such as fructose and glucose, were an unusually concentrated source of energy, and the instinct to seek out and consume them evolved in many mammals long before humans ever arose. Fruit wasn't always available, but those who ate all they could whenever it was were more likely to survive and pass on their sweet tooth to their descendants.

❿   Our love affair with sugar—and also with salt, another crucial but not always available part of the diet—goes back millions of years. But humanity's appetite for animal fat and protein is probably more recent. It was some 2.5 million years ago that our hominid ancestors developed a taste for meat. The fossil record shows that the human brain became markedly bigger and more complex about the same time. And indeed, according to Katherine Milton, an anthropologist at the University of California, Berkeley, "the incorporation of animal matter into the diet played an absolutely essential role in human evolution."

⓫   For starters, meat provided a concentrated source of protein, vitamins, minerals, and fatty acids that helped our human ancestors grow taller. The first humans were the size of small chimps, but the bones of a *Homo ergaster* boy dating back about 1.5 million years suggest that he could have stood more than six feet tall as an adult. Besides building our bodies, says Emory University's Dr. S. Boyd Eaton, the fatty acids found in animal-based foods would have served as a powerful raw material for the growth of human brains.

⓬   Because it's so packed with nutrients, meat gave early humans a rest from constant feeding. Like lions and tigers, they didn't have to eat around the clock just to keep going. But more important, unlike the big cats, which rely mostly on strength and speed to bring down dinner, our ancestors depended on guile, organization, and the social and technological skills made possible by their increasingly complex brains. Those who were smartest about hunting—and about gathering the plant foods they ate as part of their omnivorous diets—tended to be better fed and healthier than the competition. They were thus more likely to pass along their genes.

⓭   The new appetite for meat didn't mean we lost our passion for sweets, though. As Berkeley's Milton points out, the brain's growth may have been facilitated by abundant animal protein, but the brain operates on glucose, the sugar that serves as the major fuel for cellular function. "The brain drinks glucose twenty-four hours a day," she says. The sugars in fruit and the carbohydrates in edible grains and tubers are particularly good sources of glucose.

⓮   The appetite for meat and sweets were essential to human survival, but they didn't lead to obesity for several reasons. For one thing, the wild game our ancestors ate was high in protein but very low in fat—only about 4 percent, compared with up to 36 percent in grain-fed supermarket beef. For another, our ancestors couldn't count on a steady supply of any particular food. Hunters might bring down a deer or a rabbit or nothing at all. Fruit might be in season, or it might not. A chunk of honeycomb might have as many calories as half a dozen Krispy Kreme doughnuts, but you might be able to get it once a year at best—and it wouldn't have the fat.

⓯   Beyond that, hunting and gathering took enormous physical work. Chasing wild animals with spears and clubs was a marathon undertaking—and then you had to chop up the catch and drag it miles back to camp. Climbing trees to find nuts and fruit was hard work, too. In essence, early humans ate what amounted to the best of the high-protein Atkins diet and the low-fat Ornish diet, and worked out almost nonstop. To get a sense of their endurance, cardiovascular fitness, musculature, and body fat, say evolutionary anthropologists, look at a modern marathon runner.

⓰   That was the condition of pretty much the entire human race when anatomically modern humans first arose, between 150,000 and 100,000 years ago, and things stayed that way until what some anthropologists have called humanity's worst mistake: the invention of agriculture. We now had a steady source of food, but there were downsides as well. For one thing, our ancestors began gathering in much larger population centers, where bacteria and viruses could fester. Small bands of hunter-gatherers can spread disease only so far, but the birth of cities made epidemics possible for the first time.

⓱   Nutritionally, the shift away from wild meat, fruits and vegetables to a diet mostly of cultivated grain robbed humans of many of the essential amino acids, vitamins, and minerals they had thrived on. Average life span increased, thanks to the greater abundance of food, but average height diminished. Skeletons also began to show a jump in calcium deficiency, anemia, bad teeth, and bacterial infections. Most meat that people ate came from domesticated animals, which have more fat than wild game. Livestock also supplied early farmers with milk products, which are full of artery-clogging butterfat. But obesity still wasn't a problem, because even with animals to help, physical exertion was built into just about everyone's life.

⓲   That remained the case practically up to the present. It's really only in the past 100 years that cars and other machinery have dramatically reduced the need for physical labor. And as exercise has vanished from everyday life, the technology of food production has become much more sophisticated. In the year 1700, Britain consumed 23,000 tons of sugar. That was about 7.5 lbs. of sugar per capita. The United States currently consumes more than 150 lbs. of sweetener per capita, nearly 50 percent of which is high-fructose corn syrup that is increasingly used as a sugar substitute. Farmers armed with powerful fertilizers and high-tech equipment are growing enormous quantities of corn and wheat, most of which is processed and refined to be tastier and more convenient but is less nutritious. They are raising vast herds of cattle whose meat is laden with the fat that makes it taste so good. They are producing milk, butter, and cheese in huge quantities, again full of the fat that humans crave.

⑲ And thanks to mass production, all that food is relatively cheap. It's also absurdly convenient. In many areas of the United States, if you had a craving for cookies a century ago, you had to fire up the woodstove and make the dough from scratch. If you wanted butter, you had to churn it. If you wanted a steak, you had to slaughter the cow.

Now you jump into the car and head for the nearest convenience store—or if that's too much effort, you pick up a phone or log on to the Internet and have the stuff delivered to your door.

⑳ Evolving during a time of scarcity, humans developed an instinctive desire for basic tastes—sweet, fat, salt—that they could never fully satisfy. As a result, says Rutgers University anthropologist Lionel Tiger, "we don't have a cut-off mechanism for eating. Our bodies tell us, 'Fat is good to eat but hard to get.'" The second half of that equation is no longer true, but the first remains a powerful drive. As a result, we have an obesity epidemic. Indeed, says Yale public-health expert Dr. David Katz, "today's kids may be the first generation in history whose life expectancy is projected to be less than that of their parents."

Michael D. Lemonick, *Time*. Copyright © 2004 Time, Inc. Reprinted with permission.

Chunking

▷ **1.** Starting with paragraph 7, read the first sentence of every paragraph.

2. Identify the main idea of each paragraph in the margin. (Use only two or three words.)

3. Check your main ideas with a partner. You can choose different words, but you should agree on the ideas.

4. Together, group these ideas into major ideas and list them below.

Paragraphs	Major Ideas
8–13	_____
14–15	_____
16–17	_____
7, 18–19	_____
20	_____

▷ Check your work with another pair of students. Compare these ideas with the ones you predicted from the introduction.

Skimming

▶ **Highlighting** Read the article and highlight the important information corresponding to the ideas you identified above. Use your highlighting to discuss the article with a partner. Take turns explaining the information. Together, answer the following questions.

1. When and why did humans develop a taste for sugar?
2. When and why did humans develop a taste for meat?
3. Why did this diet of meat and sweets not lead to obesity?
4. What were the advantages and disadvantages of the invention of agriculture?
5. What drastic changes have taken place in the last 100 years?
6. In your own words, explain what the author means when he says, "The second half of that equation is no longer true, but the first remains a powerful drive" (paragraph 20, line 8).

Reacting to the Information

▶ Discuss the following questions, using the information you have read as well as information of your own.

1. Which of the following statements do you think the author would agree with?
   a. Our genes are to blame for the obesity problem we have today.
   b. Technology is to blame for the obesity problem we have today.
   c. Food companies are to blame for the obesity problem we have today.
2. Which would you agree with and why?
3. In general, does the information presented above make you feel more or less responsible for your eating habits? Explain.
4. Are there any changes that you can think of making to your eating habits based on the above information?

Applying the Information

▶ Using ideas generated by "How We Grew So Big," think about who/what else is to blame for the obesity that exists today. Work with a partner and make a list of all the different entities that play a role in this problem. Together, discuss the ways in which each entity is responsible and what they can do.

Schools

_____

_____

_____

_____

Surveying   ▶ Survey the following article by reading the introduction (paragraphs 1–2), the first sentence of paragraphs 3–9, and the conclusion (paragraph 10). Use your surveying to discuss:

- the point the author is making about the food industry.
- the type of information she uses to support her point.

The Gorge-Yourself Environment

❶   From giant sodas to super size burgers to all-you-can-eat buffets, America's approach to food can be summed up by one word: Big. Plates are piled high, and few crumbs are left behind. Today's blueberry muffin could, in an earlier era, have fed a family of four.

❷   Traditionally, the prescription for shedding extra pounds has been a sensible diet and increased exercise. Losing weight has been viewed as a matter of personal responsibility, a private battle between dieters and their bathroom scales. But a growing number of studies suggests that, while willpower obviously plays a role, people do not gorge themselves solely because they lack self-control. Rather, social scientists are finding, a host of environmental factors— among them, portion size, price, advertising, the availability of food, and the number of food choices presented—can influence the amount the average person consumes.

❸   Price is a powerful influence. In a series of studies, researchers at the University of Minnesota have demonstrated that the relative cost of different products has an even more potent effect on food choice than nutritional labeling. Dr. Simone French, an associate professor of epidemiology, and her colleagues manipulated the prices of high-fat and low-fat snacks in vending machines at twelve high schools and twelve workplaces.

In some cases, the snacks were labeled to indicate their fat content. "The most interesting finding was that the price changes were whopping in effect," compared with the labels, Dr. French said. Dropping the price of the low-fat snacks by even a nickel spurred more sales. In contrast, orange stickers signaling low-fat content or cartoons promoting the low-fat alternatives had little influence over which snacks were more popular.

❹   Having more choices also appears to make people eat more. In one study, Dr. Barbara Rolls, whose laboratory at Pennsylvania State University has studied the effects of the environment on eating, found that research subjects ate more when offered sandwiches with four different fillings than they did when they were given sandwiches with their single favorite filling. In another study, participants served a four-course meal with meat, fruit, bread, and a pudding—foods with very different tastes, flavors and textures— ate 60 percent more food than those served an equivalent meal of only their favorite course.

❺   To anyone who has survived Christmas season at the office, it will come as no surprise that the availability of food has an effect as well. Dr. Wansink and his colleagues varied the placement of chocolate candy in work settings over three weeks. When the candy was in plain sight on workers' desks, they ate an average of nine pieces each. Storing the sweets in a desk drawer reduced consumption to six pieces. And chocolates lurking out of sight, a couple of yards from the desk, cut the number to three pieces per person.

❻ Researchers have long suspected that large portions encourage people to eat more, but studies have begun to confirm this suspicion only in the last several years. There is little question that the serving size of many foods has increased since McDonald's introduced its groundbreaking Big Mac in 1968. For her doctoral dissertation, Dr. Lisa Young, now an adjunct assistant professor in the department of nutrition, food studies, and public health at New York University, tracked portion sizes in national restaurant chains in foods like cakes, bread products, steaks, and sodas and in cookbook recipes from the 1970s to the late 1990s.

❼ The amount of food allotted for one person increased in virtually every category Dr. Young examined. French fries, hamburgers, and soda expanded to portions that were two to five times as great as they had been at the beginning of the period Dr. Young studied. Steaks, chocolate bars, and bread products grew markedly. Cookbooks specified fewer servings (and correspondingly larger portions) for the same recipe appearing in earlier editions. "Restaurants are using larger dinner plates, bakers are using larger muffin tins, pizzerias are using larger pans, and fast-food companies are using larger drink and French fry containers," Dr. Young wrote in a paper published last year in *The American Journal of Public Health*. Even the cup holders in automobiles have grown

larger to make room for giant drinks, Dr. Young noted. She and other experts think it is no coincidence that obesity began rising sharply in the United States at the same time that portion sizes started increasing.

❽ In cultures where people are thinner, portion sizes appear to be smaller. Take France, where the citizenry is leaner in body mass and where only 7.4 percent of the population is obese, a contrast to America, where 22.3 percent qualify. Examining similar restaurant meals and supermarket foods in Paris and Philadelphia, Dr. Rozin and colleagues at Penn found that the Parisian portions were significantly less hefty. Cookbook portions were also smaller. Even some items sold at McDonald's—the chicken sandwich, for example—are smaller than their American counterparts. "There is a disconnect between people's understanding of portions and the idea that a larger portion has more calories," said Dr. Marion Nestle, chairwoman of the NYU nutrition and food policy department and the author of "Food Politics: How the Food Industry Influences Nutrition and Health." The Double Gulp, a

❾   64-ounce soft drink sold by 7-Eleven, Dr. Nestle noted, has close to 800 calories, more than a third of many people's daily requirement, but she said people were often shocked to learn this.

And, as studies by Dr. Rolls, Dr. Wansink, and others suggest, faced with larger portions, people are likely to consume more, an effect, Dr. Rolls noted, that is not limited to people who are overweight. "Men or women, obese or lean, dieters, non-dieters, plate-cleaners, non-plate-cleaners—it's pretty much across the board," she said. In one demonstration of this, Dr. Rolls and her colleagues varied the portions of ziti served at an Italian restaurant, keeping the price for the dish the same but on some days increasing the serving by 50 percent. On the days of the increase, Dr. Rolls said, customers ate 45 percent more, and while diners rated the bigger portion size as a better value, they deemed both servings appropriate. The researchers have also shown that after downing large plates of food, people do not usually compensate by eating less at their next meal.

❿   Researchers have yet to cement the link between larger portions and a fatter public. But add up the studies, Dr. Rolls and other experts say, and it is clear Americans might have more success slimming down if plates were not quite so large and a tempting snack did not await on every corner. Obviously, people have responsibility for deciding what to eat and how much, Dr. Rolls said. "The problem is," she said, "they're not very good at it."

Reporting on Studies

The above article reports on four studies done to show what factors influence how much we eat. Any report on a study should include some or all of the following five important elements:

- Goal
- Subjects
- Method
- Results
- Conclusion

▶ Scan the article to locate the information for each of the following four studies.

Study One: Effect of Price
Study Two: Effect of Variety of Choice
Study Three: Effect of Availability
Study Four: Effect of Portion Size

▶ Highlight the information corresponding to the above elements. Use what you highlighted to discuss each study. (Note that not all the elements are included in each report.)

▶ Paired Readings

▶ In an ideal world, the calories we take in should equal the calories we use. But these days we're eating too much and not burning enough. The two articles that follow present two approaches to weight reduction. Choose one of the articles and find out what is being suggested.

❶ Fitness: The One Hour/Day Way

Previewing

▶ Read the title and subtitles as well as any information in boldface. What do you think the article is about? Write your ideas in note form.

1. _____

2. _____

3. _____

Skimming

> **Reading Tip**

Remember that **skimming** is **reading quickly** to get a **general idea** of what an article is about. ▪

▶ Quickly skim the article and answer the following questions.

1. Why are people counting the number of steps they take in a day?

_____

2. What would fitness experts like to see people do?

_____

3. What do most people need to do in addition to their daily routine to keep fit?

_____

Journey to Better Fitness Starts with 10,000 Steps

By Nancy Heilmich

Mark Fenton, editor at large of *Walking Magazine*, tries to walk at least 10,000 steps during the course of his day, often with his two young children.

Abby King, an exercise researcher at the Stanford School of Medicine in northern California, usually gets in 10,000 steps, but she has

to work at it by holding walking meetings with colleagues and scheduling other forms of activity.

Both experts are tracking the number of steps they take in a day partly out of curiosity, partly for scientific reasons.

Exercise scientists across the country, including researchers at Stanford and the Cooper Institute for Aerobics Research in Dallas, are having exercise study participants wear sophisticated pedometers on their waistbands to count the number of steps and miles they walk.

The researchers' goal is to get more people to walk at least 10,000 steps a day, which is equivalent to about five miles.

King says there's nothing magical about the 10,000-step goal. Researchers are investigating the number of steps people should take for fitness.

But scientists believe that people who walk that much are probably meeting the minimum public health guideline of accumulating thirty minutes of moderate activity most days of the week, says Michelle Edwards, a health educator at the Cooper Institute.

At present only about twenty-two percent of people are active enough to get the general health benefits.

Walking is the most popular form of physical activity, experts say. As many as eighty million people are recreational or casual walkers, including those who stroll occasionally. Of those, about fifteen million are serious fitness walkers, who walk for fitness at least two days a week, Fenton says.

Experts would like to see people become more active, but they are struggling for ways to motivate them.

A New Hook

Most people have heard the walking message, says cardiologist James Rippe, considered the father of the walking movement.

But people need motivation, and what these pedometers do is give walking some "pizzazz," says Rippe, author of the 1989 book *Complete Book of Fitness Walking*.

King says that counting steps seems to be one concrete way to implement the government recommendation of accumulating thirty minutes of moderate activity most days of the week, which gives people some of the benefits of physical activity.

Too many people misinterpreted the government guideline to mean they could shuffle around the house doing light domestic activities or light gardening, King says. "That's not going to be enough."

Practically speaking, moderate-intensity exercise means that your heart rate and breathing will be faster than during lighter activities, King says.

One simple rule of thumb for walking briskly, Rippe says, is to follow Harry Truman's brisk walking style, which he described as "walking as though I have someplace to go."

But plenty of people move through the day without doing that. Many people who work in offices walk 3,000 to 5,000 steps a day, says Fenton, a former member of the U.S. national race-walking team.

At the end of the day, this group would have to walk another 5,000 to 7,000 steps, or roughly two to three miles, to reach the 10,000-step goal. In other words, in addition to their daily activity, most people need to get out and do at least a thirty-minute brisk walk.

Pedometers

To count steps, a number of pedometers are on the market, some more sophisticated than others.

Edwards says the Cooper Institute has used Digi-Walkers in two studies and is using them in a third study. Exercisers are motivated by them, she says.

Fenton says that when he started wearing a pedometer and didn't accumulate 10,000 steps by the end of the day, he was ticked off at himself and went out and walked until he had.

He says that wearing it motivates him to take the stairs instead of the elevator, do errands on foot, and walk to a farther subway stop.

Setting Goals

But how hard is it to walk 10,000 steps a day, and is it really enough?

For sedentary people, it's challenging, King says. Scientists initially work them up to 5,000 and 6,000 steps.

"If they jump directly to 10,000 steps a day, they are going to have injuries, strains, and muscle soreness from overuse," King says.

The 10,000-step goal is probably enough to get many of the health benefits of walking, Fenton says. Those who want to lose weight, get greater health gains, or become more cardiovascularly fit probably need to walk more at a higher intensity.

Fenton offers these guidelines for walkers:

- An out-of-shape person who is just getting into a walking program should build up to walking thirty minutes a day at 3 to 4 mph. That total would provide the health benefit of physical activity.

- A person who wants to lose weight should walk at 3.5 to 4.5 mph, Fenton says. "The faster you walk, the more calories you burn per minute. Walk every day for a minimum of thirty minutes. Walk at least forty-five to sixty minutes, three or four days a week."

- Those who want cardiovascular fitness should aim for 4 to 5 mph or faster if their fitness improves enough. Their goal should be two or three heavy-breathing, sweat-producing, twenty-to-forty-minute walks a week.

USA Today

Scanning for Specific Information

⮞ Reexamine the reading to find the answers to these questions. Write your answers in note form.

1. What are pedometers and what are two reasons they are important for walkers to use?

   _____

2. What is the important health reason that scientists want people to walk 10,000 steps?

   _____

3. What does "moderate-intensity exercise" mean?

   _____

4. What recommendation does Abby King make to sedentary people who are beginning to exercise?

   _____

5. What important guidelines does Mark Fenton offer people who

   a. are out of shape? _____

   b. want to lose weight? _____

   c. want cardiovascular fitness? _____

▶ Compare your answers with those of your partner. Try to agree on the same answers. Look back at the reading if you disagree.

Recapping the Information

> **Reading Tip**

Remember, highlighting is a useful strategy for finding and remembering important facts and ideas you read. ▪

▶ **A** **Highlighting** Highlight the facts you read about walking that relate to these ideas:

1. The goal of the researchers' work
2. The 10,000 step program, its purposes and benefits
3. The role of the pedometer and how it works
4. How the 10,000 step program works for different types of people

▶ **B** Working with a partner who read the *same article*, compare what you highlighted. Discuss whether you highlighted too much or too little. Add any highlighting you need to.

▶ **C** Using only what you highlighted, take turns telling each other the important information in the article. Make sure you explain the information as clearly and completely as you can, using your own words when you need to.

Reacting to the Information

▶ Discuss these questions with a partner. Explain your ideas as completely as possible.

1. According to the article, only twenty-two percent of people are active enough to get health benefits from walking. Why do you think so few people are active?
2. Do you agree that the pedometer is a good motivation technique? Why or why not?
3. Would you incorporate this type of walking into your daily routine? Why or why not?

❷ Fitness: The Six Minutes/Day Way

Previewing

▷ Read the titles and subtitles as well as any information in boldface. What do you think the article is about? Write your ideas in note form.

1. _____

2. _____

3. _____

Skimming

 Reading Tip

Remember that **skimming** is **reading quickly** to get a **general idea** of what an article is about. ■

▷ Quickly skim the article and answer the following questions.

1. What reason do people give for not exercising?

_____

2. What price is Britain paying for an unfit society?

_____

_____

3. What should people do before they do any kind of high-intensity exercise?

_____

Short Intensive Workouts are Just as Effective as Long Sessions

By Peter Zimonjic

Just six minutes of intense exercise a week does as much to improve a person's fitness as a regime of six hours, according to a study.

Moderately healthy men and women could cut their workouts from two hours a day, three times a week, to just two minutes a day and still achieve the same results, claim medical researchers.

The two-minute workout requires cycling furiously on a stationary bike in four 30-second bursts. Professor Martin Gibala, the author of the study, said, "The whole excuse that 'I don't have enough time to exercise' is directly challenged by these findings. This has the potential to change the way we think about keeping fit."

"We have shown that a person can get the same benefits in fitness and health in a much shorter period if they are willing to endure the discomfort of high-intensity activity."

No Difference

The study, published in this month's *Journal of Applied Physiology*, involved twenty-three men and women aged between 25 and 35 who were tested to see how long it took them to cycle 18.6 miles. The subjects, who all did some form of regular moderate exercise, were then given varying exercise programs three times a week.

The first group cycled for two hours a day at a moderate pace. The second group biked harder for 10 minutes a day in 60-second bursts. The last group cycled at an intense sprint for two minutes in 30-second bursts, with four minutes of rest in between each sprint.

At the end of the two weeks, each of the three groups was asked to repeat the 18.6-mile cycling test. Every subject was found to have improved to the same degree. Further tests showed that the rate at which the subjects' muscles were able to absorb oxygen also improved to the same level.

The key findings in terms of overall health showed that the two-minute workout produced the same muscle enzymes—essential for the prevention of type 2 diabetes—as riding ten times as long. That is significant in the light of growing levels of unfitness. Obesity has trebled in Britain since 1982, leading to a rise in type 2 diabetes. The Department of Health estimates that unfit Britons cost the country £2 billion a year in the treatment of heart disease and other related illnesses.

Professor Gibala, of the health department of McMaster University in Ontario, Canada, said, "We thought there would be benefits but we did not expect them to be this obvious. It shows how effective short, intense exercise can be."

Tough Going

The Sunday Telegraph put the new methods to the test by asking three employees of the Reebok Sports Club in Canary Wharf, London, to compare the workouts.

Angie Du Plessis, 35, who rode for ten minutes in 60-second sprints, said, "It felt like I had just done an hour's run. It was more than I was used to but I feel more exhilarated because it was so intense. To be honest, it was not much fun and unless I was really pressed for time I would not change my exercise regime."

Chris Mackie, 23, tried the two minutes of cycling in 30-second super-bursts and found he was exhausted very quickly. He said, "I overworked myself well beyond what I would normally do. I can't believe it. All my energy drained so quickly. It was torture, really, but I was amazed at how short a time it took me to tire myself out completely. I didn't enjoy it but it felt like it worked."

Jules Wall, 27, who rode for forty-five minutes at a moderate pace, insisted that she had also received a good workout. She said, "I am not sure I would want to go through the pain of 30-second sprints."

Caution

Our guinea pigs were all quite fit. The authors of the study caution that anyone considering taking up cycling or running at breakneck speeds should first consult their doctor or a fitness instructor.

David Crottie, a fitness expert for Reebok, was confident that the program would be effective for anyone with the correct preparation: "We have never tried it to this intensity before but I agree with the findings. Most people do not want to do it because it is so uncomfortable, but for those willing to endure the intensity it would work."

Jonathan Edwards, the Olympic triple-jump gold medalist, said, "Everyone seems to be short of time. If people could get fit in a much quicker period, I am sure that would encourage more people to do it. Going for a 40-minute run is not for everybody. The idea of going and doing a short intense workout would appeal to people and help them to embrace a healthier lifestyle."

The Sunday Telegraph

Scanning for Specific Information

◗ Reexamine the reading to find the answers to these questions. Write your answers in note form.

1. What has a recent study shown about the amount of exercise required?

   _____

2. What were the characteristics of the subjects of the study?

   _____

3. How was the effect of intense exercise tested?

   _____

4. What benefits are there to this kind of exercise?

   _____

5. How did the three Reebok Sports Club employees react to this kind of exercise?

   a. _____

   b. _____

   c. _____

6. What should people do before they start intense exercise?

   _____

7. Who would this type of exercise appeal to?

   _____

◗ Compare your answers with those of your partner. Try to agree on the same answers. Look back at the reading if you disagree.

Recapping the Information

Remember, highlighting is a useful strategy for finding and remembering important facts and ideas you read. ▪

A Highlighting Highlight the facts you read about intense exercise that relate to these ideas:

1. Definition of intense exercise
2. How the study was carried out
3. The findings of the study
4. People's reactions to the idea of intense exercise

B Working with a partner who read the *same article*, compare what you highlighted. Discuss whether you highlighted too much or too little. Add any highlighting you need to.

C Using only what you highlighted, take turns telling each other the important information in the article. Make sure you explain the information as clearly and completely as you can, using your own words when you need to.

Reacting to the Information

Discuss these questions with a partner. Explain your ideas as completely as possible.

1. What type of exercise do you do and how often?
2. If you wanted to include more exercise in your life, how difficult or easy would it be?
3. Which of the three Reebok Sports Club employees would you agree with? Why?

▶ Comparing the Readings

Retelling the Information

▶ Work with a partner who read a different article. Together, use what you highlighted and take turns explaining the information you read. Explain the ideas clearly in your own words.

Encourage your partner to ask questions or write some of the important facts you explain.

After you have both explained your information, discuss the questions in "Reacting to the Information."

Comparing the Information

▶ **A** Work with a partner who read a different article. Compare both activities by completing the chart below.

	Walking	Intense Activity
Amount per day		
Frequency		
Benefits		
Drawbacks		

▶ **B** Discuss the following questions with your partner. Explain your ideas as completely as possible.

1. Which of the above activities do you prefer? Why?
2. Which do you think can be maintained the longest? Why?

❶Vocabulary Building

Word Form   ▶ **A** Study these five words and their forms. Then choose the correct form for each part of speech in the chart below. These words are commonly found in general and academic texts.

exceed (v.)	adapt (v.)	evolve (v.)	facilitate (v.)	restrict (n.)
excess (n.)	adapted	evolved	facile	restricted
excessive (adj.)	adaptability	evolving	facility	restriction
excessively (adv.)	adaptation	evolution		restrictively

Verb	Noun	Adjective	Adverb
adapt	1. 2.	1.	
evolve	1.	1. 2.	
facilitate	1.	1.	
restrict	1.	1.	1.

▶ Compare your list with a partner.

▶ **B** Write three sentences using words from the list. Use different parts of speech.

Vocabulary in Context   ▶ **A** **Inferring Meaning** Choose the statement that best expresses what the writer meant by each of the following sentences.

1. "Everyone who doesn't exercise knows they should. And everyone who smokes knows they shouldn't."
   a. People don't know whether they should exercise and smoke or not.
   b. People have a hard time following good advice.
   c. People aren't sure what advice to follow.
2. Using a pedometer gives walking some "pizzazz."
   a. People will use a pedometer on a walk because it makes it easier to count the steps.
   b. People will use a pedometer on a walk because it makes the walk easier to do.
   c. People will use a pedometer on a walk because it is trendy and more motivating.

3. I'm "walking as though I have someplace to go."
   a. I'm deliberately walking quickly.
   b. I have to hurry to get to where I'm going.
   c. I don't have anywhere to go, so I'll take a nice leisurely walk.

4. "One in five [children] has a cholesterol level that is setting her or him up for future heart disease."
   a. Bad childhood eating habits increase the chances of disease in adulthood.
   b. Bad childhood eating habits decrease the chances of disease in adulthood.
   c. Bad childhood eating habits have no effect on the chances of disease in adulthood.

5. "We've internalized these larger portion sizes and, frankly, it's very hard to downsize."
   a. Once you've accepted larger portion sizes, it's hard to refuse them.
   b. Once you've gotten used to larger portion sizes, it's hard to reduce consuming that amount.
   c. Once you've reduced the amount you take, it's easier to get used to larger portion sizes.

▶ **B** Insert the following words back into the sentences where they fit best.

only   predictably   simply   unfortunately   yet

1. People _____ like to eat what tastes good to them.

2. _____, what tastes good to most Americans is not exactly good for them.

3. _____ about 15 percent of Americans now consume the recommended minimum of five servings a day of fruits and vegetables.

4. _____, the message nutrition specialists advocate is moderation, not elimination.

5. And, _____, as Americans choose pleasure over nutrition, we are eating more of both sugar and fat.

▶ Check your answers with a partner or with your teacher.

Using Quotes

An effective way to support a point or idea is to use a quote made by someone of authority or an expert in the field, e.g., scientists, researchers, politicians, company spokespeople, etc.

▶ **A** Identify the point that is being supported by each quotation. Then identify the source of the quote. The first one has been done as an example.

1. "The brain drinks glucose twenty-four hours a day" (How We Grew So Big, paragraph 13)

   The brain needs a lot of sugar in order to function.

   Source: Katherine Milton, anthropologist at the University of California, Berkeley

2. "We don't have a cut-off mechanism for eating. Our bodies tell us, 'Fat is good to eat but hard to get.'" (How We Grew So Big, paragraph 20)

   _____

   Source: _____

3. "Today's kids may be the first generation in history whose life expectancy is projected to be less than that of their parents." (How We Grew So Big, paragraph 20)

   _____

   Source: _____

4. "Restaurants are using larger dinner plates, bakers are using larger muffin tins, pizzerias are using larger pans, and fast-food companies are using larger drink and French fry containers." (The Gorge-Yourself Environment, paragraph 7)

   _____

   Source: _____

5. "There is a disconnect between people's understanding of portions and the idea that a larger portion has more calories." (The Gorge-Yourself Environment, paragraph 8)

   _____

   Source: _____

6. "The problem is, they're not very good at it." (The Gorge-Yourself Environment, paragraph 10)

   _____

   Source: _____

▶ Check your answers with a partner or with your teacher.

◑ **B** A technique that writers use in order to make more impact is to attribute characteristics that are normally used in one context to a completely different context.

Example: *"Fully two-thirds of U.S adults are officially overweight and about half of those have **graduated** to full-blown obesity."* Graduate normally means to finish school or college. Here it is used to mean that some of those people that were only overweight have become obese.

◑ In the following exercise, give the meaning of the boldface word in its present usage and what it normally means. Check against a dictionary if necessary.

1. But the ultimate reason for obesity may be **rooted** deep in our genes.

   _____   _____

2. Our **love affair** with sugar … goes back millions of years.

   _____   _____

3. The brain **drinks** glucose twenty-four hours a day.

   _____   _____

4. Farmers **armed** with powerful fertilizers … are growing enormous quantities of corn and wheat….

   _____   _____

5. Losing weight has been viewed as a matter of personal responsibility, a private **battle** between dieters and their bathroom scales.

   _____   _____

6. Researchers have yet to **cement** the link between larger portions and a fatter public.

   _____   _____

◑ Check your answers with a partner or with your teacher.

⬤ Expanding Your Language

Reading

▷ **A** There are many who believe that the food industry is one of the main reasons for the obesity epidemic. The author of the following article feels that we should go one step further.

Read the article and find information to discuss the following questions.

1. Who does he compare the food industry to?
2. What does he feel should be done about the food industry?
3. What reasons does he give?
4. Do you agree with him? Why or why not?

It's Time to Fight Big Food

War on fat. Battle against obesity can be won if we attack Big Food like Big Tobacco.

It's been called an epidemic—killing 440,000 North Americans a year, twenty times more deaths than from AIDS. And last month the U.S. Centers for Medicare and Medicaid Service finally lifted the rule against labeling it an illness. It is obesity.

Obesity-related deaths are predicted soon to surpass those from tobacco, and by 2020, according to the Rand Corp., one out of five dollars spent for health in the United States will go toward treating its consequences.

Let's not be confused. Obesity isn't like MS or cancer—the cause lies in front of our noses. Our high-fat, salty, sugar-laden, processed, grain-fed meat-centered diet is, literally, killing us.

Many argue that North Americans select this diet, but would a species really choose to eat what destroys it? If so, we're an evolutionary first. More likely, we are being robbed of choice.

The epidemic of obesity stems from a market ideology that sees everything as a commodity, even life's essentials. Controlled by an industry obsessed by profit, food has become a branded and highly advertised "food product." And what most fattens a company's bottom line—processed foods with additives like high fructose corn syrup—is unfortunately what fattens us.

Nutritionists now understand, for example, that high fructose corn syrup—which currently accounts for a fifth of the average youngster's daily calories—can directly contribute to obesity. Sweetened with high fructose corn syrup, one extra soft drink a day means a 60 percent greater chance of becoming obese, according to research on children.

Food companies rank second only to the auto industry in spending on ads. They take advantage of our species' weak satiation mechanism (meaning it's hard to stop!) for sugar and fat, as well as our appetite's vulnerability to the power of suggestion. The sight of food in ads whets our appetites, with children especially vulnerable, making them industry's target. A child is now exposed to 40,000 ads a year on TV alone, most of it promoting candy, soda, and snacks, according to the Kaiser Family Foundation.

Real choice means decisions based on information not manipulated by those with a vested interest in hooking us. Real choice also requires access to healthy food. Yet millions of inner-city Americans find corner stores filled with junk snacks, but no supermarkets. Little wonder, reports the U.S. Department of Health and Human Services, low-income women are 50 percent more likely to be overweight than wealthier women.

Years ago, we caught on that tobacco smoking was deadly, and moved to check an industry profiting from our demise. We legislated—getting cigarettes out of airplanes, schools, offices, television, and, as much as possible, the hands of children. We educated—producing public information campaigns about the harms of smoking. We began to protect ourselves.

We should, and can, do the same with food. Obesity is one disease for which we do not have to wait for a cure; we can act now to regain real choice. With deaths mounting, the stakes couldn't be higher.

Frances Moore Lappe and Anna Lappe, *Knight Ridder News Service*

Speaking

▷ **Debating the Issue** Several diets have been proposed to counteract overweight. Some of these are:

- the Atkins diet.
- the South Beach diet.
- the Zone.
- the Ornish diet.

▷ Choose one of these diets, or any other that you are interested in, and search the Internet or your local library for information on what the diet is and what its strengths and weaknesses are.

▷ **1.** Make notes on each idea.
   2. Practice making a three-minute report from your notes.
   3. Record your report
   4. Give the tape or audio CD to your teacher for feedback.
   5. Present your information to someone who prepared a report on a different diet.

Writing

▶ **A** **Report Writing** Use the notes from your oral presentation to write a three-paragraph report on the diet you selected.

▶ **B** **Reaction Writing** Using the information that you learned from this chapter, write about any changes that you should or could make in order to improve your present lifestyle.

❯Read On: Taking It Further

Finding More Information

Remember to write your reading journal and vocabulary log entries. ▪

▶ Do some research to find information on issues related to what was discussed in this unit. For example, you could look for information on the health effects of other lifestyle choices, such as smoking or drinking. Or you could find out whether other countries have an obesity problem and how they are dealing with it.

Discuss what you would like to read with others in a small group. Select a topic that your partner or partners will also read about. Identify some key words that you could use in your search for material—either online or at your local library.

Make a schedule for the times when you can get together to discuss what you have read. You may also want to present what you have found to your fellow students.

 For additional activities, go to the *Reading Matters* Online Study Center at *college.hmco.com/pic/wholeyfour2e.*

UNIT 3

The Environment

The world is sacred. You cannot improve it. If you try to change it, you will ruin it. If you try to help it, you will destroy it.

—*Lao Tzu*

Introducing the Topic

Man has been trying to dominate nature for as long as he has existed on this earth. But at no time has this been more extensive than now. We have dams to control rivers and planes to fight forest fires. Should we be doing this or have we gone too far? Chapter 5 explores man's role in the occurrence of "natural" disasters. Do we cause them? Is it a good idea to try to prevent them? Or does that just make things worse? Chapter 6 looks at the modern day phenomenon of megacities and what life is like in them.

Points of Interest

Quotes

▶ Read the following quotes and explain to a partner what you think the message of each is.

1. All the rivers flow into the sea, yet the sea is not full. —Ecclesiastes 1:37
2. Dakota children understand that we are of the soil and the soil is of us, that we love the birds and beasts that grew with us on this soil. —Luther Standing Bear, *My People the Sioux*
3. And with water we have made all things. —*The Koran*, Sura XXI:30
4. By the sweat of your brow you will eat your food until you return to the ground, since from it you were taken; for dust you are and to dust you will return. —Genesis 3:10

A Point of View

▶ In 1854, the "Great White Chief" in Washington D.C. (the President of the United States) made an offer of $150,000 for two million acres of Indian land and promised a reservation for the Indian people. Seattle, chief of the Suquamish and other Indian tribes around Washington State's Puget Sound (and after whom the city of Seattle is named), delivered what is considered to be one of the most beautiful and profound environmental statements ever made. He began by saying:

> "The Earth is precious. How can you buy or sell the sky, the warmth of the land? The idea is strange to us. If we do not own the freshness of the air and the sparkle of the water, how can you buy them?"

▶ Discuss the following questions.

1. What do you think Chief Seattle meant by "The idea is strange to us"?
2. What two opposing views of the environment are presented here?

5 Natural Disasters

Chapter Openers

Environment Questionnaire

▶ Which of the following are harmful (H)? Which are beneficial (B)? Which can be both? Circle *H* or *B* or both for each item below and give examples to support your answers.

1. H   B   Forest fire
2. H   B   Earthquake
3. H   B   Flood
4. H   B   Volcano
5. H   B   Landslide
6. H   B   Hurricane
7. H   B   Drought

▶ Discuss your ideas with a partner or in a small group and answer the following questions.

1. Which of the above do we try to control?
2. How successful are we?
3. Which do you consider to be manmade? natural?

Defining the Terms

▶ A lot of the terms that you will come across in this chapter are specific to the environment and what we do to it. Work in a small group. Brainstorm what you think each term means and agree on a brief definition.

1. forest degradation _____

2. ecosystem _____

3. wetland _____

4. aquifer _____

5. watershed _____

6. levee _____

7. logging _____

▶ Check your answers with your teacher or a dictionary.

Exploring and Understanding Reading

Predicting

▶ Read the title of the article that follows and answer the questions below.

1. What do you think the author will try to explain in this article?
2. Which natural disasters do you think the author will discuss?
3. In what way could humans be making these disasters worse?

Examining the Introduction

 Reading Tip

A **thesis statement** is one or two sentences (usually at the end of the introduction) that **expresses** the **focus** of the **article** as a **whole.** ■

▶ **A Identify the Introduction** Start reading the article. Stop when you think you have reached the thesis (the end of the introduction). Underline the thesis. Compare what you identified as the thesis with a partner.

▶ **B Analyze the Introduction** Based on the introduction, discuss the following with a partner or in a small group.

1. What do the two examples in paragraphs 1–2 show?
2. Which other parts of the world besides Venezuela and Central America are affected?
3. What information is given to show the huge human and financial cost?
4. Give two main reasons for why this cost is so high.
5. What are some examples of:
   a. "ecologically destructive practices" (paragraph 4)?
   b. "putting people in harm's way" (paragraph 4)?
6. What can be done to reduce the effect of natural disasters?
7. Using the thesis statement and the major ideas, orally summarize what the article will be about.
8. Does this match the predictions that you made from the title?
9. Is this an effective introduction? Why or why not?

Are Humans to Blame for Exacerbating Many Natural Disasters?

❶   A few years ago, almost 20,000,000 cubic yards of mud, trees, and boulders came barreling down from Venezuela's coastal mountain range onto the densely populated and heavily urbanized ribbon of land that hugs the Caribbean coast, killing around 30,000 people and causing about $2,000,000,000 in damages. Two years worth of rain had fallen in just two days, dislodging soil already saturated by two weeks of heavy La Niña rains. Although floods and landslides are common in this area, the devastation unearthed far more than boulders and bare soil. It exposed the perils of development in risky locations as well as inadequate disaster planning and response.

❷   Just a year earlier, Hurricane Mitch had slammed into Central America, pummeling Honduras, Nicaragua, El Salvador, and Guatemala for more than a week. As the powerful storm hung over the region, it dumped approximately eighty inches of rain. By the time it turned back out to sea, about 10,000 people had died, making it the deadliest hurricane in 200 years. Conservative estimates place its damage to the region at around $8,500,000,000— higher than the combined gross domestic product (GDP) of Honduras and Nicaragua, the two nations hardest hit. The storm set back development in the region by decades.

❸   Venezuela and Central America were not the only regions to experience such devastation in recent years. In fact, the 1990s set a record for disasters worldwide. During the decade, more than $608,000,000,000 in economic losses were chalked up to natural catastrophes, an amount greater than during the previous four decades combined. In 1998–1999, more than 120,000 people were killed and millions were displaced from their homes. In India, 10,000 lost their lives in a 1998 cyclone in Gujarat; the following year, as many as 50,000 died when a "supercyclone" hit Orissa. Vast forest fires raged out of control in Brazil, Indonesia, and Siberia. Back-to-back earthquakes in El Salvador in January 2001 erased much of the reconstruction efforts made there in the two years since Hurricane Mitch. That same month, powerful earthquakes struck Gujarat, India, and major floods submerged much of Mozambique for the second year in a row.

❹   Around the planet, a growing share of the devastation triggered by natural disasters stems from ecologically destructive practices and from putting people in harm's way. Many ecosystems have been worn down to the point where they are no longer resilient or able to withstand natural disturbances, setting the stage for "unnatural disasters"— those made more frequent or more severe due to human actions. By degrading forests, engineering rivers, filling in wetlands, and destabilizing the climate, we are unraveling the strands of a complex ecological safety net. We are beginning to understand just how valuable that safety net is.

❺   The enormous expansion of the human population and the built-up environment in the 20th and 21st centuries means that more people and economic activities are vulnerable. The migration of people to cities and coasts increases our vulnerability to the full array of natural hazards. The explosive growth of shantytowns in the cities of the developing world puts untold numbers of people at risk. These human-exacerbated disasters often take their heaviest toll on those who can least afford it—the poor.

6 To date, much of the response to disasters has focused on improving weather predictions before the events and providing cleanup and humanitarian relief afterward, both of which have helped save many lives. Yet, much more can be done. On average, $1 invested in mitigation can save $7 in disaster recovery costs, and mitigation measures are far more effective when integrated into sustainable development efforts.

7 Meanwhile, nature provides many valuable services to curb natural disasters. Healthy and resilient ecosystems are shock absorbers that protect against coastal storms and sponges that soak up floodwaters, for instance. We should take advantage of these free services, rather than undermine them. In order to stem the ever-rising social and economic costs of disasters, we need to focus on how to mitigate them by understanding our culpability, taking steps to reduce our vulnerability, and managing our impacts on nature more wisely.

8 There is an important distinction between natural and unnatural disasters. Many ecosystems and species are adapted to natural disturbance; indeed, some are necessary to maintain their health and vitality, even their continued existence. Numerous forests and grasslands, for example, depend on periodic natural fires to burn off dead vegetation, restore soil fertility, and release seeds.

9 Likewise, river systems need periodic flooding, and plants and animals across the landscape have adapted to this regime. Fish use the flood plain as a breeding ground and nursery for their young. Many plants need floods to germinate and absorb newly available dissolved nutrients. Migratory birds also rely on the bounty that floods bring. Soils, too, benefit from the regular addition of nutrients and organic matter, and underground aquifers are refilled as floodwaters are slowly absorbed into the ground. By disrupting the natural flooding regime, we cut off the interactions between a river and its surrounding landscape that make them more diverse and productive. Natural flooding is so beneficial that some of the biggest fish and crop harvests come the year after a flood. Little wonder that flood plains and deltas have attracted human settlement for millennia and have been the cradles of civilizations.

10 Just as not every natural disturbance is a disaster, not every disaster is completely natural. We have altered many natural systems so dramatically that their ability to bounce back from disturbance has been greatly diminished. Deforestation damages watersheds, contributes to climate change, and raises the risk of fires. Destruction of coastal areas eliminates nature's shock absorbers for coastal storms. Such human-made changes end up making naturally vulnerable areas—such as hillsides, rivers, coastal zones, and low-lying islands—even more vulnerable to extreme weather events.

11 Droughts, and the famines that often follow, may be the most widely understood—if underreported—examples of unnatural disasters. They are triggered partly by global climate variability (both natural and human-induced) and partly by resource mismanagement such as deforestation, overgrazing, and the over-tapping of rivers and wells for irrigation. Droughts are not as well reported as storms and floods, nor are they usually included in disaster-related financial loss data. Yet, they affect major portions of Africa and Asia and are projected to continue worsening in the coming years as a result of climate change. According to data prepared by the Center for Research on the Epidemiology of Disasters and published in the *World Disasters Report*, droughts and famines accounted for forty-two percent of disaster-related deaths between 1991 and 2000.

⓬   China's Yangtze River dramatically shows the consequences of the loss of healthy ecosystems. Flooding in 1998 caused more than 4,000 deaths, affected 223,000,000 people, inundated 61,000,000 acres of cropland, and cost well over $36,000,000,000. Heavy summer rains are common in southern and central China, and flooding often results. In 1998, however, as the floodwater continued to rise, it became clear that other factors besides heavy rains were at play. One influence was the extensive deforestation that had left many steep hillsides bare. In the past few decades, eighty-five percent of the forest cover in the Yangtze basin has been cleared by logging and agriculture. The loss of forests, which normally intercept rainfall and allow it to be absorbed by the soil, permitted water to rush across the land, carrying valuable topsoil with it. As the runoff raced across the denuded landscape, it caused floods.

⓭   In addition, the Yangtze's natural flood controls had been undermined by numerous dams and levees, and a large proportion of the basin's wetlands and lakes, which usually act as natural sponges, had been filled in or drained. The areas previously left open to give floodwaters a place to go have filled instead with waves of human settlements. All these changes reduced the capacity of the Yangtze's watershed to absorb rain and greatly increased the speed and severity of the resulting runoff.

⓮   Flooding and landslides following deforestation are not limited to developing countries. In the U.S. Pacific Northwest, where hundreds of landslides occur annually, a study found that ninety-four percent of them originated from clearing trees and logging roads. The torrents of water and debris from degraded watersheds caused billions of dollars in damage in 1996 alone.

⓯   Paradoxically, clearing natural forest also intensifies drought by allowing the soil to dry out more quickly. Such droughts helped fuel the record-breaking fires in Indonesia and Brazil in 1997–1998. These massive fires occurred in tropical forests that are normally too moist to burn. When fragmented by logging and agricultural clearing, the forests dried to the point where fires set deliberately to clear land were quickly able to spread out of control. In Indonesia, industrial timber and palm oil plantation owners took advantage of a severe El Niño drought to expand their areas and, in 1997–1998, burned at least 24,000,000 acres, an area the size of South Korea.

⓰   The smoke and haze from Indonesia's fires choked neighboring countries, affecting about 70,000,000 people. The economic damage to the region has been conservatively estimated at around $9,300,000,000. Schools, airports, and businesses were shut down. Many crops were lost to the drought and fires, and the haze impaired the pollination of other crops and wild plants, the ecological repercussions of which will unfold for many years. If harm to fisheries, biodiversity, orangutans, and long-term health were included, the damage figure would be far higher.

⓱ In contrast to human-made unnatural disasters that should be prevented, but are not, considerable effort is spent trying to stop natural disturbances that are actually beneficial. Our usual approach to natural disturbances is to try to prevent them through shortsighted strategies using methods that all too often exacerbate them. The result is disasters of unnatural proportions. In the United States, for instance, fire suppression has long been the policy, even in fire-dependent forest and grassland ecosystems. The result has been the buildup of debris that fuels very hot fires capable of destroying these ecosystems, as well as the homes that are increasingly built there. The record-setting expense of fires and fire suppression in the United States—nearly $1,400,000,000 in federal agency costs in 2000—is a telling reminder of the consequences of such wrongheaded policies. Recent events have rekindled the debate and are providing the stimulus to rethink American fire policies.

⓲ Likewise, a common response to floods is to try to prevent them by controlling rivers. Dams and levees, for instance, are built to change the flow of rivers. Contrary to popular belief, though, containing a river in embankments, dams, channels, reservoirs, and other structures does not reduce flooding. Instead, it dramatically increases the rate of flow and causes even worse flooding downstream. The Rhine River in Europe, for example, is cut off from ninety percent of its original floodplain in its upper reaches and flows twice as fast as it did before the modifications. Flooding in the basin has grown significantly more frequent and severe due to increased urbanization, river engineering, and poor floodplain management.

⓳ The great Midwest flood of the upper Mississippi and Missouri rivers in 1993 provided another dramatic and costly lesson on the effects of treating the natural flow of rivers as a problem. The flood was the largest and most destructive in modern U.S. history. It set records for amounts of precipitation, river levels, flood duration, area of flooding, and economic loss. Financial costs were estimated at $19,000,000,000. The floodwaters breached levees spanning around 6,000 miles. In hindsight, many now realize that the rivers were simply attempting to reclaim their floodplain. Not surprisingly, 1993 was a record breeding year for fish as the rivers were restored, temporarily, to more natural functioning.

⓴ Today's problems reflect the cumulative impacts of more than a century of actions by public and private interests to expand agriculture, facilitate navigation, and control flooding on the Mississippi and its tributaries. Nearly half of the 2,345-mile-long Mississippi flows through artificial channels. Records show that the 1973, 1982, and 1993 floods were substantially higher than they might have been before structural flood control began in 1927 after a major flood.

㉑ Throughout the huge Mississippi River basin, the construction of thousands of levees, the creation of deep navigation channels, extensive farming in the floodplain, and the draining of over 17,000,000 acres of wetlands (more than an eighty-five percent reduction in some states) have cut into the ability of the Mississippi's floodplains to absorb and slowly release rain, floodwater, nutrients, and sediments. Separating fish from floodplain breeding grounds and upstream reaches has virtually eliminated some species and caused many others to decline. The commercial fish catch in the Missouri River, the Mississippi's largest tributary, fell eighty-three percent between 1947 and 1995.

㉒   Flood control and navigation structures have also adversely affected the Mississippi Delta and the Gulf of Mexico. Because these structures trap sediments, rather than allow them to be carried downstream to replenish the delta, as they have done for millennia, the delta areas are subsiding as water floods wetlands and threatens coastal communities and productive fisheries.

㉓   But perhaps the best example of the cost of man's ecologically disruptive practices as well as his interference with nature is on the other side of the globe, in Bangladesh. Annual floods are a natural and beneficial cycle in this low-lying coastal nation, which encircles the meandering deltas of the Ganges, Brahmaputra, and Meghna rivers. The people of Bangladesh have long adapted their housing, land use patterns, and economic activities to these *barsha* (beneficial floods). However, the summer of 1998 brought a *bonna* (devastating flood)— the most extensive flood of the 20th century. Two-thirds of the country became inundated for months. Floodwaters reached near-record levels and did not recede for months. All told, 1,300 people died; 31,000,000 were left temporarily homeless; and almost 10,000,000 miles of roads were heavily damaged. Overall damage estimates exceed $3,400,000,000—or ten percent of the nation's GDP.

㉔   A number of factors precipitated Bangladesh's *bonna*. It is true that there was heavy rainfall upriver in the Himalayas of northern India and Nepal. However a lot of this rain fell on heavily logged areas, which exacerbated the disaster, as did the runoff from extensive development upstream that helped clog the region's rivers and floodplains with silt and mud. Furthermore, one main reason why so much of Bangladesh was submerged for so long was that extensive embankments built in the last ten years as part of the nation's Flood Action Plan actually prevented drainage because water that topped the embankment during the flood's peak could not drain as the river receded. The structures also dried out the backwaters that once fertilized fields and provided fish after the floods receded.

㉕   In the future, climate change is expected to bring about rising sea levels and increased rainfall and cyclone activity. Unless something is done soon, countries like Bangladesh will become even more vulnerable, with possibly twenty percent of the nation's land area becoming submerged. It doesn't help that large expanses of stabilizing mangroves have been removed from shores in recent years to make way for shrimp ponds, exposing the coast to additional inundation.

Janet N. Abramovitz is a senior researcher at the Worldwatch Institute, Washington, D.C., focusing on ecosystem services, forests and forest products, biodiversity, freshwater ecosystems, consumption, and social equity.

Chunking

◐ Read the first sentence of every paragraph after the introduction. With your partner, group the paragraphs that discuss the same main idea (chunk). List the main ideas and the corresponding paragraphs below.

Paragraph Groups	Main Ideas
_____	Introduction
_____	_____
10–16	Causes of "unnatural" disasters
_____	_____
_____	_____
_____	Conclusion

Analyzing Chunks of Text

> **Reading Tip**

Well-organized articles consist of **several main ideas** with **related subordinate ideas**. This can be compared to a tree with its main branches and smaller branches. Identifying the main ideas and the subordinate ideas and organizing them into an idea tree makes understanding and using the information in an article much easier. ▪

◐ **Idea Trees** Each major chunk that you identified above contains a number of related subordinate ideas. Identify the subordinate ideas as follows:

◐ **1.** Scan the chunk on "causes of unnatural disasters" and identify the paragraphs that contain the following subordinate ideas.

_____ alteration of natural systems

_____ examples of "unnatural" disasters

_____ loss of ecosystems—flooding

_____ loss of ecosystems—fires

2. Check the paragraphs you chose with a partner.

3. Scan the other three chunks and identify the subordinate ideas that each section contains. Write your own idea trees.

4. Compare your idea trees with a partner. Your wording may be different but the paragraphs you chose should be the same.

Understanding Details

◐ Use the idea trees you made to help you find the information for answering the following questions. Underline the information. Answer the questions in your own words.

1. What are some ways that we have altered the earth's natural systems?

_____

2. a. What are droughts and famines examples of?

_____

2. b. Why are they not as well reported as other disasters?

_____

3. a. How does deforestation lead to flooding?

_____

b. How can deforestation lead to fire?

_____

4. Why is the suppression of natural fires not a good idea?

_____

5. What are some of the negative consequences of controlling floods?

_____

6. In what ways is the problem in Bangladesh an example of the consequence of ecologically disruptive practices as well as interference with nature?

_____

▶ Check your answers with a partner or in a small group.

Reviewing the Information

▶ Work with a partner to orally review the following:

- The difference between natural and "unnatural" disasters
- What man has done to lead to "unnatural" disasters
- The benefits of some natural disasters
- The consequences of controlling natural disasters

Applying the Information

▶ Tsunami, which are giant sea waves resulting from earthquakes beneath the ocean floor, are considered to be among the deadliest of natural disasters. In light of what you have read so far, discuss the type of damage that can be caused as well as how it can be prevented or minimized. Work in groups of 3–4.

1. What is a tsunami?
2. How could some damage from tsunami be prevented and more lives saved?

Skimming

▶ The Boxing Day tsunami that took place on December 26, 2004, is considered to be one of the deadliest natural disasters in recorded history. Read through the following article quickly to answer the questions below. Use the headings and subheadings as well as the charts and diagrams to help you locate the information.

1. What caused the tsunami?
2. Where did it happen?
3. Which countries were most affected?
4. How many lives were lost?
5. How much damage was caused?
6. What measures should be put in place for the future?

The Boxing Day 2004 Tsunami

❶   At 7:58:53 A.M. local time, approximately 100 miles off Banda Aceh on the island of Sumatra, Indonesia, the largest earthquake since 1960 occurred, registering 9.0 on the Richter scale. The earthquake was the result of the Indian tectonic plate sliding under the Burma tectonic plate. The resultant tsunami, one of the deadliest natural disasters in recorded history, is estimated to have released the energy of 23,000 Hiroshima-type atomic bombs. It hit the shores of Indonesia, Sri Lanka, Thailand, India, and Africa with a sequence of waves moving at speeds of up to 500 miles per hour and with an estimated impact of approximately 4.5 tons on a person of average weight and height. It is likely to remain clearer in our minds than almost any other disaster. The subsequent relief effort is unsurpassed in its intensity, with the involvement of so many countries and in money raised; only Band Aid and Live Aid in the Ethiopian famine of 1984–1985 have made similar impacts. The 2004 tsunami was a truly significant global event, and not simply because of its size and scale.

What Happened and Why

❷   *What is a tsunami?* Tsunami are giant sea waves caused by large-scale and sudden disturbance of seawater. The popular name for a tsunami—whose plural, too, is tsunami—is "tidal wave," which is incorrect, as it has nothing to do with tides. *Tsunami* is a Japanese word meaning "harbor wave." A tsunami is almost always a secondary effect of an earthquake and results from large and rapid movements of the sea floor covering an area of several hundred kilometers. Earthquakes result from movements along plate boundaries. Most occur along subduction—or destructive—plate margins, where denser oceanic crust is dragged beneath lighter continental crust in a series of irregular movements. These generate shock waves at their focus, which we feel as earthquakes. Earthquake size and intensity depends on the degree of movement and the depth at which they occur; intense, shallow earthquakes are felt more severely. Tsunami occur where earthquake intensity exceeds 6.5 on the Richter scale and where the focus is less than 50 kilometers deep, otherwise shock intensity is absorbed by the surroundings. The key factor is the degree of displacement of the sea floor; the larger and more shallow the earthquake, the greater the intensity of the tsunami. The severity and scale of the earthquake that resulted in the Boxing Day tsunami is especially rare. The massive thrust of tectonic plates probably heaved the Indian Ocean floor toward Indonesia by about 15 meters, permanently altering the geography of islands such as Sumatra. The earthquake force was such that it made the earth wobble on its axis and cut day length by fractions of a second.

How Do Tsunami Behave?

❸   In open water, tsunami are difficult to detect; they can be mistaken for a large swell. Opinions differ about their speed, but the recent tsunami reached a known speed of 800 kilometers/hour. Once generated, the waves formed a ripple effect, advancing across the Indian Ocean (see Figure 1), affecting different countries at different times and in different ways depending on shoreline shape and configuration. Thus,

- tsunami waves that struck Banda Aceh, only 15 minutes from their origin, and parts of Sri Lanka were 15 meters high on impact.
- islands in the Maldives experienced only a four-meter sea swell rather than a crashing wall of water.

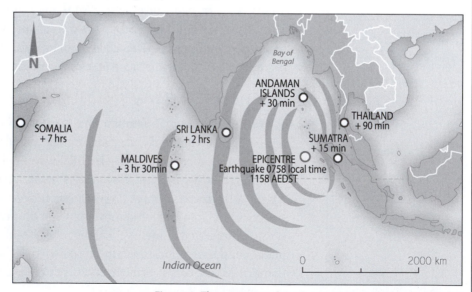

Figure 1 The progress of the tsunami across the Indian Ocean

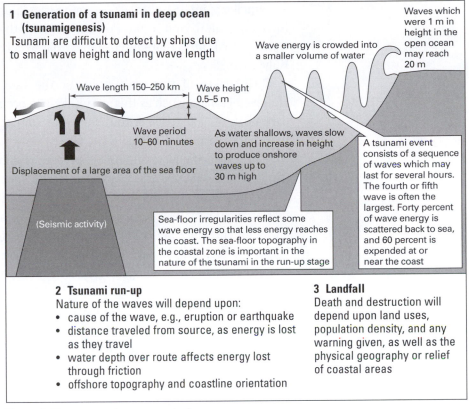

1 Generation of a tsunami in deep ocean (tsunamigenesis)
Tsunami are difficult to detect by ships due to small wave height and long wave length

Wave length 150–250 km

Wave height 0.5–5 m

Wave period 10–60 minutes

Displacement of a large area of the sea floor

(Seismic activity)

Wave energy is crowded into a smaller volume of water

Waves which were 1 m in height in the open ocean may reach 20 m

As water shallows, waves slow down and increase in height to produce onshore waves up to 30 m high

Sea-floor irregularities reflect some wave energy so that less energy reaches the coast. The sea-floor topography in the coastal zone is important in the nature of the tsunami in the run-up stage

A tsunami event consists of a sequence of waves which may last for several hours. The fourth or fifth wave is often the largest. Forty percent of wave energy is scattered back to sea, and 60 percent is expended at or near the coast

2 Tsunami run-up
Nature of the waves will depend upon:
- cause of the wave, e.g., eruption or earthquake
- distance traveled from source, as energy is lost as they travel
- water depth over route affects energy lost through friction
- offshore topography and coastline orientation

3 Landfall
Death and destruction will depend upon land uses, population density, and any warning given, as well as the physical geography or relief of coastal areas

Figure 2 How tsunami are generated

As wave fronts approach the shore (see Figure 2), energy is concentrated and wave height increases. In approaching a coastline, the wave changes considerably. Where the first part of the wave is a trough, a "draw-down" occurs, whereby the sea appears to "fall" or recede well below normal levels. Many victims in Thailand and India were those who went to observe what appeared to be a withdrawal of the sea far beyond the normal shoreline.

4   In the 1960 Chilean earthquake, sea level prior to the tsunami fell by 40 meters. However, this phenomenon does give those who have been educated about tsunami the chance to recognize what is happening and escape its effects. Invariably, the first wave is not the largest; only as waves approach the shore and are slowed by the rising sea floor do they begin to "stack up," so that the fourth or fifth wave is often the largest. As many television broadcasts have shown, much damage was done by subsequent waves across Asia.

How Significant Was the Tsunami as a Hazardous Event?

5   The earthquake that caused the Boxing Day tsunami measured 9 on the Richter scale of earthquake intensity. This scale is logarithmic; an earthquake of intensity scale 2 is ten times greater in force than one that is intensity scale 1, and so on. Put into context, the Boxing Day earthquake was over 100 times more intense than that which caused major damage in Kobe in 1995.

❻ Earthquakes of this scale occur at the rate of about one per year. However, tsunami such as this are unlikely to occur annually because most earthquakes occur deep within the earth's crust and do not cause such vertical displacement. Globally, the largest destructive margin is along the edge of the Pacific plate and ninety percent of damaging tsunami occur in the Pacific basin, one third of these in the deep sea trenches bordering Japan, the Aleutians, and South America. Japan itself experiences four or five large tsunami per century. Tsunami in southeast Asia are less common; although the plate boundary moves frequently, few [earthquakes] are so shallow or vertical in nature. The scale of the Boxing Day tsunami has enabled seismologists and geophysicists to recognize this as a one-in-one-hundred-year event.

❼ Two previous events emphasize the significance of the Boxing Day tsunami:

• The earthquake that triggered the tsunami was not the biggest known; that record belongs to the 1960 Chilean earthquake which measured 9.5 on the Richter scale.

• The impacts of the 2004 tsunami may be the worst on record, but the 1976 earthquake in Tangshan, China, killed between 250,000 and 650,000 people.

What Impacts Did the Tsunami Have and How Did These Vary Spatially?

❽ Of all the countries affected (see Figure 3), Indonesia was the hardest hit with Banda Aceh making the most impact on people's minds (even though many may never have heard of Banda Aceh, capital of Aceh province in northwestern Sumatra, before the tsunami). There, more than fourteen percent of the population has been confirmed dead.

❾ *Social impacts* One of the greatest impacts has been on orphaned children. The UN children's agency, UNICEF, estimates that 1.5 million children were affected—orphaned, injured or traumatized. In Aceh alone, an estimated 35,000 children have been affected.

❿ *Economic impacts* It is difficult to assess economic impact; many of those whose lives were disrupted were subsistence workers or those in the informal economy. There are no figures to calculate this loss; images of smashed fishing boats can only hint at the economic devastation of those areas affected. However, at least one million people are estimated to have lost their livelihoods in Sri Lanka and Indonesia alone. Flooded land, erased

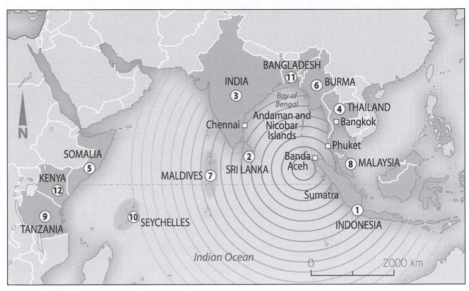

Death Toll as of February 2005

1	Indonesia	236,169	5	Somalia	150	9	Tanzania	10
2	Sri Lanka	31,147	6	Burma	61	10	Seychelles	3
3	India*	16,513	7	Maldives	82	11	Bangladesh	2
4	Thailand	5,395	8	Malaysia	68	12	Kenya	1
							Total	289,601

*including Andaman and Nicobar Islands

Figure 3 Impacts of the Boxing Day tsunami on different countries

homes, lost vehicles, smashed boats—all add up to a picture of personal economic devastation for those affected.

⑪   Stock markets, too, have felt the effects of the tsunami. The stock market in Jakarta fell sharply in January after Indonesian analysts doubled the likely cost of rebuilding from the tsunami. Some economic analysts believe that the 1997 Asian economic crisis was due to costs of the 1995 Kobe earthquake, which placed insurance companies under huge strain. The Indonesian government estimates that five-year rebuilding costs for Banda Aceh province alone are approximately US $1.9 billion.

⑫   *Environmental impacts* Across Indonesia, whole sections of coastline have been drastically altered. In many areas where the tsunami had a lot of energy or was moving laterally to the shoreline, it has washed away beaches and rock, leaving underground material exposed to the sea and air. Witnesses speak of some islands and coral reefs being washed away or drastically changed. In Indonesia, the earthquake seems to have "submerged" the Aceh region, and created lakes and wetlands that may prove to be permanent and which have made some areas impassable to survivors and aid workers.

What Are the Prospects for the Future?

⑬   *A warning system* With hindsight, a warning system seems essential. None of the countries affected had a tsunami warning mechanism or tidal gauges to alert people. The Maldives received their warnings via news footage on CNN. Perhaps the most insensitive statement following the tsunami came from the US Geological Survey (USGS), who claimed that a tsunami warning center in southeastern Asia could have saved most of the people who died.

⑭   Pacific Rim countries have had a tsunami warning system in place for four decades. The United States has warning centers in Hawaii and Alaska operated by the USGS. However, large tsunami are rare in the Indian Ocean; people have not been educated to flee inland after earthquake tremors, and there are no monitors in the region. Only Kenya was in a position to respond to warnings—ten hours after the event.

⑮   Donor countries and nations affected by the tsunami have now agreed that the United Nations should begin work on an early warning system in the Indian Ocean. UN agencies are starting work now and say that a basic system could be ready in 12–18 months with money pledged by Japan, the European Union, and others.

⑯   A warning system involves installing a pressure sensor on the ocean floor which measures the weight of water above it. If a tsunami passes overhead, pressure increases and the sensor sends signals to a buoy on the sea surface, which in turn sends a signal to a satellite, which alerts a staffed early warning center. The United States, Germany, and Australia have already offered technologies for a communications center. Certainly, had a warning system been in place, even those in Banda Aceh, just fifteen minutes from the tsunami's origin, could have made some progress away from the shoreline and coastal area.

⑰   *How effective might a warning system be?* The biggest challenge will be how to communicate localized warnings to isolated communities. An operator in a warning center in Jakarta might know about an impending tsunami, but how can fishermen in Sumatra, or people on Nicobar Island, be warned effectively? In many remote areas of southeast Asia, TV, radio, even a telephone, is not an option. The only answer is that education about tsunami should accompany any warning system.

⑱   *Modifying vulnerability or modifying the event* In addition to a warning system, decision-makers faced with hazardous situations have to think about hazard reduction—either by modifying vulnerability to the hazard or modifying the event. Modifying vulnerability involves modifying the degree of exposure for those most at risk. Japan has employed a system of coastal land-use planning that is designed to reduce the impacts of tsunami. Such planning is designed to reduce the vulnerability for a tsunami akin to the 2004 tsunami in Asia. In this model, the beach and the forest are used to absorb the impact of the on-shore wave; evacuation routes and development are located away from where the event might happen.

⓳   It is, of course, not possible to modify a tsunami any more than it is possible to control an earthquake. However, means of modifying the event itself—that is, the point at which the wave reaches the shore—have been effected in Japan. There tsunami protection includes:

• a breakwater of sufficient height to break a large on-shore wave.
• a beach area, restricted from any further human development, which acts as an inundation barrier.
• a coastal evacuation route, elevated above inundated land.
• building designs that resist tsunami impacts.

⓴   *The value of mangroves* It would be difficult to know to what extent such measures could be applied in the poorer regions of southeast Asia. Indeed, it may not be possible to develop the hard engineering solutions. But there are other ways by which a natural resource such as mangroves can be used to minimize the impacts of tsunami. The worst damage this time was in places with no natural protection from the sea; communities behind intact mangrove forests were largely spared. Mangrove forests acted like a shield and bore the brunt of the tsunami. Many studies have found that mangroves help protect coastlines from erosion, storm damage, and wave action by acting as buffers and catching alluvial materials. They also protect coral reefs and sea grass beds from damaging siltation and pollution. Now however, powerful tourist and aquaculture industries have rapidly encroached onto beaches and cleared the intertidal areas to provide better views, wider beaches, or the brackish water environment in which shrimps and prawns thrive. Mangroves once covered up to seventy-five percent of the coastlines of tropical and subtropical countries. Today, less than fifty percent remain.

㉑   The message for decision makers therefore may be not to rely so much on advanced technology but rather to use what nature has given us. Protecting what is left of the mangroves might be the best way of ensuring that future tsunami do not create the devastation that we are facing today.

Adapted from Bob Digby, *GEODate*

Note Taking   ◯ Work in a group of three. Choose one of the main sections, underline the important information, and use what you underlined to make notes using the divided page format outlined on page 31. You can use the subheadings as supporting ideas or choose your own. Take turns explaining the information using your notes and the relevant figures.

Applying the Information   ◯ Using information from both readings, discuss the following:

To what extent can the 2004 tsunami be considered an "unnatural" disaster?

◯ Vocabulary Building

Word Form   ◯ **A** Study these five words and their forms. Then choose the correct form for each part of speech in the chart below. These words are commonly found in general and academic texts.

estimate (v.)   displace (v.)   expose (v.)   intensify (v.)   maintain (v.)
overestimate (v.)   displacement   exposed   intensity   maintenance
estimate (n.)   displaced   exposure   intense   maintainable
estimation (n.)   displaceable   exposable   intensely   maintainability
estimator (n.)   intenseness
estimable (adj.)   intensive
estimated (adj.)

Verb	Noun	Adjective	Adverb
displace	1.	1.	
		2.	
expose	1.	1.	
		2.	
intensify	1.	1.	1.
	2.	2.	
maintain	1.	1.	
	2.		

◯ Compare your lists with a partner.

◯ **B** Write three sentences using words from the list. Use different parts of speech.

Vocabulary in Context

⊙ **Inferring Meaning** The following sentences are all taken from the reading "Are Humans to Blame for Exacerbating Many Natural Disasters?" Use the context to infer the meaning of the words in boldface.

1. … almost 20,000,000 cubic yards of mud, trees, and boulders came **barreling** down from Venezuela's coastal mountain range onto the densely populated and heavily urbanized **ribbon** of land that **hugs** the Caribbean coast …

   barreling _____

   ribbon _____

   hugs _____

2. During the decade, more than $608,000,000,000 in economic losses were **chalked up** to natural catastrophes, an amount greater than during the previous four decades combined.

   chalked up _____

3. Healthy and resilient ecosystems are **shock absorbers** that protect against coastal storms and sponges that soak up floodwaters, for instance.

   shock absorbers _____

4. By degrading forests, engineering rivers, filling in wetlands, and destabilizing the climate, we are **unraveling the strands** of a complex **ecological safety net**.

   unraveling the strands _____

   ecological safety net _____

5. We have altered many natural systems so dramatically that their ability to **bounce back** from disturbance has been greatly diminished.

   bounce back _____

6. Our usual approach to natural disturbances is to try to prevent them through **shortsighted** strategies using methods that all too often exacerbate them.

   shortsighted _____

⊙ Check your answers with a partner.

Expanding Your Language

Reading

▷ The 2004 tsunami was one of the worst disasters in recent history but, as with other disasters, there were incredible tales of heroism and survival. Read the following to find out how one family survived.

How Hero Saved His Family from Killer Wave

"When the tsunami struck, I tied my family to trees. I'd seen it in a movie as a kid."

Ferocious waves crashed around Stephen Boulton as he waded through swirling water toward his screaming wife and kids. Battling against the current, he carried his hysterical family to the shore and lashed them to trees with their beach towels. There, they would be safe—above the wave sweeping so many other people to their deaths.

Thanks to Stephen's heroism, his wife and three children managed to survive the Asian tsunami disaster.

"In the midst of the panic, I suddenly remembered this black and white movie I'd seen as a kid," says Stephen, a part-time firefighter. "There had been a tidal wave and people tied themselves to trees. Thankfully, the same thing worked for us."

It had all started out as a dream holiday. Plumber Stephen, from Balfron, Great Britain, had planned and saved for it for months. "We'd moved earlier last year. Then I lost my job and also had a stomach operation. So we needed a break. I'd been to the Maldives before and knew how nice it was. Ironically, I also chose it because the beaches are so safe."

Stephen, his wife Ray, thirty-three, and their children Ashley, thirteen, Euan, four, and two-year-old Iona arrived on the island of Kandooma on Christmas Day and, because of the long flight, went straight to bed. "We woke at 7 A.M.," says Stephen. "The kids were thrilled because they were getting their presents and I was excited because it was my birthday."

Over breakfast, Ray mentioned there had been a tremor that morning, though the rest of the family had slept through it. Stephen says, "I thought nothing of it. We went to the beach, left our bags under some trees, and headed for the water." There was no sign that anything was less than perfect so Stephen, Ray, and the children started splashing about on the shore, then headed for a pier. "I was going to take a running jump off the end of it with Ashley," says Stephen. "But as we got to the end, something told me not to jump. I'm not religious but I still can't explain what stopped me."

If they had jumped in, they would have been swept out to sea because the water was already frothing, with dangerous undercurrents. "As I looked down, I noticed the water was white rather than clear and I wondered if it was some strange tidal effect. Then I realized the water was rising and big waves were rolling in."

Not realizing just how big, Stephen told Ashley to head back to the beach and move their bags. But when water started crashing over a six-foot harbor wall, he knew these were no ordinary waves. "The water came in so suddenly that before we knew it, it was up to our chests," he says. "I shouted to Ashley to get to higher ground and I linked arms with Ray. We started wading through horrendous currents to the trees, clambering up with Iona and Euan on our backs." If either of them had fallen, the currents would have carried them and their children away.

Stephen used all his strength to get over to Ashley, so they were all together—and only then did he realize the scale of the disaster. "I'd watched the Discovery Channel and worked out that this was a tsunami. That meant there would be more, even bigger waves, so I had to get the family to safety quickly." Ray says, "Stephen was amazing. He just clicked into firefighter mode, calmed us all down, and then set about saving our lives." He grabbed his family's wet beach towels and started strapping each of them into the branches of the trees, above the rising water. The children were hysterical and feared they wouldn't make it. Ray says, "We were sitting in a tree, surrounded by swirling water and debris."

Just as they were giving up hope, the water suddenly receded. Stephen says: "It was like someone had pulled a plug and the tide just swept out, carrying everything—people, beach chairs, bungalows. It was just awful."

When he realized his family was safe, Stephen climbed down and set about trying to help other survivors. He dashed back to the hotel, breaking a toe as he waded through the filthy water, and coordinated a head count to find out who was missing. While he was there, Stephen found the family's passports in a bag—and Euan's favorite monkey toy. "You should have seen Euan's face when I brought it back. He didn't realize the danger he'd been in—he was just happy to see his toy."

Stephen helped the hotel manager find supplies in case no help came for a few days. Then an island official warned everyone that an even bigger wave was on the way. All the women and children were to be put on boats, so they could ride it out. "When we said goodbye, it was like something out of the Titanic film," Stephen recalls. "Ray was crying her eyes out and begging me to get on with her. But I couldn't do that because it wasn't fair."

After a tense, hour-long wait, it became clear that the giant wave wasn't coming ... and Stephen was reunited with his family. They were whisked away by speedboat to another island that had suffered only minimal damage and, the following day, caught the first available flight back to Britain. Stephen, Ray, and their kids arrived at Gatwick barefoot, still wearing their swimming suits and T-shirts. "It was freezing but I was just glad we had survived," says Stephen. "It was only after we'd flown back to Glasgow and I was driving home that I felt like I'd done my job and could finally relax. Then the emotions, and the tears, came out."

Ray is sure that she and the kids would have died if it weren't for Stephen's bravery.

"He is our hero," she says simply. "I know that if it wasn't for him, we would have been dead now." However, modest Stephen claims that he only did what had to be done. "I did what every father would do," he says. "No dad would let go of his kids."

Damien Fletcher, *The Mirror*

Discussion Questions

🔘 Discuss the following:

1. How did Stephen know what to do?
2. What does the way he acted say about Stephen's personality?
3. What effect do you think this experience had on Stephen? his wife? his kids?
4. Have you ever been in a similar situation? If yes, explain what happened.

Speaking

🔘 **Speaking From Experience** Prepare a three to five minute talk about somebody you consider to be a hero(ine). To prepare for this, follow these steps.

🔘 **1.** Write some notes giving:
   • general background information about the person.
   • his/her personality.
   • what he/she accomplished.
   • why you consider this person to be your hero(ine).

2. Practice telling the story from your notes. Include as many facts as possible.

3. Time yourself as you try to speak as clearly and naturally as possible.

4. Present your talk to a small group.

Writing

▶ **Summary Writing** The main purpose of summary writing is to communicate the important ideas to someone who has not read the information. It is an important skill to develop both for academic and professional life. In order to write a good summary it is necessary to:

- understand what you read.
- select only the important ideas and information.
- write the important information in your own words.

▶ **A** To practice summary writing, you will write a summary of the article "Are Humans to Blame for Exacerbating Natural Disasters?" To prepare for the summary, follow these steps.

▶ **1.** Read the article quickly one more time.

2. Review the idea tree that you made for the article (page 101).

3. Make any changes that you think are necessary.

4. Add any details/examples that you think are necessary.

5. Select the main ideas that must be included in order to give an accurate representation of the article.

6. Select the subordinate points and details that need to be included for clarity.

7. Discuss what you selected with a partner or in a small group.

8. Decide on how to group the ideas into paragraphs and on the order of the paragraphs.

> **Writing Tip**

A **summary** does not have an introduction with a thesis statement. Instead, it **starts** with an **introductory sentence or two** that gives the author, the title, the source, the focus and, if possible, the approach and/or point of view of the author. ■

▶ **B** To write the summary, follow these steps.

▶ **1.** Decide what to include in the introductory sentence(s).

2. Compare your choices with a partner and, together, write the introductory sentence(s).

3. Write the summary using what you prepared in part A above.

4. Give your summary to your teacher for feedback.

Online Study Center For additional activities, go to the *Reading Matters* Online Study Center at *college.hmco.com/pic/wholeyfour2e*.

6 Urban Growth and Water Supply

Chapter Openers

Discussion Questions

▷ Discuss the following questions in small groups of three or four.

1. How would you define the term megacity? To which cities could this term apply?
2. Do you think the number of megacities in the world is increasing? If yes, where?
3. What are the advantages of living in a megacity?
4. What are the disadvantages of living in a megacity?
5. Would you prefer to live in a city or in the country? Why?

Ranking

▷ **A The World's Ten Largest Cities** The table on the next page lists the populations of the world's largest cities in 1950 and 2003. Try to guess which city corresponds to which population and list the cities in descending order in the appropriate column.

Bombay, India
Buenos Aires, Argentina
Calcutta, India
Chicago, USA
Delhi, India
Dhaka, Bangladesh
Essen, Germany
London, England
Los Angeles, USA
Mexico City, Mexico
Moscow, USSR
New York, USA
Paris, France
Sao Paolo, Brazil
Shanghai, China
Tokyo, Japan

City	1950 Population (millions)	Rank in 1950	City	2003 Population (millions)	Rank in 2003
	12.3			26.7	
	8.7			18.9	
	6.9			18.6	
	5.4			17.4	
	5.4			17.0	
	5.3			14.4	
	5.3			14.1	
	5.0			13.8	
	4.9			13.5	
	4.4			13.0	

▶ Compare your ranking with a partner. Check your ranking against the table on page 275.

▶ **B** Discuss the following questions with your partner.

1. How many megacities (over 10 million) were there in 1950? In 2003?
2. How does the location of the world's largest cities in 1950 compare with that in 2003?
3. What reason(s) can you give for this transition?
4. What problems can this increase in megacities cause?

▶Exploring and Understanding Reading

Using Charts and Graphs

▷ One of the major problems resulting from population growth and the growth of megacities is a shortage of water. Use the charts below to answer these questions.

1. What human activity requires the most water?
2. Do all major regions of the world have equal access to freshwater?
3. Do countries within the same major region have equal access to fresh water?
4. How has water use changed during the twentieth century (1900–2000)?

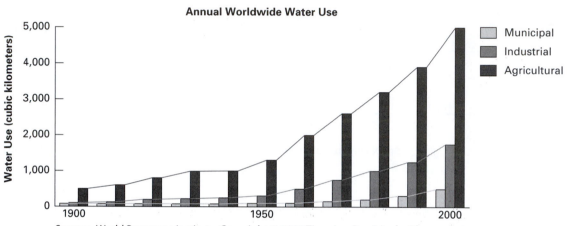

Annual Worldwide Water Use

Source: *World Resources Institute. Copyright © 1997 Time, Inc. Reprinted with permission.*

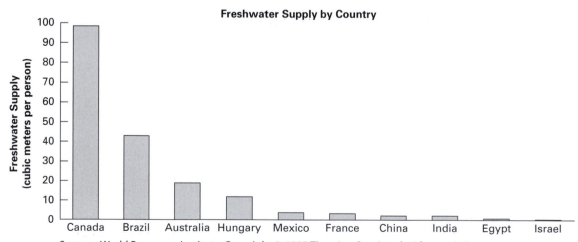

Freshwater Supply by Country

Source: *World Resources Institute. Copyright © 1997 Time, Inc. Reprinted with permission.*

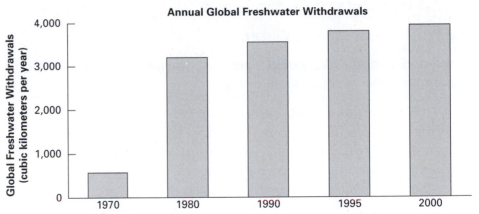

Source: UNEP Global Environmental Outlook 3. © 2002 Time, Inc. Reprinted with permission.

▶ Check your answers with a partner or in a small group.

Previewing

▶ Read the title and subtitle only of the following article. List three or four ideas that you expect will be explained in the article.

_____   _____

_____   _____

Skimming

▶ Read paragraphs 1–3 quickly and complete the following.

1. _____ Number of people living without access to safe drinking water

2. _____ Number of people living without access to basic sanitation facilities

3. _____ Number of people who die every year due to diseases caused by unsanitary water

4. _____ Rate at which children are dying due to preventable water-borne diseases

5. _____ Proportion of the earth made up of water

6. _____ Percentage of water available for human use

7. _____ Percentage of water available for drinking and other personal use

8. _____ Increase in global water demand 1950–1990 compared to increase in population

▶ Compare your answers with a partner or in a small group.

The World Shortage of Water

Between 1950 and 2000, global water demand more than tripled—and despite conservation measures, it is still rising.

❶ At a recent G8 summit, delegates met to discuss, among other issues, how to provide safe drinking water to the 1.5 billion of the world's citizens who live without it. Everyone within the summit gates enjoyed the free and plentiful bottled mineral water. "It's obscene," says one journalist who attended the conference, held near the source of one of the world's most famous bottled water brands. "How can they not see that holding the summit in this place and talking about water in Africa is tasteless? It's beyond comprehension."

❷ In fact, although many people might agree that, "Clean water is a universal human right," the world is sharply divided in terms of access to safe water. Those who can afford it are consuming ever-increasing numbers of designer water bottles, while half the world's population lacks basic sanitation facilities, according to the United Nations (UN). Diseases caused by unsanitary water kill 5 to 12 million people a year, most of them women and children. A child dies every eight seconds from a preventable water-borne disease.

❸ Two thirds of the earth is made up of water. The only problem is it is either salty or frozen. More than 97 percent of the world's water is in its oceans and of the remaining 3 percent, approximately 2 percent is locked up in the polar icecaps. After agriculture and industry have taken what they need, only one-hundredth of one percent of the planet's water remains readily accessible for drinking and other personal use. The World Resources Institute (WRI) estimates that 2.3 billion people currently live in "water-stressed areas." Hydrologists cite much of Africa, northern China, pockets of India, Mexico, the Middle East, and parts of western North America as regions facing severe water shortages. Some of the world's largest cities, including Mexico City, Bangkok, and Jakarta, have severely over-pumped their groundwater aquifers. Between 1950 and 1990, global water demand tripled, even though the total population only doubled. And despite conservation measures, it is still rising. According to UN estimates, water scarcity will affect two out of every three people by 2025.

❹ This imbalance is largely due to industrial agriculture, but it is also a product of unequal development in standards of living versus sound water management. Additionally, scientists at Harvard University point out that global warming could significantly harm water availability. A warmer atmosphere could lead to higher rates of evaporation, causing droughts and more severe weather. Warmer water may also promote detrimental algae and microbial blooms, which may lead to more water-borne illnesses. And ironically, as the climate heats up, people will want to use more water for drinking, bathing, and watering plants.

❺ "The next world war will be over water," says Vice President Ismail Serageldin of the World Bank. Even now, some competition is beginning to build between (and within) nations over finite water resources. Egypt has watched warily as Ethiopia has built hundreds of dams on the Nile. Syria and Iraq have squabbled over water projects with Turkey, and some of Israel's many conflicts with Jordan and the Palestinians have been over water issues. Botswana raised a public outcry after Namibia announced emergency drought plans to divert water from the Okavango River.

6   In much of the Third World, municipal water systems often serve only cities or primarily upper- and middle-class residents (who typically pay very low fees for use). As a result, as Christian Aid journalist Andrew Pendleton puts it, "The only water that is available to many poor people free of charge lies in festering pools and contains killer diseases such as cholera." Pendleton continues, "If poor parents want to ensure their children will not die as a result of diarrhea, they must pay through the nose for water from private vendors or tankers."

> In some areas of Mexico City, the land level has dropped twenty meters because water in the underlying aquifer has been pumped out.

7   In Haiti's capital, Port-au-Prince, only 10 percent of homes have tap water, even though the local groundwater reserves are thought to host enough capacity for every resident. The public water system struggles from serious disrepair and a chronic lack of funding. Recently, some entrepreneurs began drawing water from a network of private wells and trucking it to tank owners, who then sell the precious liquid to families at a huge profit. Paul Constance of the Inter-American Development Bank says it is not uncommon for "legal or illegal private providers to make handsome profits by trucking or carting water into the poorest neighborhoods." Many people have to carry water bottles great distances.

8   Overuse of groundwater has also led to serious consequences. Over-pumping and rising sea levels have resulted in falling, and salt-water-invaded, water tables. Initial treatment of the 300,000 contaminated groundwater sites in the United States will cost up to $1 trillion over the next thirty years, according to the National Research Council. In some parts of Mexico City the land level has dropped by twenty meters because water in the underlying aquifer has been pumped out. Water scarcity is also a serious threat to natural ecosystems. "Watersheds with the highest biological value, as measured by the number of bird and fish species, are also generally the most degraded," says Carmen Revenga of the WRI. In the United States, 37 percent of freshwater fish are at risk of extinction, 51 percent of crayfish and 40 percent of amphibians are imperiled or vulnerable, and 67 percent of freshwater mussels are extinct or vulnerable to extinction.

9   One strategy that humans have used to improve their access to water since ancient times has been to build dams. Build a barrier across a river to stop the water escaping to the sea. It's worked for thousands of years but it delivers mixed results. For instance, Egypt's Lake Nasser, a reservoir of Nile River water behind the Aswan High Dam, loses up to 10 km^3 per year to evaporation caused by the sun. That is enough water to submerge 1.2 million hectares of cropland under 60 cm of water. Reservoirs lose additional water that seeps into the soil, a problem that is made worse if the canals that carry the water from the reservoir are unpaved. The Imperial Irrigation District in California, for example, estimates it could save enough water to irrigate 4,000 hectares simply by lining a delivery canal with concrete. And reservoirs silt up. The rivers feeding the lakes behind dams carry suspended solids which settle to the bottom of the lake when the water stops moving. Lake Mead is the huge water store held back by the Hoover Dam on the border of Nevada and Arizona. Eventually, Lake Mead will fill up with sediment and the Hoover Dam will become a very expensive waterfall.

❿ Another strategy is to use the water that is all around. We can't drink the sea water or use it for watering crops unless we take the salt out. This can be done, but it costs a lot. In the summer of 2000, there were 11,000 desalination plants around the world, with 60 percent of them in the arid Middle East. According to one expert, less than 0.2 percent of the world's water supply currently comes from desalination. That's mostly because it costs up to $2.50 a cubic meter to produce.

⓫ The bigger desalination plants operate on variations of the distillation process. Seawater is boiled, the steam is condensed, and the dissolved salts in the seawater are left behind. This method is expensive because of the cost of energy needed to raise cool seawater to the boiling point. For countries such as Saudi Arabia, which sit on vast reserves of oil, this is not such a critical issue. For nations that are short of water and cheap energy, desalination is not an option. However, as desalination technology improves, the cost will come down. When it reaches about thirty cents per cubic meter it will be economically viable for many more people, although it's unlikely to be cheap enough for agricultural use. And 70 percent of all water is used for growing crops.

⓬ Some people in developing countries are increasingly turning to bottled water to meet their daily needs. World consumption of bottled water is growing at 7 percent a year, with the largest increases in the Asia Pacific region. *U.S. News & World Report* recently concluded, "The drive toward bottled water and filters will, however, widen the gap between the haves and have-nots." For one thing, as Pendleton points out, poor people in need may be charged more per gallon of clean water than those in developed nations. Many families in Ghana spend 10 to 20 percent of their income on water.

⓭ Also, since many countries lack the infrastructure to recycle used water bottles, the containers end up further polluting the local water sources. In Nepal, for example, water bottles tossed aside by trekkers have caused a serious litter problem, because the government can't afford to cart them out of remote areas. Many activists have also protested aggressive bottling operations in the developing world. In Brazil, Nestlé offers Latin Americans a brand of bottled water called Nestlé Pure Life. But as Paul Constance points out, "Though it looks much like the bottled mineral water long offered in restaurants and upscale supermarkets, Pure Life is different. It is drawn from local water sources, has an aggressively low price, and is marketed specifically 'to meet the needs of people who have daily difficulty with access to quality water.'" One Pure Life bottling plant was established on a popular and ecologically sensitive mineral spring, prompting fierce opposition.

⑭   Clearly, the world is in a water crisis. Watersheds and municipal systems must be secured from rising threats. Scientists and engineers can do some amazing things, but one thing they can't do is increase the amount of water available to us on our planet. As a result, many water analysts agree that the world must use the water it has more efficiently. Sandra Postel, among others, asserts that the world must double the benefit from every unit of fresh water in order to meet its growing needs.

⑮   The answer lies not in finding more water, but in making better use of what we have already. What does work is the kind of careful conservation practiced by an increasing number of water users. That's not a widely accepted practice, because water is free or heavily subsidized by governments in most parts of the world. Yet simply charging higher fees for water can be a first step toward conservation. Municipalities from Mexico City to New York City to Singapore are doing just that. In the Muslim world though, water is considered a gift of God, and governments are reluctant to put a price on it.

⑯   Fortunately that's not the only way to achieve conservation. Industrial water recycling, begun on a large scale in the 1970s, has proven to be an effective conservation measure. It is also in everyone's interest. It lowers an industrial plant's water bill (sometimes by as much as 90 percent), the stress on resources is reduced, and pollution is cut. In Japan and western Germany, total industrial water use has not risen in more than two decades, despite a large increase in the number of factories. American steelmakers, which once consumed 280 tons of water for every ton of steel made, now use only 14 tons of new water. The rest is recycled.

⑰   This idea of a "multi-use" policy on water is also happening for municipal water use. Instead of regarding sewage as "waste," for example, it can be transformed into nutrient-rich irrigation matter. Seventy percent of the domestic water discharged from communities in Israel is now used for irrigation. "Sewage farming" may sound unappealing, but it makes sense. Cities have also saved from 10 to 25 percent of their water through the repair of leaky pipes, recycling of wastewater for urban irrigation, and fines for water waste. Mexico City replaced 650,000 of its toilets with smaller, six-liter models and saved enough water each day to serve hundreds of thousands of households. When a drought hit Melbourne, Australia, in the early 1980s, the city cut its water use 30 percent by launching a television campaign and restricting residential consumption. Even after the end of the dry spell, Melbourne's water demand has grown modestly, thanks in part to a user-pays system.

⑱   In agriculture, the wonder machine of the age is not the giant hydroelectric dam but a simple length of perforated pipe hooked up to a pump. This basic tool of drip irrigation, also called micro-irrigation, is an Israeli-devised technique in which small amounts of water are applied directly to plant roots through pipes buried along rows of crops. The method is 95 percent efficient—meaning that almost all the water is applied to nurturing the plant—compared with as little as 20 percent in traditional irrigation. Not much water is lost to evaporation or runoff.

⑲   The benefits of drip-irrigation, six-liter toilets, or low-flow showerheads may seem small but, drop by drop, they make a difference. Until every lake, river, and stream is as prized as a desert oasis, the world can expect ever-widening conflicts over water.

The time to start conserving and protecting the planet's most vital resource is long before the well of life runs dry.

Adapted from "Running Dry," *Canada and the World,* and "The World's Water Crisis," *E: The Environmental Magazine.*

Tellback

 Tip

Tellback is a useful reading strategy that helps you get the **general idea** and **some details quickly.** ■

▶ Work with a partner. Read paragraphs 4–5. Close your book and tell your partner whatever you remember. Repeat with paragraphs 6–7, 8, 9, 10–11, 12–13, 14–15, 16–18, and 19. Take turns being the first to speak.

Identifying Main Ideas

▶ Based on the tellback, make a list of the ideas being discussed in the article.

_____

_____

_____

_____

▶ Check your list with a partner. Make any changes that you consider necessary.

Scanning for Details

▶ Answer the following questions in your own words. Use the list of main ideas you made to help you locate the information.

1. Why is there is such an imbalance in water availability?

   _____

2. How will global warming add to the problem?

   a. _____

   b. _____

   c. _____

3. What is happening as a result of the limited water supply?

   _____

4. a. Who pays more for clean water in most Third World countries?

   _____

   b. Who do they get the water from?

   _____

5. Identify three consequences of the overuse of groundwater.

   a. _____

   b. _____

   c. _____

6. a. What is the main function of dams?

   _____

   b. What are three reasons why a dam is not a perfect solution?

   _____

7. Why is desalination expensive?

   _____

8. a. What is the main problem with bottled water?

   _____

   b. What other problems are there?

   _____

9. Why is there little incentive for conservation?

   _____

10. a. What is the "multi-use" policy on water?

   _____

   b. How can it be applied to industrial use?

   _____

   c. How can it be applied to municipal use?

   _____

11. What are some other ways that municipal water use can be cut down?

   _____

12. What is the difference between drip irrigation and traditional irrigation in terms of:

a. Method _____

b. Efficiency _____

◉ Check your answers with a partner or in small group.

Recapping the Information

◉ Summarize in note form:

1. Reasons for the water shortage in so many parts of the world (other than an increase in population)

_____

_____

2. Consequences of the water shortage (other than that people do not have enough to drink)

_____

_____

◉ Compare your notes with a partner or in a small group.

◐Paired Readings

◉ The following readings are about the water situation in two very different parts of the world: Mexico City and Jordan. Choose one of the readings and work with someone who has chosen the same reading.

1 The Sinking City

Predicting   Answer the following using your own knowledge and the information you have read so far.

1. Why do you think Mexico City has a water problem?

_____

2. What are the consequences?

_____

Skimming   Read the article quickly to verify your predictions. Make any necessary changes.

Water Crisis as Mexico City Sinks Faster than Venice

❶   Standing in his office high above Latin America's largest city, the water board operations chief Alejandro Martinez smiles as he considers one of the ironies of Mexico City's development. Five hundred years ago, it was a compact Aztec citadel set in a broad highland lagoon. Today it is a vast metropolis sprawling across a dried-up lakebed.

❷   Mexico City's underlying aquifer is now collapsing at a staggering rate beneath the streets. While Venice slips into the Adriatic at a fraction of an inch each year, Mexico City is lurching downwards by as much as a foot a year in some areas. Over the past century, it has dropped 30 feet. Chugging the equivalent of one Olympic-sized swimming pool full of water every minute, the city's strained aquifers are dragging much of the capital's rich heritage down with them, while the twenty million residents face problems that include water-borne diseases, power outages, and the threat of riots.

❸   The result of a head-on collision between booming demand and finite resources, Mexico City provides a sneak preview of a situation that the United Nations warns could become widespread in coming decades as the world's megacities continue to grow unchecked and unplanned. Mr. Martinez told *The Independent*, "The difficulties that we are confronting today could be faced by other cities in the future. ... We have to look for new and alternative technologies to find a solution to the problem of producing water and avoid a crisis in the short term."

❹   Once a thriving city of *chinampas*, or floating gardens, linked to land by an elaborate system of causeways, the abundant water of Lake Texcoco was gradually drained to make way for the colonial capital after the Spanish Conquest in 1519. Despite rapid growth, the city continued to meet its water needs in the nineteenth century from springs, shallow wells, and remaining surface water. The first strains began to show with massive migration in the 1940s; the capital began swallowing up one satellite town after another as it grew by seven percent a year. Faced with shortfalls as the underlying sand and clay aquifers failed to keep pace with demand, city authorities tapped into two neighboring river systems. The cost is massive because both systems are on the other side of the mountains surrounding Mexico City.

❺   The city now has five pumping stations working around the clock to draw water vertically up three-quarters of a mile from the neighboring Cutzamala River basin and from the lower catchment area of the River Lerma. Paying about $50,000 a day in water rights alone, the system consumes the same amount of electricity as Puebla, a city of 1.3 million people to the southeast. Now comprising 350 neighborhoods packed into a smog-wreathed metropolitan area more than twice the size of greater London, the city swills a massive 10.5 million gallons of water each day.

❻   Used by residents and by water-intensive industries such as beer brewing and soft-drink bottling, the ever-expanding metropolis's supplies are again running short. In several shantytowns on the outskirts, a growing army of bucket-wielding residents are forced to queue for water from a fleet of tanker trucks that fan out across the city each day as authorities admit to a growing shortfall. Mr. Martinez said, "In the past eight years, the supply of water has remained constant, while the population has grown. The network currently fails to reach about two percent of the city, mostly in outlying areas on higher ground."

❼   In the leafy park surrounding the imposing Monument to the Revolution, there is an old cast-iron well casing that has continued to hold as the city around it has sunk. Once flush with street level, the plain black pillar now stands 26 feet high, serving as an unusual photograph stop for amazed tourists. Crawling through cross-town traffic to the Avenida de la Reforma—a central thoroughfare that cuts through the city's upscale business district—a towering column topped with a golden angel comes into view. Built in the early 1900s to celebrate the centenary of the Mexican War of Independence, twenty-three steps were recently added to reach its base as the city fell away around it. A short ride away in the north of the city, the yellow-domed Basilica of Our Lady of Guadalupe is also in trouble. Built more than two centuries ago to honor the patron saint of New Spain, the shrine tilted so heavily beneath the weight of millions of pilgrims that it was declared unsafe in the 1970s and a new basilica was built next to it. The listing building now serves as a museum.

❽   But collapsing heritage is just the tip of the iceberg. Below street level, the ongoing subsidence is making the water distribution even worse. The city's 8,300-mile network of water pipes routinely fracture, losing up to forty percent of precious potable water supplies, according to some estimates. And thus the vicious cycle continues.

Tim Gaynor, *The Independent*

Finding Main Ideas

▷ Work with someone who chose the same reading. Together, make a list of the reasons for and consequences of Mexico City's water problem. Read again carefully and highlight the supporting explanations and examples for each main idea. Compare what each of you highlighted. Make any changes you think are necessary.

Recapping the Information

▷ Using what you highlighted, take turns telling the important information to your partner. Make sure you explain as clearly and completely as you can.

❷The Thirsty Kingdom

Predicting   ▷ Answer the following using your own knowledge and the information you have read so far.

1. Why do you think Jordan has a water problem?

_____

2. What are the consequences?

_____

Skimming   ▷ Read the article quickly to verify your predictions. Make any necessary changes.

In Jordan, the Feared Mideast Water Shortage is Already Reality

❶   In the arid Middle East, there is always talk of a future water shortage. In Jordan, it's already happening. Streams are drying up, and water levels across the desert Arab kingdom are falling. A rationing system means citizens get water from public supplies just two days a week. For the government, the water shortage means constantly seeking loans and grants to find ways to stretch the water there is. For the public, the shortage is the source of daily conversation, arguments, and schemes to get more.

❷   That Jordanians are used to the water shortage can be seen in Ghalia Haddad's recollection of the water dribbling off in the middle of her shower one day. "I dried my hair with a towel, put on my jeans, stopped at a nearby supermarket and bought bottled water to continue my bath," said the thirty-five-year-old architect. The reason for the severity of the shortage is simple: Jordan lacks the rivers of nearby Syria, Turkey, Iraq, and Egypt— and it doesn't have the money oil-rich Persian Gulf countries use to pay for desalination of seawater.

❸   Not that other Middle Eastern states are not without water problems. For example, Lebanon's broken down system means it can't deliver water regularly even though it has plenty. But Jordan is the only country rationing year round because of shortages, meaning each household gets just 22 gallons a day. It's not much, because the average Jordanian household is nine people, and the water must be used for showers, toilet-flushing, cooking, house-cleaning, and drinking. It compares poorly to the 65 gallons available per household in Saudi Arabia and 78 gallons in Israel.

❹   With rain being Jordan's only assured renewable water source, the government began pumping water from a handful of underground aquifers across the country in 1989. Now Jordan is using 35 billion cubic feet of water yearly, even though its renewable water resources amount to only 23 billion cubic feet. Water scarcity is most evident during the long summer when it is common to see neighbors arguing over accusations of water thefts from rooftop tanks on houses.

❺   During heat waves, there also are fights with private suppliers who triple the usual price for 1,300 gallons of water to 20 Jordanian dinars, or about $30—in a country where the per capita annual income is $1,100. "It is sometimes impossible to persuade these devils to fill up the (rooftop) bins even if you lure them with a tip," said Fadi Badaro, a car-wash clerk. "It is a nightmare." Water looting is not confined to homes. Herdsmen are known to have used submachine guns to pierce water pipes to quench the thirst of their cattle. And some Jordanians hook up their homes to the state's network without obtaining a permit. "It is difficult to pinpoint the source of the loss," said Munther Haddadin, the water and irrigation minister, showing charts that say fifty percent of pumped water is stolen or leaks from eroded pipelines dating to the 1940s.

❻   Elias Salameh, a water expert at the University of Jordan, points to "soft management" as a contributing factor to water scarcity. Licenses for wells have been carelessly handed out to farmers. For example, the number of wells near the shrinking oasis of Azraq, where Lawrence of Arabia once lived in southeastern Jordan, has risen from 50 in the 1970s to 800.

❼   Farmers are resisting suggestions to change to crops that require less water and can be planted in winter. Consumption is soaring, and water is never cut off in wealthy districts (housing government officials) and much is wasted on swimming pools and irrigating public parks. Lewis Lucke, director of Jordan programs for the U.S. Agency for International Development, said the problem can be eased "not by using less water, but by using water more efficiently."

❽   Germany, Japan, and the United States have spent $500 million on Jordanian water projects since 1990, but Haddadin, the water minister, said it was barely enough to "keep our nose above the water." The 1994 peace treaty with Israel was touted as one solution to the problem because it promised Jordan additional water, but that will come from future projects. One such proposal calls for construction of a $5 billion canal linking the

Red Sea with the Dead Sea, where desalination plants would be linked with pipelines to Amman and Israel.

❾ Salameh, the water expert at the University of Jordan, is a pessimist. He thinks the water shortage is incurable. "We will always be vulnerable and a series of drought years will expose our water crisis," he said.

Jamal Halaby, *Associated Press Online*

Finding Main Ideas

▶ Work with someone who chose the same reading. Together, make a list of the reasons for and consequences of Jordan's water problem. Read again carefully and highlight the supporting explanations and examples for each main idea. Compare what each of you highlighted. Make any changes you think are necessary.

Recapping the Information

▶ Using what you highlighted, take turns telling the important information to your partner. Make sure you explain as clearly and completely as you can.

Comparing the Readings

Retelling the Information

▶ **A** Work with someone who read a different article. Using what you highlighted, explain the situation in each area.

▶ **B** Discuss the following:

1. What is the role played by mismanagement and bad planning in each case?
2. According to the readings, is the prognosis for the future optimistic or pessimistic?
3. Do you agree with the prognosis? Why or why not?
4. What solutions do you think are possible?

Reacting to the Information

▶ Most of the following statements are from readings in this chapter. Think about each one and discuss your reaction with a partner or in a small group.

1. It's obscene. How can they not see that holding the summit in this place [Evian, France] and talking about water in Africa is tasteless? It's beyond comprehension.
2. Clean water is a universal human right.
3. The next world war will be over water.
4. The drive toward bottled water and filters will, however, widen the gap between the haves and have-nots.
5. Whisky is for drinking, water is for fighting.
6. I dried my hair with a towel, put on my jeans, stopped at a nearby supermarket, and bought bottled water to continue my bath.
7. Water is a gift of God and should not be priced.

⟩Vocabulary Building

Word Form   ▶ **A** Study these five words and their forms. Then choose the correct form for each part of speech in the chart below. These words are commonly found in general and academic texts.

reside (v.)   confine (v.)   migrate (v.)   promote (v.)   stress (v.)
resident (n.)   confinement   migration   promotion   stressful
residence (n.)   confining   migrant   promoter   stressor
residential (adj.)   immigrant   promotable   stressed
residing (adj.)   migrant   stressing
                                          immigrate   stress
                                                                                  stressfully

Verb	Noun	Adjective	Adverb
confine	1.	1.	
migrate 2.	1. 2. 3.	1.	
promote	1. 2.	1.	
stress	1. 2.	1. 2. 3.	1.

▶ Compare your lists with a partner.

▶ **B** Write three sentences using words from the list. Use different parts of speech.

Using Examples

▶ An effective way to support a point or idea is to use an example. In the following exercise, identify the point that is being supported by each example from "The World Shortage of Water."

1. Egypt has watched warily as Ethiopia has built hundreds of dams on the Nile. Syria and Iraq have squabbled over water projects with Turkey, and some of Israel's many conflicts with Jordan and the Palestinians have been over water issues. Botswana raised a public outcry after Namibia announced emergency drought plans to divert water from the Okavango River. (paragraph 5)

_____

2. In Haiti's capital, Port-au-Prince, only ten percent of homes have tap water, even though the local groundwater reserves are thought to host enough capacity for every resident. (paragraph 7)

_____

3. In the United States, 37 percent of freshwater fish are at risk of extinction, 51 percent of crayfish and 40 percent of amphibians are imperiled or vulnerable, and 67 percent of freshwater mussels are extinct or vulnerable to extinction. (paragraph 8)

_____

4. Egypt's Lake Nasser (paragraph 9)

_____

5. In Nepal, for example, water bottles tossed aside by trekkers have caused a serious litter problem, because the government can't afford to cart them out of remote areas. (paragraph 13)

_____

6. Mexico City replaced 650,000 of its toilets with smaller, six-liter models. (paragraph 17)

_____

▶ Compare your answers with a partner or in a small group. The words you use might be different but you should agree on the ideas.

Expanding Your Language

Speaking

▶ **A What's Your Opinion?** Think about the following.

The River Nile is the longest river in the world. It has two main tributaries, the White Nile, which starts in Lake Victoria, and the Blue Nile, which rises in Lake Tana. Lake Tana is in Ethiopia, while Lake Victoria is shared by Kenya, Tanzania, and Uganda. The two tributaries meet in Khartoum, Sudan, and continue on as the River Nile through the rest of Sudan and into Egypt. The Nile flows from the south to the north of Egypt and ends its journey at the Mediterranean Sea.

▶ Should any one country maintain control over the Nile? If not, how should control be shared?

▶ **B Debate** There are many who now believe that governments are unable to adequately control and distribute water. They feel that water should go into private hands. What is your position on this?

Brainstorm a list of ideas in support of your position. Work with a partner who has the same position and add to your list. Think of as many reasons or examples as you can to defend your position. Prepare to talk for one minute for each point you want to make.

Debate your position with two students who chose another position. Take turns presenting your points. Listen carefully to your partners and ask questions about the information. Share your conclusions with your classmates.

Writing

▶ **A Reaction Writing** Write about your reaction to the statement, "Water is a gift of God and should not be priced," or to another idea that caught your attention in this chapter.

▶ **B Position Writing** Use the information generated in the debate above to write a position paper. Follow these steps.

▶ **1.** Write a short introduction that ends with a clear statement of your position.

2. Write 2–3 paragraphs, one for each of your main ideas. Make sure you provide enough supporting information.

3. Write a short conclusion.

▶Read On: Taking It Further

**Reading
Journal**

▷ Many books have been written about what we are doing to the environment. For example, *The Sacred Balance*, by David Suzuki. Go to the local library and find that book or a similar one. Choose a section to read and report on.

**Surfing the
Web**

▷ Think of a country or region that you are interested in. Check the Internet for information on the water situation in that area. Key words to use in conjunction with the area you have chosen could be "water crisis," "water wars," "water shortage," etc. Use the information you find to make a five-minute oral report. Remember to identify main ideas and make brief notes on each. Present your report to a group of three or four others.

 *Online Study Center*   For additional activities, go to the *Reading Matters* Online Study Center at *college.hmco.com/pic/wholeyfour2e*.

The Age of Communications

A civilization is judged by its quality, not by its speed.

—*Edman*

Introducing the Topic

How is today's communications technology changing our world? With cell phones and e-mail constantly available, are our private lives and personal time disappearing? In this unit we will find out about some of the communications issues that people are debating today. In Chapter 7, we will find out how e-mail and the Internet revolution are changing views about privacy. With increased use of the Internet, what private information is becoming public? Do the benefits of access outweigh the dangers? Chapter 8 explores the spread of cell phone use. Why are cell phones popular? How does cell phone use affect our daily lives?

Points of Interest

Questionnaire

▶ **A** **More or Less** Is it *more* or *less* possible for people today to do the following than it was twenty years ago? Circle *M* for more or *L* for less. Be prepared to explain your choices.

1. M L   Make contact with people in different societies.

2. M L   Find time to write a long letter to a friend.

3. M L   Find out what your coworker really thinks about your boss.

4. M L   Overhear a private conversation.

5. M L   Carry out business on the weekend.

6. M L   Find out what a person's credit rating is.

7. M L   Keep personal information about yourself a secret from people you don't know.

▶ **B** Discuss your ideas with a partner or small group and answer the following questions.

1. What technology makes it possible to do each of the things in the above list?
2. What are the advantages and disadvantages of today's communications technology?

What is Your Opinion?

▶ With the advances in technology, surveillance devices have become smaller and more widespread. Which of the following applications do you agree with and why?

1. A mother inserting a camera inside her child's teddy bear in order to monitor the nanny
2. A son attaching a recorder next to his mother's hospital bed to make sure she is being well treated by the nurses
3. A store installing cameras in the light fixtures of their changing rooms to make sure none of their merchandise is stolen
4. A manager installing software in all the office computers that allows him/her to monitor his/her employees
5. A father installing a camera in his daughter's cell phone in order to know exactly where she is

▶ Discuss your ideas with a partner or small group.

The Internet: Blessing or Curse

◗ Chapter Openers

Agree or Disagree

◗ Which of the following personal information would you be willing to make public and to whom?

1. _____ The PIN code to access your bank account

2. _____ Your Social Security, Medicare, or driver's license number

3. _____ Your telephone number and address (including e-mail)

4. _____ The amount of money you make on an annual basis

5. _____ The types of purchases you make and the amount of money you spend on each type

6. _____ Your medical history, including genetic analyses

7. _____ Your political or religious affiliation

◗ Do you think that, over the past few decades, private information has become more open to the public? If so, what are the advantages and disadvantages of this?

Quotes

◗ Read each of these quotes on the topic of privacy. Decide if you agree or not and why.

1. "Privacy is not something that I'm merely entitled to. It's an absolute prerequisite." —*Marlon Brando, actor*

2. "Today … the only place sacred from interruption is the private toilet." —*Lewis Mumford, philosopher*

3. "Government has no place in the bedrooms of its citizens." —*Pierre Elliot Trudeau, former Canadian Prime Minister*

4. "I am opposed to writing about the private lives of living authors and psychoanalyzing them while they are alive." —*Ernest Hemingway, writer*

◗ Discuss your ideas with a partner or in a small group.

▶ Exploring and Understanding Reading

Predicting

▶ Predict whether you think it is easy (*E*) or difficult (*D*) for the following things to happen. Be prepared to give reasons or examples to support your answers.

1.   E   D   Someone uses your credit card number and charges $3,000 to your account.

2.   E   D   Someone gets information from your medical files and sends you brochures on health products you may want to buy.

3.   E   D   Someone uses the motor-vehicle registration records on your car to find your home address.

4.   E   D   Someone reroutes your telephone calls to another number without your knowledge.

5.   E   D   Someone sends an e-mail message that destroys the files on your computer.

▶ Compare your answers and explain your reasoning with a partner. Return to these questions after you have finished reading the introduction to the next reading and discuss your answers again.

Previewing

▶ Quickly read the title, quotes, and all the boxes contained in the reading. Based on your preview, make a list of four ideas that you expect will be explained in the article.

1. _____

2. _____

3. _____

4. _____

Examining the Introduction

▶ **A Highlighting** The introduction to this article consists of the first thirteen paragraphs (1–13). Read the introduction and find and highlight the following facts.

 Tip

Remember, **one** of the **purposes** of an **introduction** is to **interest you** in the topic. Often writers do this by way of a story or a striking example told in a personal way. ■

1. The type of work that the author does
2. The problems that the author experienced with his credit card
3. The type of book that he and his wife wrote
4. The damage that the hacker did to the author's telephone number
5. The measures the phone company took to counteract the hacker
6. The author's feelings about giving out private information

7. The feelings that most people have about privacy

8. Some important questions about the topic of privacy

▶ Discuss the facts you highlighted with a partner. What information surprised you or interested you? What ideas do you agree or disagree with?

▶ **B Finding the Connection and Purpose** Answer the following questions.

> **Reading Tip**

A writer uses the **first person**, a **personal style**, to communicate and establish a **connection** with the reader. To be effective, the writer must establish a credible connection. ■

1. a. What information does the writer give using the first person "I"?

   _____

   b. How many paragraphs are written in the first person?

   _____

2. What information establishes the writer as an authority on this topic?

   _____

3. Paraphrase (restate in your own words) the thesis or author's purpose in writing this article.

   _____

▶ Work with a partner or a small group to compare your answers.

Invasion of Privacy

Our right to be left alone has disappeared, bit by bit, in Little Brotherly steps. Still, we've got something in return—and it's not all bad.

By Joshua Quittner

❶ For the longest time, I couldn't get worked up about privacy: my right to it, how it's dying, how we're headed for an even more wired, under-regulated, over-intrusive, privacy deprived planet.

❷ I mean, I probably have more reason to think about this stuff than the average John Q. All Too Public. A few years ago, for instance, after I applied for a credit card at a consumer-electronics store, somebody got hold of my name and vital numbers and used them to get a duplicate card. That somebody ran up a $3,000 bill, but the nice lady from the fraud division of the credit card company took care of it with steely digital dispatch. (I filed a short report over the phone. I never lost a cent. The end.)

❸ I also hang out online a lot, and now and then on the Net someone will impersonate me, spoofing my e-mail address or posting stupid stuff to bulletin boards. It's annoying, I suppose. But in the end, the impersonators get bored and disappear. My reputation, such as it is, survives.

4   I should also point out that as news director for Pathfinder, Time Inc.'s mega info mall, and a guy who makes his living on the Web, I know better than most people that we're hurtling toward an even more intrusive world. We're all being watched by computers whenever we visit websites; by the mere act of "browsing" (it sounds so passive!) we're going public in a way that was unimaginable a decade ago. I know this because I'm a watcher too. When people come to my website, without ever knowing their names, I can peer over their shoulders, recording what they look at, timing how long they stay on a particular page, following them around Pathfinder's sprawling offerings.

5   None of this would bother me in the least, I suspect, if a few years ago my phone hadn't given me a glimpse of the nightmares to come. On Thanksgiving weekend in 1995, someone (presumably a critic of a book my wife and I had just written about computer hackers) forwarded my home telephone number to an out-of-state answering machine, where unsuspecting callers trying to reach me heard a male voice identify himself as me and say some extremely rude things. Then, with typical hacker aplomb, the prankster asked people to leave their messages (which to my surprise many callers, including my mother, did). This went on for several days until my wife and I figured out that something was wrong ("Hey … why hasn't the phone rung since Wednesday?") and got our phone restored.

6   It seemed funny at first, and it gave us a swell story to tell on our book tour. But the interloper who seized our telephone line continued to hit us even after the tour ended.

And hit us again and again for the next six months. The phone company seemed powerless. Its security folks moved us to one unlisted number after another, half a dozen times. They put special PIN codes in place. They put traces on the line. But the troublemaker kept breaking through.

7   If our hacker had been truly evil, there would probably have been even worse ways he could have threatened my privacy. He could have sabotaged my credit rating. He could have eavesdropped on my telephone conversations or siphoned off my e-mail. He could have called in my mortgage, discontinued my health insurance, or obliterated my Social Security number. Like Sandra Bullock in *The Net*, I could have been a digital untouchable, wandering the planet without a connection to the rest of humanity.

8   Still, I remember feeling violated at the time and as powerless as a minnow in a flash flood. Someone was invading my private space—my family's private space—and there was nothing I or the authorities could do. And as I watched my personal digital hell unfold, it struck me that our privacy—mine and yours—has already disappeared, not in one Big Brotherly blitzkrieg but in Little Brotherly moments, bit by bit.

9   Losing control of your telephone, of course, is the least of it. After all, most of us voluntarily give out our phone number and address when we allow ourselves to be listed in the White Pages. Most of us go a lot further than that. We register our whereabouts whenever we put a bank card in an ATM machine or drive through an E-Z Pass lane on the highway. We submit to being photographed every day—twenty times a day on average if you live or work in New York City—by surveillance cameras. We make public our interests and our purchasing habits every time we shop by mail order or visit a commercial website.

10 I don't know about you, but I do all this willingly because I appreciate what I get in return: the security of a safe parking lot, the convenience of cash when I need it, the improved service of mail-order houses that know me well enough to send me catalogs of stuff that interests me. And while I know we're supposed to feel just awful about giving up our vaunted privacy, I suspect (based on what the pollsters say) that you're as ambivalent about it as I am.

11 Popular culture shines its klieg lights on the most intimate corners of our lives and most of us play right along. If all we really wanted was to be left alone, explain the lasting popularity of Oprah and Sally and Ricki tell-all TV. Memoirs top the best-seller lists, with books about incest and insanity and illness leading the way. Perfect strangers at cocktail parties tell me the most disturbing details of their abusive upbringings. Why?

12 "It's a very schizophrenic time," says Sherry Turkle, professor of sociology at the Massachusetts Institute of Technology, who writes books about how computers and online communication are transforming society. She believes our culture is undergoing a kind of mass identity crisis, trying to hang on to a sense of privacy and intimacy in a global village of tens of millions. "We have very unstable notions about the boundaries of the individual," she says.

> It's a very schizophrenic time. We have very unstable notions about the boundaries of the individual.
>
> —Sherry Turkle, *Massachusetts Institute of Technology*

13 If things seem crazy now, think how much crazier they will be when everybody is as wired as I am. We're in the midst of a global interconnection that is happening much faster than electrification did a century ago and is expected to have consequences at least as profound. What would happen if all the information stored on the world's computers were accessible via the Internet to anyone? Who would own it? Who would control it? Who would protect it from abuse?

14 Small-scale privacy atrocities take place every day. Ask Dr. Denise Nagel, executive director of the National Coalition for Patient Rights, about medical privacy, for example, and she rattles off a list of abuses that would make Big Brother blush. She talks about how two years ago, a convicted child rapist working as a technician in a Boston hospital riffled through 1,000 computerized records looking for potential victims (and was caught when the father of a nine-year-old girl used caller ID to trace the call back to the hospital). How a banker on Maryland's state health commission pulled up a list of cancer patients, cross-checked it against the names of his bank's customers, and revoked the loans of the matches. How Sara Lee bakeries planned to collaborate with Lovelace Health Systems, a subsidiary of Cigna, to match employee health records with work-performance reports to find workers who might benefit from antidepressants.

15 At least a third of all Fortune 500 companies regularly review health information before making hiring decisions. And that's nothing compared with what

How You're Spied On

Everyday events that can make your life a little less private

Bank Machines
Every time you use an automated teller, the bank records the time, date, and location of your transaction.

Prescription Drugs
If you use your company health insurance to purchase drugs, your employer may have access to the details.

Employee ID Scanners
If you rely on a magnetic-stripe pass to enter the office, your whereabouts are automatically recorded.

Browsing the Web
Many sites tag visitors with "magic cookies" that record what you're looking at and when you have been surfing.

Mail-Order Transactions
Many companies, including mail-order houses and publishers, sell lists of their customers. Why do you think you're getting that Victoria's Secret catalog?

Cellular Telephone
Your calls can be intercepted and your access numbers cribbed by eavesdroppers with police scanners.

Credit Cards
Everything you charge is in a database that police, among others, could look at.

Registering to Vote
In most states, voter-registration records are public and online. They typically list your address and birth date.

Making a Phone Call
The phone company doesn't need a court order to note the number you're calling—or who's calling you.

Electronic Tolls
In many places, drivers can pay tolls electronically with passes that tip off your whereabouts.

Supermarket Scanners
Many grocery stores let you register for discount coupons that are used to track what you purchase.

Sweepstakes
These are bonanzas for marketers. Every time you enter one, you add an electronic brushstroke to your digital portrait.

Satellites
Commercial satellites are coming online that are eagle-eyed enough to spot you—and maybe a companion—in a hot tub.

Surveillance Cameras
They're in banks, federal office buildings, 7-Elevens, even houses of worship; New Yorkers are on camera up to twenty times a day.

Sending E-Mail
In offices, e-mail is considered part of your work. Your employer is allowed to read it—and many bosses do.

awaits us when employers and insurance companies start testing our DNA for possible imperfections. Farfetched? More than 200 subjects in a case study published last January in the journal *Science and Engineering Ethics* reported that they had been discriminated against as a result of genetic testing. None of them were actually sick, but DNA analysis suggested that they might become sick someday. "The technology is getting ahead of our ethics," says Nagel.

16 But how did we arrive at this point, where so much about what we do and own and think is an open book?

17 It all started in the 1950s, when, in order to administer Social Security funds, the U.S. government began entering records on big mainframe computers, using nine-digit identification numbers as data points. Then, even more than today, the citizenry instinctively loathed the computer and its injunctions against folding, spindling, and mutilating. We were not numbers! We were human beings! These fears came to a head in the late 1960s, recalls Alan Westin, a retired Columbia University professor who publishes a quarterly report, *Privacy and American Business*. "The techniques of intrusion and data surveillance had overcome the weak laws and social mores that we had built up in the pre-World War II era," says Westin.

18 The public rebelled, and Congress took up the question of how much the government and private companies should be permitted to know about us. A privacy bill of rights was drafted. "What we did," says Westin, "was to basically redefine what we meant by 'reasonable expectations of privacy.'"

19 The result was a flurry of new legislation that clarified and defined consumer and citizen rights. The first Fair Credit Reporting Act, passed in 1970, overhauled what had once been a secret, unregulated industry with no provisions for due process. The new law gave consumers the right to know what was in their credit files and to demand corrections. Other financial and health privacy acts followed, although to this day no federal law protects the confidentiality of medical records.

20 As Westin sees it, the public and private sectors took two very different approaches. Congress passed legislation requiring that the government tell citizens what records it keeps on them while insisting that the information itself not be released unless required by law. The private sector responded by letting each industry—credit-card companies, banking, insurance, marketing, advertising—create its own guidelines.

21 That approach worked—to a point. And that point came when mainframes started giving way to desktop computers. In the old days, information stored in government databases was relatively inaccessible. Now, however, with PCs on every desktop linked to office networks and then to the Internet, data that were once carefully hidden may be only a few keystrokes away.

22 Suddenly someone could run motor-vehicle-registration records against voting registrations to find six-foot-tall Republicans who were arrested during the past year for drunk driving—and who own a gun. The genie was not only out of the bottle, he was also peering into everyone's bedroom window. (Except the windows of the very rich, who can afford to screen themselves.)

23 "Most people would be astounded to know what's out there," says Carole Lane, author of *Naked in Cyberspace: How to Find Personal Information Online*. "In a few hours, sitting at my computer, beginning with no more than your name and address, I can find out what you do for a living, the names and ages of your spouse and children, what kind of car you drive, the value of your house and how much tax you pay on it."

24 Lane is a member of a new trade: paid Internet searcher, which already has its own professional group, the Association of Independent Information Professionals. Her career has given her a fresh appreciation for what's going on. "Real privacy as we've known it," she says, "is fleeting."

25 Now, there are plenty of things you could do to protect yourself. You could get an unlisted telephone number, as I was forced to do. You could cut up your credit cards and pay cash for everything. You could rip your E-Z Pass off the windshield and use quarters at tolls. You could refuse to divulge your Social Security number except for Social Security purposes, which is all that the law requires. You'd be surprised how often you're asked to provide it by people who have no right to see it.

㉕ That might make your life a bit less comfortable, of course. As in the case of Bob Bruen, who went into a barbershop in Watertown, MA, recently. "When I was asked for my phone number, I refused to give them the last four digits," Bruen says. "I was also asked for my name, and I also refused. The girl at the counter called her supervisor, who told me I could not get a haircut in their shop." Why? The barbershop uses a computer to record all transactions. Bruen went elsewhere to get his locks shorn.

㉗ But can we do that all the time? The computer and its spreading networks convey status and bring opportunity. They empower us. They allow an information economy to thrive and grow. They make life easier. Hence, the dilemma.

㉘ The real problem, says Kevin Kelly, executive editor of *Wired* magazine, is that although we say we value our privacy, what we really want is something very different: "We think that privacy is about information, but it's not—it's about relationships." The way Kelly sees it, there was no privacy in the traditional village or small town; everyone knew everyone else's secrets. And that was comfortable. I knew about you, and you knew about me. "There was a symmetry to the knowledge," he says. "What's gone out of whack is we don't know who knows about us anymore. Privacy has become asymmetrical."

㉙ The trick, says Kelly, is to restore that balance. And not surprisingly, he and others point out that what technology has taken,

> We think that privacy is about information—it's not. It's about relationships.
>
> —Kevin Kelly, executive editor, *Wired* magazine

technology can restore. Take the problem of "magic cookies"—those little bits of code most websites use to track visitors. We set up a system at Pathfinder in which, when you visit our site, we drop a cookie into the basket of your browser that tags you like a rare bird. We use that cookie in place of your name, which, needless to say, we never know. If you look up a weather report by keying in a zip code, we note that (it tells us where you live or maybe where you wish you lived). We'll mark down whether you look up stock quotes (though we draw the line at capturing the symbols of the specific stocks you found). If you come to the *Netly News,* we'll record your interest in technology. Then, the next time you visit, we might serve up an ad for a modem or an online brokerage firm or a restaurant in Akron, Ohio, depending on what we've managed to glean about you.

㉚ Some people find the whole process offensive. "Cookies represent a way of watching consumers without their consent, and that is a fairly frightening phenomenon," says Nick Grouf, CEO of Firefly, a Boston company that makes software offering an alternative approach to profiling, known as "intelligent agents."

㉛ Privacy advocates like Grouf—as well as the two companies that control the online browser market, Microsoft and Netscape— say the answer to the cookie monster is something they call the Open Profiling Standard. The idea is to allow the computer user to create an electronic "passport" that identifies him to online marketers without revealing his name. The user tailors the passport to his own interests, so if he is passionate about fly fishing and is cruising through L.L. Bean's website, the passport will steer the electronic-catalog copy toward fishing gear instead of, say, roller-blades.

32 The advantage to computer users is that they can decide how much information they want to reveal while limiting their exposure to intrusive marketing techniques. The advantage to website entrepreneurs is that they learn about their customers' tastes without intruding on their privacy.

33 Many online consumers, however, are skittish about leaving any footprints in cyberspace. Susan Scott, executive director of TRUSTe, a firm based in Palo Alto, CA, that rates websites according to the level of privacy they afford, says a survey her company sponsored found that forty-one percent of respondents would quit a webpage rather than reveal any personal information about themselves. About twenty-five percent said that when they do volunteer information, they lie. "The users want access, but they don't want to get correspondence back," she says.

34 But worse things may already be happening to their e-mail. Many office electronic-mail systems warn users that the employer reserves the right to monitor their e-mail. In October, software will be available to Wall Street firms that can automatically monitor correspondence between brokers and clients through an artificial-intelligence program that scans for evidence of securities violations.

35 "Technology has outpaced law," says Marc Rotenberg, director of the Washington-based Electronic Privacy Information Center. Rotenberg advocates protecting the privacy of e-mail by encrypting it with secret codes so powerful that even the National Security Agency's supercomputers would have a hard

time cracking it. Such codes are legal within the United States but cannot be used abroad—where terrorists might use them to protect their secrets—without violating U.S.

Protect Yourself

- **Just say no to telemarketers**
  If you don't want to get an unlisted telephone number (cost: $1.50 a month), practice the mantra, "I don't take phone solicitations." Once you buy, you're put on a chump list that's sold to other marketers.

- **Consider removing your name from many direct-mail and telemarketing lists**
  Write to: Direct Marketing Association, Mail/Telephone Preference Service, P.O. Box 9008 (mail) or P.O. Box 9014 (phone), Farmingdale, NY 11735

- **Pay cash whenever possible**
  The less you put on your credit cards, the fewer details anyone has about your buying habits.

- **Be wary about buying mail order**
  Many mail-order companies sell their customer lists. So call the company to check its procedures (unless you like catalogs).

- **Give your Social Security number only when required by law**
  Many organizations, from school to work, use it as your ID number. Resist them. (Experts say it often helps if you can tell someone in authority about your concerns.)

- **Think twice before filling out warranty cards or entering sweepstakes**
  These are data mines for marketers. Besides, most products are guaranteed by your sales receipt. And have you ever won anything in a sweepstakes?

- **Be careful when using "free blood-pressure clinics"**
  Typically, your data will be used by marketers and pharmaceutical companies.

- **Avoid leaving footprints on the Net**
  You're being watched even as you browse. And search engines index your postings to public forums such as Usenet by your name.

export laws. The battle between the Clinton Administration and the computer industry over encryption export policy has been raging for six years without resolution, a situation that is making it hard to do business on the Net and is clearly starting to fray some nerves. "The future is in electronic commerce," says Ira Magaziner, Clinton's point man on Net issues. All that's holding it up is "this privacy thing."

36   Rotenberg thinks we need a new government agency—a privacy agency—to sort out the issues. "We need new legal protections," he says, "to enforce the privacy act, to keep federal agencies in line, to act as a spokesperson for the federal government, and to act on behalf of privacy interests."

37   *Wired*'s Kelly disagrees. "A federal privacy agency would be disastrous! The answer to the whole privacy question is more knowledge," he says. "More knowledge about who's watching you. More knowledge about the information that flows between us—particularly the meta information about who knows what and where it's going."

38   I'm with Kelly. The only guys who insist on perfect privacy are hermits like the Unabomber. I don't want to be cut off from the world. I have nothing to hide. I just want some measure of control over what people know about me. I want to have my magic cookie and eat it too.

Chunking

> **Reading Tip**

Remember to **use** your **surveying skills** and read the beginning of each paragraph to quickly see which ones develop a single idea. ■

▶ Survey the article from paragraphs 14 through 38. Write the idea that links the following groups of paragraphs. Numbers 1 and 5 have been done as examples.

1. Paragraphs 14–15   *Abuses of privacy in the field of health*

2. Paragraphs 16–20   _____

3. Paragraphs 21–24   _____

4. Paragraphs 25–26   _____

5. Paragraphs 27–29   *How to have the right amount of privacy*

6. Paragraphs 30–33   _____

7. Paragraphs 34–35   _____

8. Paragraphs 36–38   _____

▶ Work with a partner to compare your ideas.

Note Taking

Listing information in **note form** is a useful reading strategy that sensitizes you to the connections among ideas as you analyze and restate ideas in your own words. ▪

▶ **A Reporting the Facts** The author of "Invasion of Privacy" explains a number of important issues through the use of facts and examples that are central to each.

▶ **1.** Choose *one* of the following sets of important ideas:

Paragraphs 16–24

Paragraphs 25–35

2. On a separate sheet of paper, prepare notes based on the information in the section of the reading you chose. Use the divided-page system shown in the example on page 31 to make your notes.

3. Work with a partner who prepared notes on the *same set of paragraphs*. Take turns verifying the completeness and correctness of your notes. If necessary, refer to the reading.

▶ **B Sharing the Information** Work with a partner who prepared notes for a *different* section of the reading. Use your notes to explain the information to your partner.

▶ **C Answering Questions from Notes** Using the information from both sets of notes, work with your partner to complete the following.

1. Name three areas in peoples' lives where, because of advances in today's technology, the right to privacy could be compromised.

    a. _____

    b. _____

    c. _____

2. Give two examples of how private information can be discovered and used in a negative way.

    a. _____

    b. _____

3. According to the author, what has been the history of private information gathering? Complete the following time line by listing important events under each time period.

1950s	1960s	1970	Introduction of PCs	Today

Social Security numbers entered on mainframes by U.S. government

4. List the facts that show we have conflicting attitudes about the need for privacy.

Maintain Privacy at All Costs

a. _____

b. _____

c. _____

Forgo Privacy for Convenience

a. _____

b. _____

c. _____

Paired Readings

The readings that follow are about two specific uses/benefits of the Internet. Pick an article and work with someone who has chosen the same one.

1 Benefits of Online Crime?

Predicting

A Read the title and predict what use/benefit this article will discuss and for whom.

What: _____

For whom: _____

B Read the first paragraph. Does it confirm your predictions? If not, change your predictions accordingly.

Skimming

Skim the entire article quickly and answer the following questions.

1. How fast are these "cybersleuth" companies growing?
2. What types of problems do they deal with?
3. What areas have the highest crime rate?

Fighting Crime One Computer at a Time

❶   A lot of perfectly respectable small businesses are raking in money from Internet fraud. From identity theft to bogus stock sales to counterfeit prescription drugs, crime is widespread on the Web. But what has become the Wild West for cybercriminals has also developed into a major business opportunity for cybersleuths.

❷   One of the most well-known is Kroll Ontrack, a technology services provider that Kroll, an international security company based in New York, set up in 1985. Others include ICG Inc. in Princeton, NJ, Decision Strategies in Falls Church, VA, and Cyveillance in Arlington, VA, all started in 1997. "As more and more crime is committed on the Internet, there will be growth of these services," said Rich Mogull, research director of information security and risk at Gartner Inc., a technology-market research firm in Stamford, CT.

❸   ICG, for example, has grown to thirty-five employees and projected revenues of $7 million this year from eight employees and $1.5 million four years ago, said Michael Allison, its founder and chief executive. ICG, which is a licensed private investigator, uses both technology and more traditional cat-and-mouse tactics to track down online troublemakers for major corporations around the world. These include spammers and disgruntled former employees as well as scam artists. "It's exciting getting into the hunt," Mr. Allison, a forty-five-year old British expatriate, said. "You never know what you're going to find. And when you identify and finally catch someone, it's a real rush."

❹   Mi2g, a computer security firm, said online identity theft cost businesses and consumers more than $5 billion last year worldwide, while spamming drained $3.5 billion dollars from corporate coffers. Those numbers are climbing, experts say. "The Internet was never designed to be secure," said Alan E. Brill, senior managing director at Kroll Ontrack. "There are no guarantees."

❺   Kroll has seven crime laboratories around the world and is opening two more in the United States. "It's common to think that we're all former hackers," Mr. Allison said about the industry, and his company in particular. "But it's not true. The people who work here wear ties. Shaving is compulsory. We have former marines, FBI agents, and graduate students. We're a real white-shoe sort of operation." ICG's clients, many of whom he will not identify because of privacy agreements, include pharmaceutical companies, lawyers, financial institutions, Internet service providers, digital entertainment groups, and telecommunications giants.

❻   One of the few cases that ICG can talk about is a spamming problem that happened at Ericsson, the Swedish telecommunications company, a few years ago. Hundreds of thousands of e-mail messages promoting a telephone-sex service inundated its servers hourly, crippling the system, according to the company. "They kept trying to filter it out," said Jeffrey Bedser, chief operating officer of ICG. "But the spam kept on morphing and getting around filters."

❼   While no solution is exactly the same for online detective cases, a general search for a spammer typically involves thousands of webpages, Usenet groups, and message boards. Sometimes, all the searching comes up empty. "There is no hard-and-fast guarantee to identify everyone," Mr. Allison said. "There were cases that I'd hoped we get a result for and just didn't."

❽   It is especially difficult these days, he says, because of cloaking software, such as Anonymizer, that is used to hide the movements of a Web user, as well as the "hijacking" of third-party computers that are then used to carry out illicit activity without the owners of the computers knowing what is happening. In the Ericsson case, Mr. Bedser and his team plugged the spam message into search engines and located other places on the Web where it appeared; some e-mail addresses turned up, which led to a defunct e-fax website; that website had in its registry the name of the spammer, who turned out to be a middle-aged man living in the Georgetown section of Washington.

❾   Several weeks later, the man was sued. He ultimately agreed to a $100,000 civil settlement, though he didn't go away, Mr. Bedser said. "The guy sent me an e-mail that said, 'I know who you are and where you are,'" he recalled. "He also signed me up for all kinds of spam and I ended up getting flooded with e-mail for sex and drugs for the next year."

❿   Over the years, Mr. Allison estimates that ICG has tracked down more than 300 spammers, 75 of which its clients brought to civil court, and 12 of which went to criminal referrals. Mr. Allison says ICG's detective work is, for the most part, unglamorous—sitting in front of computers and "looking for ones and zeros." Still, there are some private-eye moments. Computer forensic work takes investigators to corporate offices all over America, sometimes in the dead of night. Searching through suspect hard drives—always with a company lawyer or executive present—they hunt for "vampire data," or old e-mails and documents that the computer users thought they had deleted long ago.

⓫   In some cases, investigators have to use subterfuge. Once, an ICG staff member befriended a suspect in a "pump-and-dump" scheme—in which swindlers heavily promote a little-known stock to get the price up, then sell their holdings at artificially high prices—by chatting with him electronically on a chess website. Investigators often adopt pseudonyms when they interact on a message board. "We like to masquerade as women," Mr. Allison said. "Typically, we'll use names like Pat, Terry, or Casey so it's ambiguous."

⓬   It is when investigators start coaxing identities and backgrounds out of people under false pretenses that privacy experts start to worry. "There's a lot of work that involves what is kindly called social engineering and what could just as easily be called fraud," said Stewart A. Baker, head of the technology department at the law firm Steptoe & Johnson. "You have to have evidence that holds up to scrutiny in court." There are areas that ICG and other leading sleuthing companies will not touch, such as celebrities, politics, sex, and matrimonial issues. "It's dirt digging," said Mr. Allison.

⓭   Before Mr. Allison opened ICG, he worked as a public information officer for the British government and also spent time running background checks for Wall Street firms. In 1991, he started International Business Research, which grew into ICG six years later. The Internet boom almost guarantees an unending supply of cybercriminals. "They're like mushrooms," Mr. Allison said.

⓮   Right now, the most crowded fields of criminal activity are the digital theft of music and movies, illegal prescription-drug sales, and "phishers," identity thieves who pose as financial institutions like Citibank or Chase and send out fake e-mail messages to people asking for personal account information. The Anti-Phishing Working Group, an industry association, estimates that five to twenty percent of the recipients respond to these messages.

⓯   In 2003, 215,000 cases of identity theft were reported to the Federal Trade Commission, an increase of thirty-three percent from the year before. Bad news for consumers, a growth opportunity for ICG. "The bad guys will always be out there," Mr. Allison said. "But we're getting better and better. And we're catching up quickly."

Scanning for Details

▶ Read each question and look for the answers in the article. Mark the question number in the margin to show where the answer is located. Highlight the information. Use what you highlighted to answer the question in your own words.

1. Why are these services expected to grow?

_____

2. Approximately how much money was lost to Internet crime in the year prior to when the article was written?

_____

3. a. What types of people work at these "cybersleuth" companies?

   _____

   b. What types of companies do they serve?

   _____

4. a. What problem was Ericsson having?

   _____

   b. How was the culprit caught?

   _____

   c. Did he stop? Explain.

   _____

5. What are some ways ICG catches culprits?

   _____.

6. What is the conclusion of the article?

   _____.

▶ Discuss your answers with your partner.

Tellback

▶ Read the article one more time and highlight additional information that you think is interesting. Use what you highlighted to talk about the article. Take turns explaining the information to each other.

2 Friendship Online?

Predicting

▶ **A** Read the title and predict what use/benefit this article will discuss and for whom.

What: _____

For whom: _____

▶ **B** Read the first paragraph. Does it confirm your predictions? If not, change your predictions accordingly.

Skimming

▶ Skim the entire article quickly and answer the following questions.

1. What are these digital "buddies" programmed to do?
2. Why are they so effective?
3. How fast are they spreading?

Web Friend or Faux?

Lifelike digital "buddies" are spreading the word—about products.

1   When none of her friends is online, eleven-year-old Olga Szpiro sends her artificial ones an instant message to chat. "hey ... welcome back!" one replies. "what can i do for u?" But unlike Olga, these friends don't just socialize. They sell. One markets movie tickets. Another talks up a reality television show. A third pushes magazine subscriptions. In a culture inundated with advertising, companies have discovered a new way to connect with consumers and make their messages stand out amid the din. They are using digital "buddies" to spread word of their products on the Internet.

2   The buddies are software applications also known as "bots." They're programmed to make friends and small talk, and they're very good at it. They take cues from a human acquaintance's questions and answers and search databases for conversational fodder. Bot-speak can be formulaic and stilted. It can also be witty, provocative, and startlingly lifelike.

3   Buddies are not mere motor mouths. The more elaborate ones have quirks, preferences, yearnings—virtual personalities. Their presence on the Web represents a powerful new dimension in marketing. It's easy to ignore a billboard or flip past a magazine ad, and many TV viewers reach for the remote the instant a commercial appears. Web-based buddies, on the other hand, make a direct, even intimate, connection with people. They allow companies to reach potential customers one on one, typically in the privacy of their homes. The marketing message need not be heavy-handed or obvious: It can be artfully insinuated into light badinage between buddies.

❹   At least a dozen companies have deployed bots, using software developed by ActiveBuddy Inc., a New York company. Hooking up with human pals through instant message services, they urge people to buy Ford trucks, check out the eBay auction site, and take in *Lord of the Rings*. Appearing in Szpiro's personal message list every time she goes online to chat with one of her Los Angeles classmates, they are indefatigable and ever-present.

❺   Most buddies are programmed with personalities that appeal to their target audiences. ELLEgirl Buddy, the Internet ego of teen magazine *ELLEgirl*, is a redheaded sixteen-year-old who likes kickboxing, the color periwinkle, and French class. Googly Minotaur, a buddy for the British progressive rock band Radiohead, affected a British demeanor with words like "mate." The Austin Powers buddy, which promotes the summer film *Goldmember*, interjects the movie character's favorite phrases—"yeah, baby" and "grrr"—into conversation.

❻   Some buddies are even programmed to express emotions—sadness, frustration, desire. In the year since it debuted, people have told SmarterChild, the demo buddy for ActiveBuddy, "I love you" more than nine million times, the company reports. Every time, it's responded, "I love you." Though most users understand they are communicating with a computer, some engage in deep conversation with buddies, talking to them as they would to friends. College students look them up late at night. Teenagers consult them about fashion faux pas and weight problems.

❼   Such exchanges reveal how technology can assume a lifelike character in people's minds, even when it's just an elaborate advertisement. "People forget in very profound ways that they are talking to nothing," said Sherry Turkle, director of MIT's initiative on technology and self. Computers first chatted in the mid-1960s, when Massachusetts Institute of Technology professor Joseph Weizenbaum created a software program called Eliza. Designed to converse in the manner of a psychotherapist, Eliza asked people questions by rephrasing their previous statements. The "patient" typed questions on a keyboard. Eliza's answer appeared on the screen moments later.

❽   In a typical exchange, a user said that she was "depressed much of the time."

"I am sorry to hear you are depressed," Eliza replied.

"It's true. I am unhappy," the person typed.

"Do you think coming here will help you not to be unhappy?" Eliza asked.

Some of Eliza's chat partners thought they were communicating with a human being. A few even formed emotional bonds with the program. Disturbed by these reactions, Weizenbaum lost his enthusiasm for artificial intelligence and wrote a book warning of its potential dangers.

9 The technology has only grown more sophisticated since then. Today's buddies operate through instant message services such as America Online's AIM and Microsoft's MSN Messenger, which allow people to communicate in real time at their keyboards. A buddy can't crash into someone's cyberspace; they have to be invited. Users maintain online lists of friends and send them instant messages by clicking on their screen names. People add digital buddies to their lists after learning of them by word of mouth or from websites.

10 When a user clicks on a buddy's screen name, a computer server receives the message. By analyzing key words, it interprets what the user is saying and formulates an appropriate response. Typically, a buddy's speech content is tailored to the products or services of its sponsoring company. The Sporting News offers sports scores. Agent Reuters looks up stock quotes. Bots can promote causes as well as companies. The Virginia Tobacco Settlement Foundation recently launched an anti-smoking buddy that says, among other things, "Smoking can really make you sick."

11 When developers created the software for buddies, they focused on delivering information, not making chitchat, said Stephen Klein, ActiveBuddy's chief executive. But after launching their demo buddy last year, company officials discovered that users engaged it in lengthy chat sessions, sometimes submitting more than a hundred messages in one sitting. So programmers tweaked the software to improve its chat capabilities.

12 Buddies don't always understand a user's submission and sometimes ask for clarification, but their responses often seem quite human. Tell SmarterChild that you are sad, and it replies that "there are plenty of things to feel good about ... listen to music, go for a walk, learn something new, read a book, be creative." Use vulgar language and it asks you to "play nice." Request a kiss and it obliges with three Xs.

13 More than eight million people have added SmarterChild to their personal message lists, creating almost a cult following. Hundreds of users have posted their conversations with the bot online. One fan website, Imaddict.com, displays portions of several dozen conversations with the buddy.

"So will you go out with me?" one user asked.

"You're human, I'm a machine," the buddy replied. "I don't think that would work out."

⓮   ActiveBuddy's bots save details about each user—names, birth dates, even instances when the person used offensive language. When the buddy recalls these facts, it could appear to the user that it is taking a genuine interest in him or her. "We're programmed to respond to certain signals as though in the presence of a life form," said MIT's Turkle. "These objects are pushing our buttons."

⓯   ELLEgirl Buddy lives in San Francisco with her mother, father, and older brother. Her favorite book is *Catcher in the Rye*. Her favorite television show is *Buffy the Vampire Slayer*. And her favorite band is No Doubt. When she grows up, she wants to design handbags, own a bookstore café, and work overseas as a foreign correspondent. "i looove making my own clothes," ELLEgirl Buddy says in an instant message. "i use gap tees a lot. you just shrink em and add ribbons. insta-chic! i like kickboxing, reading ... i like 2 curl up with a book and an extra-chocolaty mocha. yum!" The buddy—launched in mid-February to drive users to the website for *ELLEgirl* magazine—responds to questions as a sixteen-year-old girl would. It has programmed answers to questions about ELLEgirl Buddy's family, school, and aspirations. The bot's personality is so developed that some girls see it as a cyber-confidant, writing to it about bad haircuts and image problems. "It's something you wouldn't ask a computer," said Judy Koutsky, senior director of ELLEgirl.com. "It's almost like a girlfriend." Online subscriptions to the magazine were seven times higher in May than the month before the launch, in part because of the buddy, Koutsky said.

Christine Frey, *Los Angeles Times*

Scanning for Details

🔘 Read each question and look for the answers in the article. Mark the question number in the margin to show where the answer is located. Highlight the information. Use what you highlighted to answer the question in your own words.

1. What are the characteristics of "bots"?

_____

2. a. What types of personalities are they programmed with?

_____

   b. What types of emotions can they express?

_____

3. a. Do the users treat these "bots" as machines? Explain.

_____

   b. What personality was Eliza impersonating and what effect did "she" have?

   _____

4. What is the principle behind the operation of these "bots"?

   _____

5. What type of information does ActiveBuddy save and what effect does this have?

   _____

6. What is the conclusion of the article?

   _____

▶ Discuss your answers with your partner.

Tellback   ▶ Read the article one more time and highlight additional information that you think is interesting. Use what you highlighted to talk about the article. Take turns explaining the information to each other.

▶Comparing the Readings

Reacting to the Information   ▶ **A** Work with a partner who read a different article. Use what you highlighted to talk about the information in your article.

▶ **B** **Ethical Issues** Based on the information in the two articles, and your own opinion, think about the following questions.

1. What does the success of programs like "bots" say about society today?
2. Do you think it is ethical for companies to use such advertising techniques?
3. Do you think "cybersleuthing" is another form of invasion of privacy?
4. If yes, does the fact that criminals are being caught justify the actions of the investigators?
5. Comment on the following statements.
    a. "It's ("bot" program) almost like a girlfriend." ("Web Friend or Faux?" paragraph 15)
    b. "There's a lot of work that involves what is kindly called social engineering and what could just as easily be called fraud." ("Fighting Crime One Computer at a Time," paragraph 12)

▶ Discuss your opinions in a small group.

Applying the Information

▶ **Problems and Solutions** Discuss each of the following situations with a partner. Analyze the situation and decide whether it is a problem or not. If it is a problem, brainstorm some possible solutions. If not, give the reasons for your opinion.

1. You subscribe to a cable company that has a monitor program. Using this program, the company can find out exactly what programs and channels you are watching. This information can be checked against your address and other demographic information. Using this information, advertisers could direct specific commercials at TV viewers in your house.

2. A politician running for office uses a computer program that can analyze demographic and lifestyle information of voters in a given district. The politician's campaign organization can use this information to tailor the content and style of the politician's message. In addition, the program can help identify people who could make big contributions to the politician's campaign.

3. You have a bank card that allows you to take money out of the bank at any time of the day or night. You can also use the card to buy things at many different types of stores. The bank card company automatically records the transaction every time you use the card. A software company has made a program that can analyze this data and make it available to anyone who wants to buy it. With this information, banks or other institutions can rate you and use the ratings to decide your value as a customer.

4. You go to the bank to withdraw money from your account and discover that the bank has frozen your account. Your credit card is no longer valid. It seems that your identity has been stolen and the thief has made thousands of dollars of purchases in your name. The thief even applied for and received a bank loan using your name.

❯Vocabulary Building

Word Form

▶ **A** Study these five words and their forms. Then choose the correct form for each part of speech in the chart on the next page. These words are commonly found in general and academic texts.

appreciate (v.)	alternate (v.)	clarify (v.)	discriminate (v.)	transform (v.)
appreciation (n.)	alternative	clarification	discrimination	transformed
appreciable (adj.)	alternatively	clarifying	discriminative	transforming
appreciative (adj.)	alternating	clarity	discriminatingly	transformable
appreciably (adv.)	alternative		discriminating	transformation

Verb	Noun	Adjective	Adverb
alternate	1.	1.	1.
		2.	
clarify	1.	1.	
	2.		
discriminate	1.	1.	1.
		2.	
transform	1.	1.	
		2.	
		3.	

▷ Compare your lists with a partner.

▷ **B** Write three sentences using words from the list. Use different parts of speech.

Vocabulary in Context

▷ **A** **Expressions** Use the context of the reading to understand the meaning of each expression in boldface below. Use each expression in a sentence of your own.

1. ICG, which is a licensed private investigator, uses both technology and more traditional **cat-and-mouse tactics** to track down online troublemakers. ("Fighting Crime ..." paragraph 3)

_____

2. It's exciting getting into the hunt. You never know what you're going to find. And when you identify and finally catch someone, it's **a real rush**. ("Fighting Crime ..." paragraph 3)

_____

3. There are areas that ICG and other leading sleuthing companies will not touch, such as celebrities, politics, sex, and matrimonial issues. "It's **dirt digging**," said Mr. Allison. ("Fighting Crime ..." paragraph 12)

_____

4. The Internet boom almost guarantees an unending supply of cybercriminals. "They're **like mushrooms**." ("Fighting Crime ..." paragraph 13)

_____

5. A buddy can't **crash** into someone's cyberspace; they have to be invited. ("Web Friend …" paragraph 9)

_____

6. When developers created the software for buddies, they focused on delivering information, not **making chitchat**. ("Web Friend …" paragraph 11)

_____

7. Use vulgar language and it asks you to "**play nice**." ("Web Friend …" paragraph 12)

_____

8. We're programmed to respond to certain signals as though in the presence of a life form. These objects are **pushing our buttons**. ("Web Friend …" paragraph 14)

_____

◐ Compare your answers with a partner. Take turns reading your sentences aloud. Check with your teacher if you are not sure about what any of the expressions mean.

◐ **B Word Choice** One technique that writers use to provide variety is to use different words to describe the same person or idea. From the reading "Invasion of Privacy," find and circle the word or words used for the following items.

1. the hacker who changed the telephone number

2. gives information quickly

3. look through

4. a haircut

5. record

6. learn

◐ Work with a partner to compare your answers. Check them with your whole class.

Expanding Your Language

Speaking

A Two-Minute Taped Talk Make a two-minute audio recording about the ideas in the notes you wrote for a section of this chapter's reading (see page 151). To make your recording, follow these steps.

1. Review your notes.
2. Practice explaining the information. Include as many of the important facts as you can within the time frame you have to speak.
3. Time yourself as you try to speak as clearly and naturally as possible.
4. Record yourself telling the information.
5. Give your tape to your teacher for feedback.

B Debating the Issue What is your position on the statement, "Privacy should be maintained at all costs"? Follow these steps to debate the issue.

1. Choose your position.
2. Work with a partner who shares your position and identify 3–4 points supporting your position.
3. Develop your points by finding explanations, examples, etc. (Use your own experience whenever possible.)
4. Take turns practicing presenting and explaining your points.
5. Debate against those who prepared opposing arguments.

Writing

A Reaction Writing React in writing to the ideas presented in either one or both articles, "Web Friend or Faux" or "Fighting Crime One Computer at a Time." Use the questions in "Reacting to the Information" (page 161) to help you.

B Topic Writing Review the chapter's discussion questions and your notes. Use the information from these exercises and from the readings to help focus your ideas, then complete the following steps.

1. Write a list of ideas for each of the following in your journal notebook.
   - The convenience of Internet access for shopping and other services
   - The benefits of Internet access for information and communication
   - The problem of criminal activity and access to private information via the Internet
   - The problem of depending too much on the Internet

2. Work with a partner and explain your ideas to each other.

3. Write a draft of a three-paragraph essay with these main ideas.

   Paragraph 1: The benefits of the Internet

   Paragraph 2: The drawbacks of the Internet

   Paragraph 3: Do the benefits outweigh the drawbacks?

4. Show your draft to a partner for peer review.

5. Rewrite your draft and give the final writing to your teacher.

Online Study Center   For additional activities, go to the ***Reading Matters*** Online Study Center at *college.hmco.com/pic/wholeyfour2e.*

8 Cell Phones: Blessing or Curse

◗Chapter Openers

Discussion Questions

◗ Discuss the following questions in a small group.

1. Do you have a cell phone? If not, why not?
2. What proportion of people around you have cell phones?
3. If you had to choose between a cell phone and a land phone, which would you choose and why?
4. Do you think people are becoming too dependent on cell phones? Explain.
5. Should everyone in the world have access to cell phones? Why or why not?
6. In what situations is having a cell phone essential? When is it a nuisance or an unnecessary distraction?

Scanning

◗ There are many reports about cell phones in the news. Scan these short summaries of news reports from NPR (National Public Radio) Online and highlight information that shows that cell phones are:

- helpful.
- problematic.
- neither.
- both.

Cell Phone Rally

In an effort to unseat Philippine president Joseph Estrada, Filipinos sent thirty million cell phone "text messages" daily—more than anywhere else in the world. Activists are using the technology to organize rallies and respond instantly to the latest corruption charges.

Cell Phone Courtesy

San Diego is trying a new campaign to encourage more courteous use of cell phones. Cell phone maker Nokia and the San Diego city government are teaming up to post signs asking cell phone users to turn off their ringers, or their phones, in public places such as churches, libraries, and movie theaters.

The FBI and Cell Phones

The Federal Bureau of Investigation is trying to gain an extended authority to precisely track cellular phones and where their users are. The FBI says it needs to be able to pinpoint criminal use of cell phones, but industry officials and privacy advocates oppose the plans, citing how much the new measures to track cellular phones would cost, and that it would violate the privacy of cell phone users.

Cell Phones in Cars

With cell phone sales increasing dramatically, there has been a sharp rise in the number of car accidents caused by drivers talking on their cell phones. In Brooklyn, Ohio, a new city ordinance is banning motorists from that activity, and police will begin ticketing motorists who don't have both hands on the steering wheel.

Cell Phone Cameras

As the man in front of him at the grocery store began yelling at a cashier who could not process his credit card, Gary Dann flipped open his camera phone and pressed a few buttons, pretending to look up a number. Moments later, as the man paid in cash, his snarling picture appeared on Dann's website complete with an unflattering caption. Dann, 23, who lives in Philadelphia, keeps an online journal of his cell phone snapshots.

▶ Work with a partner or in a small group to discuss the reasons for your choices. Decide on the most helpful and the most problematic uses of cell phones. Be prepared to discuss your ideas with others in the class.

Exploring and Understanding Reading

Previewing   ▶ Read the title and section headings of the following article. Answer the following.

1. What is the focus of the article?

_____

2. What three areas will be discussed?

_____

_____

_____

▶ Discuss what you know about cell phones and each of these areas before you start reading the article.

Skimming

▶ Read the article quickly. What general conclusions can you make about the following statements?

1. Cell phones cause cancer.
2. Cell phone use while driving is dangerous.
3. Cell phone users are a nuisance to those around them.

▶ Discuss your conclusions with a partner or in a small group.

Cell Phone: A Convenience, a Hazard, or Both?

❶   When a new technology takes off, it seems to fly with the speed of light. So it is with cell phones, now owned by well over half the population and soon to be found in more than ninety percent of American households. The latest trend is to replace one's land line with a cell phone, but that action seems a bit premature, given the erratic nature of many cell phone connections.

❷   Still, the potential is there, and when you can carry a phone wherever you go, you can spend many more hours on the phone than you would if a land line was all you had. This raises critical questions that have been asked for nearly a decade with little resolution. How safe are they? What effect do they have on quality of life? Recent bans in New York State and elsewhere on the use of hand-held phones while driving only begin to address these questions, and with limited effectiveness.

A Cause of Cancer?

❸   Right up front, I must say that it is not possible to prove definitively that anything is safe. Science can only produce evidence that makes it highly unlikely that a hazard exists. Widespread fears that cell phones could increase the risk of brain cancer began in January 1993 when David Raynard, whose wife talked on a cell phone "all the time" and subsequently died of brain cancer, appeared on *Larry King Live* and told viewers he was suing the cell phone industry on the grounds that it was responsible for his wife's illness. Since then, more than a dozen studies have been conducted here and abroad. None have found any credible evidence for a link between cell phone use and any kind of cancer. To be sure, all the studies had limits, and if a relationship exists it may take thirty or forty years of cell phone use to show it, not the ten years or less covered by the studies.

❹   But there is also biology to consider. Do cell phones generate the kinds of radiation that could conceivably cause cancer? Dr. Robert L. Park of the

American Physical Society addressed that question last year in an editorial in *The Journal of the National Cancer Institute*. "All known cancer-inducing agents—including radiation, certain chemicals, and a few viruses—act by breaking chemical bonds, producing mutant strands of DNA," Dr. Park wrote. "Not until the ultraviolet region of the electromagnetic spectrum is reached, beyond visible light, beyond infrared, and far, far beyond microwaves, do photons have sufficient energy to break chemical bonds. Microwave photons heat tissue, but they do not come close to the energy needed to break chemical bonds, no matter how intense the radiation." In other words, cell phones, which operate with radio frequencies in the microwave range, do not emit ionizing radiation, the type that damages DNA. So I would say at this point, cancer is the least of one's worries when it comes to using cell phones.

A Road Hazard?

❺   Cars, trucks, and vans these days come equipped with a host of electronic devices that can easily distract the most conscientious of drivers, and the future promises even more. Just try tuning the radio while driving a car that has been produced in the last five or ten years and it becomes clear. Distractions abound that can interfere with safe driving. A study supported by the Automobile Association of America Foundation and  conducted by the University of North Carolina Highway Safety Research Center revealed that distractions outside the vehicle, such as gawking at accidents, other drivers, pedestrians, animals, and even road construction were the primary distraction culprits in road accidents. After visual distractions came adjusting the radio or sound system and interacting with passengers. Talking on a cell phone was the least prominent distraction in serious crashes, accounting for 1.5 percent of 5,000 accidents, the same as eating and drinking or smoking.

❻   But the researchers believe the role of cell phones was most likely underreported. Publicity about the risks of phoning while driving may have made drivers in accidents less willing to admit to talking on the phone.

Furthermore, without knowing how many cell phone calls result in crashes (as opposed to how many radio adjustments), it is impossible to rank the risk accurately. In Japan, where the police have kept track of accidents caused by the use of cell phones, cell phone-related crashes plummeted by 75 percent after 1999 when the country banned the use of hand-held phones while driving. In New York, where a similar ban took effect in November 2001, the law is still widely ignored. Had I not shouted to an elderly woman crossing a Brooklyn street with the light the other day, she would have been hit by a minivan turning the corner driven by a woman talking on her hand-held cell phone and apparently totally unaware of the pedestrian.

7 But restrictions on hand-held phones address only part of the hazard—that of having to juggle a phone while steering, braking, and shifting. Instead, the effects of a phone conversation on the brain are likely to be more important, and those effects apply equally to hand-held and hands-free phones. Studies of brain function during multitasks like driving and talking on a phone have shown that the brain's ability to attend to each task is significantly diminished. One study cited by Dr. Paul Green of the University of Michigan Transportation Research Institute showed that hands-on or hands-off, the risk of a crash is about four times as great when a driver is talking on the phone as it is when the phone is not in use. "Requiring the use of hands-free phones may reduce the risk associated with retrieving and holding the phone," Dr. Green said, "but the main problem is that the act of answering the phone can happen at an inopportune time—in heavy traffic, for example."

8 He noted that a phone conversation was not the same as talking to a passenger, who might notice a potential road hazard even before the driver does and stop talking and perhaps even warn the driver. But the person at the other end of a phone call has no idea what is happening on the road and keeps chatting. A smart driver will interrupt the call when a hazard arises, but only if the driver notices it in the first place. Having a phone in a car is a good idea. It can relieve anxiety in unavoidable delays and be lifesaving in an emergency. But safety-conscious drivers would be wise to avoid using it for casual conversations and should always pull off the road when dialing, talking, or answering it.

A Nuisance Factor?

9 Finally, there is the question of common courtesy. Most cell phone users seem to think the person on the other end is deaf. They all but shout into their phones, disturbing everyone within 25 feet or more. It is especially annoying in places where there is no escape from someone else's cell phone conversation, such as airport gates where you may be trying to read, work, or doze in peace. Phones outside of homes, once housed in booths, are now separated by partitions to prevent others from listening to or being disturbed by a phone conversation. But there are no barriers around cell phone users. They should take a moment to find a private place for long business or personal calls.

❿   I suppose I should have been amused by my unavoidable eavesdropping on a cell phone conversation on the street involving a young woman who was trying to find out from her boyfriend why he had stopped calling her. But, in fact, I was annoyed, because I had other things to think about that were far more important to me.

Jane E. Brody, *The New York Times,* October 1, 2002, p. F7. Copyright © 2002 by The New York Times Co. Reprinted with permission.

Scanning for Details

▶ **Understanding Results from Studies** Read each question and look for the answers in the article. Mark the question number in the margin to show where the answer is located. Highlight the information. Use what you highlighted to answer the question in your own words.

1. Why is it not yet a good idea to replace a land line with a cell phone?

   _____

2. What questions has the increased use of cell phones raised?

   _____

3. Explain where the idea that cell phones cause cancer originated.

   _____

4. a. Since then, what have studies shown?

   _____

   b. Are the results from these studies final? Explain.

   _____

5. a. What agents cause cancer and how?

   _____

   b. Why is it unlikely that there is a connection between cell phones and cancer?

   _____

6. List the possible driver distractions identified in the study carried out by the University of North Carolina Highway Safety Research Center from most (a) to least (c) distractive.

   a. _____

   b. _____

   c. _____

7. Give two reasons why researchers felt the results concerning cell phones were not accurate.

   a. _____

   b. _____

8. What is the significance of the information from Japan?

   _____

9. What additional effect is there other than that of just having to hold the phone and drive?

   _____

10. What does the study done by Dr. Paul Green show about

    a. the difference between hands-on and hands-off phones?

       _____

    b. the difference between talking to a passenger and talking on a cell phone?

       _____

11. Why is cell phone use annoying to others?

    _____

12. What is the main difference between public phones and cell phones?

    _____

▶ Compare your answers with a partner or in a small group.

Inferring Opinion

▷ Writers do not always express their opinion explicitly. Sometimes they present information in such a way that the reader is led to a particular conclusion. Now that you have read the article in more detail, discuss with a partner what the writer wants us to conclude about each of the three areas discussed:

- Cell phones cause cancer.
- Cell phone use while driving is dangerous.
- Cell phone users are a nuisance to those around them.

1. Do you agree with the writer? Why or why not?
2. Do you think the writer would agree with the following statements?
   a. Cell phone use while driving should be banned.
   b. Cell phone conversations in confined public places should be banned.
3. Do you agree with these statements? Why or why not?

Surveying

▷ **A** Read the following article quickly and bracket the sections in which the author is drawing the following conclusions.

1. Cell phones force us to hear information which should be private to others.
2. Cell phones force us to hear embarrassing information.
3. Cell phones have changed our definition of personal "space."
4. Cell phones allow us to violate our own privacy.
5. Cell phones are breaking the everyday contact we have with people around us.
6. Cell phones have made the people around us invisible.
7. Cell phones enable us to live in our own virtual community.

▷ **B** Highlight the examples that correspond to each conclusion.

▷ **C** Use what you highlighted to talk about the article.

Cell Phones Have Transformed How We Communicate

The blessing and the curse of the cell phone turned out to be in the way it has enabled us to live in our own virtual community and opt out of the community around us.

❶   The flight ends, the ritual begins. Wheels down, cell phones up. Within seconds, the woman standing behind me in a crowded plane aisle has called her office and begun a cranky and noisy inquisition. Has the memo gone out warning "Ken was not a suitable candidate for trafficking director"?

2   Mind you, I don't know this woman. Nor do I know Ken. Nor do I know what a trafficking director is. But there she is, publicly sharing office gossip, not to mention Ken's future, with at least six people on either end of her substantial voice range.

3   This was by no means the only cell snippet of a life story to come my way through the mobile airwaves. Nor was it the most outrageous. In just the past few weeks, there was the woman who got on the train in Boston with a shaky relationship—"I did not leave my things at your place on purpose"—and got off in New York with no relationship. There was the father in Cincinnati whose son's SAT scores—540 in math, 480 in English—were audibly not what he hoped for. There was the doctor in the grocery store discussing a CAT scan of a patient in Milwaukee.

4   By now we have all had little bits of dialogue float past us on the street. A *tete-a-tete* is now a *tete-a-tous*. What once was told in quiet now wafts by any open ear. Cell stories have become the oral equivalent of indecent exposure. But this morning, with poor Ken's fate hanging in the airplane, my annoyance went on speed dial. It occurred to me the line between what's public and what's private must have been inadvertently severed when the first phone line was disconnected from the wall.

5   Text messaging has taken off in Japan in part because it's considered unutterably rude to blather on in public. North Americans seem to have no such problem. I've seen them all: the blowhard blaring into his hand-held, the gossip giggling over her screen phone, the discreet mumbler muttering seemingly to himself. And with this chatter has gone a basic principle of civilized urban life—of decorum, privacy, manners. The invention of the cell phone has confirmed people's illusory sense of their own personal space. To someone wired to the wider world, my space versus your space no longer exists.

6   Is it barely a generation since phones became mobile? Once, the phone booth was the place where people could protect their privacy. Now, cell-phoners strip in public. And city folks who long ago cultivated a way of avoiding eye contact are now supposed to avoid ear contact. No one's embarrassed anymore to discuss intimate details of their lives in front of strangers. I've heard people instructing their wives on beers to buy and their brokers on stocks to sell. I've waited at pedestrian crossings as young women shamelessly dissected their absent dates and young men boasted of their conquests—naming names. I've tried to concentrate on a newspaper on a train while the woman in front of me reassured a succession of callers that she was on her way back to their apparently anxious arms.

7   On the politically sensitive Washington-to-New York run, as well as various commuter lines, Amtrak introduced "quiet cars" for those who want to travel undisturbed by the conversational patter of others. But too often these are invaded by business travelers who want to put every minute of their time to profitable use: they spend the entire journey striking deals, wheedling clients, and leaving messages for distant assistants. A friend tells me of an acquaintance who recently overheard two lawyers discussing the details of a merger—involving her company!

❽   Of course, people have always had a yen for sharing a little too much— the garrulous granny on a crosstown bus loudly describing her ailments to the lady on the next seat in the mistaken assumption that everyone was as deaf as she was. Once upon a time, people with cell phones would be among the first to roll their eyes at such behavior. Nowadays, they're the ones who infringe on our peace—and their own, if only they were aware.

❾   Indeed, cell technology has transformed into all sorts of odd behavior. We now have people who perform running commentary on the minutiae of their daily lives as they travel down a grocery line—"Honey, I'm at the avocados"—or round the corner. A favorite New Yorker cartoon tracks a cell phone narrator through three panels: "I'm boarding the train. I'm on the train. I'm leaving the train."

❿   At the same time, it has cut down the number of small personal encounters that make strangers feel as if they inhabit the same world. It might not be a safety hazard to talk to one person while ordering coffee from another, but what was the woman's message to her hair-stylist when she talked on the phone while he cut her hair? You're invisible?

⓫   The same applies to those who are not strangers. Not a day goes by, I've found, without my spotting a couple on the street, sometimes even holding hands—one of them ignoring the other and chatting on the cell phone. Last week, while standing on the corner trying to hail a cab, I hit the jackpot: a couple quite visibly together, walking side by side, each of them animatedly engaged in separate conversations. Why bother to be together, I wondered, if you'd rather be talking to someone else?

⓬   The blessing and the curse of the cell phone turned out to be in the way it has enabled us to live in our own virtual community and opt out of the physical community around us. We never have to be exclusively where we are, on the road or a mountaintop or the aisle of an airplane. Even the area code that once described a piece of geography has been dislocated. We can keep in constant contact with a wandering teenager or a wandering employee—but we never know precisely where they are.

⓭   The diminished sense of place and the increased sense of anonymity have together transformed privacy in the cell story age. It is easier to hang your feelings or your son's SAT scores out in public if the people around you are invisible. U.S. Supreme Court Justice Louis Brandeis once, famously, described privacy as "the right to be let alone." But Brandeis didn't have a cell phone. The original fear was that someone would invade your space, dig into the personal details of your life. But what do you call it when someone invades your space with personal details of *their* life?

Memo to the woman on the plane with the cell phone: I'm here and I'm listening.

Memo to Ken: Better buff up that resume.

Adapted from Ellen Goodman, *The Gazette,* and Shashi Tharoor, *Newsweek*

Applying the Information

▶ **A** With a partner or in a small group, use information from the article above, as well as your own information, to discuss how cell phones violate our privacy and change the way we communicate.

▶ **B** Relate your own experience to the information in the article by discussing the following questions.

1. Have you found yourself in a situation where you heard information that you felt you should not be hearing?
2. How did you feel/react?
3. Have you yourself used a cell phone in a way that you later felt was inappropriate? Describe what happened.
4. What is your response to the question at the end of the article: "But what do you call it when someone invades your space with personal details of *their* life?"

A Different Point of View

▶ So far we have focused on how cell phones are regarded in the United States. The following article will look at cell phones in the developing world. Before you read the article, discuss the following.

1. Should cell phones be made easily accessible in the developing world?
2. In what way(s) would the role played by cell phones there be different from that in developed countries?
3. Do you think people will have the same reactions with regards to privacy? Explain.

Previewing

▶ Read the title and subtitle, then answer these questions.

1. To what two items is the cell phone being compared?
2. What do you expect the focus of the article will be?
3. What type of information do you think this article will give?

Surveying

Reading Tip

Some paragraphs are **just linking** paragraphs. They either **conclude** a section or **introduce** the next or both. ■

▶ Read the first three paragraphs and the first sentence of every paragraph after that. Identify the thesis and the main ideas of the article. Rephrase these in your own words.

Thesis

_____

_____

Main Ideas	**Paragraphs**
1. _____	_____
2. _____	_____
3. _____	_____

▶ Compare your answers with a partner or in a small group.

A World of Difference

To westerners, the cell phone may be just a toy and sometimes a nuisance. But to the dispossessed migrant workers—the poor of the developing world—it is a lifeline.

❶   In the past few years, the cell phone has become one of the most commonplace pieces of technology in the world. What began as a cumbersome and costly tool for the high-flying western executive has grown into a cheap and accessible device with an almost universal appeal. This is, in fact, the first digital device to fall into so many hands so fast. Unlike all its predecessors and, no doubt, many of its successors, too, the cell phone has found its way to the young and the old, the rich and the poor, men and women all around the world.

❷   The purposes to which the cell phone is put, the meanings it assumes, the ways in which it is used, and the attitudes it provokes seem to be as varied as its users. Some people see the cell phone as a terrible invasion of both their private lives and their public space; others love to feel in touch with anyone at any time. For some, the cell phone is a key to a new kind of independence, the means to a life unbound from the office desk or the family; others see it instituting a new kind of dependency, entrapping them in a world of connectivity without escape. Many people argue that the cell phone is establishing new kinds of networks on unprecedented scales; for others, it is merely reducing people's circles to the local list contained on their own Sim card.

3 Such differences of opinion are by no means special to regions of the world, or even nationalities: the attitudes of a group of young people in Birmingham are likely to be as wide-ranging as those of a group of people from all corners of the world. But a few broad observations about cell phone use on a global scale can be made without the risk of too much oversimplification.

4 For a start, it is easy for westerners to treat the cell phone as an unnecessary toy. In lands of telecommunications aplenty, this may indeed be true. But for people across the developing world, where getting a fixed phone line remains a bureaucratic impossibility, the cell phone revolution has allowed them to leapfrog from archaic forms of communication straight into the digital era—and that is changing the fabric of their daily lives. To them, access to a phone is often something new and something to be cherished.

5 The mobile phone has made an enormous difference to, for example, sub-Saharan Africa, a region to which, in the course of just five years, wireless technologies have brought far more telephones than the old wired system brought in the whole of the twentieth century. In 2004, Rwanda already had five times as many cell phones (134,000) as fixed telephone lines (23,000), according to the International Telecommunications Union. As in Rwanda, people elsewhere across Africa are coming to appreciate and rely upon the magic of the cell phone—communicating with a distant friend while under a baobab tree in Mali, for example, or on the Kenyan savanna. In Senegal, farmers use them

in their annual, age-old battle against plagues of locusts, calling each other and the authorities to keep track of the progress of insect "hopper bands." In Somalia, men in loincloths flash their cell phones as they guide camels to port. Masai warriors in Tanzania pull phones from their red "shuka" robes to call gem brokers when they find glimmering purple-blue tanzanite, a rare gemstone found only in the shadow of Mount Kilimanjaro.

6 In Latin America, the number of cell phones has tripled since 1999, and one in five people now owns one. In Caracas, Venezuela, where half of the city's population lives in non-wired slums, cell phones with pay-as-you-go cards have provided communication services to many residents for the first time. In Peru, as in many other countries in the region, there are more cell phones than fixed phone lines. Tiny villages in the western Amazon jungle, like Iquitos, are now among the more remote outposts in South America's expanding cellular phone system, part of a global network that is beginning to penetrate even the poorest and most undeveloped corners of the world.

❼   A few kilometers downriver from Iquitos, Andres Alvarado hops off a boat and walks up a muddy path to a hollowed-out log on a wooden stand. He beats the log with a stick, sending a series of low-pitched tones into the rain forest. "This is what they call the 'telephone of the jungle,'" says Alvarado, a tricycle taxi-driver and tourist guide. Moments later, as children of the Bora Indian tribe come bounding down the path to answer the "telephone," Alvarado's belt begins beeping: It's his cell phone. Alvarado uses it to round up clients for his tricycle taxi. And earlier this year, it beeped with the most important call of his life. "My mother-in-law called me from the delivery room," Alvarado recalled. His wife had gone into labor with their first child, and he raced to the hospital on his tricycle. "We all thought we were going to have a girl, but it turned out to be a boy." He flashed the news from the hospital to his sister in Lima, Peru, via his cell phone, the kind of call that might seem routine in North America but which still carries for him an aura of science fiction.

❽   Furthermore, being connected in the developing world means much more than just shopping on eBay. Information technology evangelists believe that such technology can help bring better education and health care to rural areas, and make them wealthier, too. "Poor people are poor because they're stuck in an environment that is stifling," said Iqbal Z. Quadir, a former New York investment banker who returned to his native Bangladesh in 1996 to build a rural cellular network with Grameen Bank. "If they are connected, the environment changes and everyone's life gets better." Mr. Quadir's GrameenPhone lends money to village women like thirty-year-old Hosne-ara to buy cellular telephones. Hosne-ara, who lives in the mud-and-thatch-hut village of Porabari, 15 km north of the Bangladeshi capital of Dhaka, bought a Nokia handset with the loan and is in turn selling fellow villagers time on the phone. They use it for calling relatives abroad, checking rice and poultry prices, arranging bank transfers, or consulting doctors in distant cities. It also earns Hosne-ara some $600 a year—twice the annual per capita income in Bangladesh. Today, GrameenPhone's rural resellers connect 2,800 villages and pocket on average $2 a day—equivalent to a large chunk of average income.

9   People who, not long ago, had to make a day's journey to use a telephone are generally rather less dismissive of cell phones than those to whom the devices provide one more of many means of communication.

10   Second, it seems that the cell phone is received very differently in what might be described as collective, sociable cultures than in those with a rather more individualistic style. In Thailand, for example, or even in Italy, where people have always tended to live interconnected, even communal lives, the use of cell phones is high, and few objections are raised to the volumes at which people speak, the contexts in which they make or take their calls, or the nature of the conversations they might overhear. Calls received in cinemas in a city such as Bangkok, or even in monasteries in the Thai countryside, meet with little of the disapproval that frequently awaits them in the West. In the United States, where complaints and misgivings about cellular phones run high, levels of cell phone use are so low that, for the first time in a hundred years, America finds itself trailing behind the technological state of play in so much of the rest of the world.

11   There are several technological and economic reasons for America's reluctance to engage with the cell phone. But the importance placed by many Americans on privacy, autonomy, and personal space are hardly incidental when it comes to explaining this unprecedented lag.

12   Finally, opinions and uses of the cell phone tend also to depend on the most obvious of all its attributes—its mobility. The cell phone thrives wherever there is movement: with the vast populations drifting to the cities of China; illegal migrant workers establishing themselves within the European Union; Kenyan taxi drivers looking for new fares; people crammed together on commuter trains; and demonstrators on the streets of Manila, Caracas, or the many other cities that have seen the cell phone used as the effective tool for movements of the political kind.

13   If the land-line telephone "arrived at the exact period when it was needed for the organization of great cities and the unification of nations," as Herbert Casson wrote in *The History of the Telephone*, it seems that the cellular phone has come to suit a new era of mobility. Even people who go nowhere face new instabilities as circulations of commodities, money, and information gain a new sense of momentum, and traditional structures of employment, family, community, and cultural life are disturbed. The cell phone encourages such movements, and can also help to repair the connections they may break.

Adapted from Sadie Plant, *New Statesman;* Hector Tobar, *The Gazette;* Wayne Arnold, *The New York Times;* and *Time*

Note Taking   ▶ Read the paragraphs corresponding to each main idea. Highlight the important information. Use what you highlighted to make notes on the article. Use the following framework.

Main Ideas	Supporting Points/Details

Introduction

A. Facilitating Communication

                                            a. Sub-Saharan Africa

                                            b. Latin America

                                                Example:

                                            c. Effect on Standard of Life

B.

C.

Conclusion

▶ Use your notes to discuss the article. Take turns explaining the information.

Giving Your Opinion   ▶ Read the following two statements. Explain what they mean. Discuss which you agree with more and why.

1. Spreading the use of cell phones is part of the western world's battle over the potentially lucrative market among Africa's one billion inhabitants. It should wait until "other crucial needs of Africans have been met," among them, education, healthcare, and safe drinking water, writes Moudjibouthe Daouda in the monthly *Africultures*.

2. "Poor people are poor because they're stuck in an environment that is stifling," said Iqbal Z. Quadir, a former New York investment banker who returned to his native Bangladesh in 1996 to build a rural cellular network with Grameen Bank. "If they are connected, the environment changes and everyone's life gets better." (paragraph 8, above)

ⓓVocabulary Building

Word Form

▷ **A** Study these five words and their forms. Then choose the correct form for each part of speech in the chart below. These words are commonly found in general and academic texts.

generate (v.)   confirm (v.)   consult (v.)   establish (v.)   induce (v.)
generator (n.)   confirmation   consultative   establishment   induced
generation (n.)   confirmed   consultation   established   induction
generatable (adj.)   consultancy   establishing

Verb	Noun	Adjective	Adverb
confirm	1.	1.	
consult	1. 2.	1.	
establish	1.	1. 2.	
induce	1.	1.	

▷ Compare your lists with a partner.

▷ **B** Write three sentences using words from the list. Use different parts of speech.

Vocabulary in Context

▷ The author of "Cell Phones Have Transformed How We Communicate" uses a very effective technique to bring her message across. She uses terminology normally reserved for one context in a completely different context.

Example: But this morning, with poor Ken's fate hanging in the airplane, my annoyance **went on speed dial**.

"Speed dial" is one of the features now available on most phones. Here, the term is being used to mean that she became annoyed immediately.

▷ Identify similar expressions in the following sentences. Write down their original meaning and what they are referring to in this particular context.

1. By now we have all had little bits of dialogue float past us on the street.

   Original meaning: _____

   Meaning in this context: _____

2. To someone wired to the wider world, *your* space no longer exists.

Original meaning: _____

Meaning in this context: _____

3. Now, cell-phoners strip in public.

Original meaning: _____

Meaning in this context: _____

4. Last week, while standing on the corner trying to hail a cab, I hit the jackpot.

Original meaning: _____

Meaning in this context: _____

5. It occurred to me the line between what's public and what's private must have been inadvertently severed when the first phone line was disconnected from the wall.

Original meaning: _____

Meaning in this context: _____

▶ Compare your answers with a partner or in a small group. Check with your teacher if necessary.

Expanding Your Language

Speaking

▶ **A Giving Advice** Read each of the following scenarios. How would you handle or give advice on handling the situation? Use the suggestions that are given or decide on a solution of your own. Write your ideas in note form.

1. You are in a restaurant enjoying an intimate dinner with a friend. A man at the next table is talking on a cell phone so loudly that it is disturbing you. You feel increasingly uncomfortable and would like to get away. You feel that you shouldn't have to listen to this conversation in a public place.

Some possibilities:

a. Ask the person to move or leave and take his phone conversation out of the dining room.

b. Ask the waiter to tell this customer to turn off the cell phone.

c. Ask the waiter to move you to a table far away from this person.

Your action or advice:

_____

2. You are traveling at high speed down a superhighway, with your friend at the wheel, when the cell phone rings. Your friend reaches over to answer the phone. You decide to take action.

   Some possibilities:

   a. Hand the phone over so that your friend can carry on the conversation while driving.

   b. Answer the phone yourself and take a message so that your friend can make the call when the car is stopped.

   c. Ask your friend to pull over to the side of the highway and stop the car while on the phone.

   Your action or advice:

   _____

3. You are visiting a wilderness area with a few friends. Your friends suggest climbing a mountain that requires a certain level of expertise. You are afraid that you and your friends do not have enough supplies and other equipment and may not be able to complete the climb safely. Your friends tell you not to worry because they have a cell phone and can call for help if they get in trouble. What is your reaction?

   Some possibilities:

   a. Insist that they not climb until they have the supplies and equipment they need.

   b. Agree to climb with them.

   c. Decide to climb only if they talk to a park official for advice before climbing.

   Your action or advice:

   _____

▶ **Discussion** Work with a partner or a small group to discuss your answers. Explain your choices. Present your suggestions to the class as a whole.

▶ **Role Play** Choose one of the three scenarios and decide on the roles involved with a partner or others in a small group. Together, write the conversations among the people in their roles. Practice your role plays. Prepare to present your role plays to others in a small group.

▶ **B Interviewing** What do people think about the advantages and disadvantages of cell phones? To find out, interview other students or people outside of class. Find out about their cell phone use and experience. To carry out the interviews, follow these steps.

▶ **1.** On your own: Make a short list of interesting questions (four or five) on the topic.

2. In small groups: Choose the five most interesting questions.

3. Whole class: Compare the questions written in each of the groups.

4. In small groups: Write the questions you will use on pages of your own. Leave spaces to take notes.

5. Interview: Alone or with a partner, choose three people and interview them.

6. Report: Discuss the responses with the group you worked with in step 4. Report to the class a few interesting or surprising findings from your interviews.

Writing

▶ **A Topic Writing** Write about the growing popularity of cell phones and how their popularity will change our culture and communications, both positively and negatively.
Follow these steps:

▶ **1.** Outline the details on the following main ideas of the topic. Use your notes to help you remember important facts.

A. Growing Popularity
   Places
   Statistics
B. Positive Uses
   Personal Communication
   Business Communication
   Other Uses
C. Negative Consequences
   Lack of Privacy
   Annoyance
   Dangerous Habits

2. Using your outline as a guide, write a paragraph about each of the three ideas.

3. Reread this first draft and check to see that the topic of each paragraph is clearly stated in the first sentence. Make any changes needed.

4. Reread the second draft and change the order of the information—or add information—for a final draft.

5. Submit the final draft to your teacher.

B Reaction Writing Some cities have instituted bans on cell phone use in public places such as theaters, banks, and subways similar to bans on smoking. Do you agree with such legal restrictions? Use the information in this chapter as well as your own experience to write your reaction in paragraph form.

Read On: Taking It Further

Reading Journal

Some very interesting books about privacy have been written both in the past and more recently. Some books, such as *1984* and *Brave New World*, present fictional worlds in which personal identities and freedoms are threatened. Others, such as *The Cuckoo's Egg*, present incredible stories of hackers who subvert the Internet for their own purposes. Consult with your teacher about these or other topics related to this unit. With your teacher's guidance, choose a selection to read and report on.

Newspaper and Magazine Articles

Check the media in print or on the Internet over a few days and find an interesting article about cell phones, privacy, or a related communications technology topic that interests you. Prepare to present the information in that article to a partner or in a small group.

Follow these steps:

1. Skim the article quickly to get the general idea of the information.

2. Ask the journalist's questions—*who, what, where, when,* and *why*—to pinpoint information that is interesting for your audience to hear about and that can be readily explained.

3. Highlight the important facts. Make notes if it will help you to explain more easily.

4. Practice your presentation.

5. Present your information.

Online Study Center   For additional activities, go to the ***Reading Matters*** Online Study Center at *college.hmco.com/pic/wholeyfour2e*.

Economics

In God We Trust

*—Motto written
on U.S. currency*

Introducing the Topic

In North America, personal satisfaction and a sense of self-worth are often equated with tangible things we can buy—things such as the latest model car or expensive clothes—rather than intangible things such as developing close relationships or taking pride in a job well done. Certainly money is a necessity, but does it necessarily define who we are, how we live, and what our values are? This unit examines the topic of business and economics. Chapter 9 will delve into the economic issues that people have to face in their daily lives: the value of work, money, and community life. In Chapter 10, we will look at ethical issues in today's business world.

▶Points of Interest

Reacting to the News

▶ Read this short excerpt from a news article about happiness and social values and discuss the following questions.

1. Faced with the choices that Tashi Wangyal had, what would your choice be?
2. What questions would you ask to establish the importance of happiness and well-being in people's lives? For example, "How much time do you give yourself to relax everyday?"

Thimphu, Bhutan—Five years ago, Tashi Wangyal had it all: a master's degree in philosophy from Cambridge University, a beautiful girlfriend, and an attractive job offer as a consultant in London. But the scholarship student, then twenty-five years old, threw it all away for a $120-a-month job in his native Bhutan, the isolated Buddhist kingdom perched in the Himalayas. The decision confounded his university friends, but Mr. Wangyal can find plenty of understanding at home. Despite Bhutan being among the poorest nations in the world, almost all of its scholarship students overseas return home after graduation. One reason they cite: Along with improvements in health care, education, and the environment, the Bhutanese government has pursued the more elusive goal of promoting its nation's happiness.

"The more I traveled and lived abroad, the more I learned to appreciate what we had at home," Mr. Wangyal says.

A few years ago, Bhutan's government threw out the usual indicators measuring progress, instead using an innovative model—called "gross national happiness"—that now has researchers and think tanks around the world taking note. Bhutan's concept embraces everything from protecting natural resources to promoting a strong national culture and ensuring democratic governance—with the goal of creating a foundation of happiness for citizens.

It isn't only Bhutan that is questioning the value of measuring material wealth without regard to a more comprehensive notion of fulfillment. The World Values Survey, a group of international social scientists, released a report last year that ranked well-being by society. The study, which analyzes the impact of values and beliefs on political and social life, concluded that people from Puerto Rico register the greatest sense of well-being; the United States came in at number 15. (Bhutan wasn't among the eighty-one societies surveyed.)

How You Doing?

Well-being rankings of eleven of the eighty-one societies, based on combined "happiness" and "life satisfaction" scores, are listed below.

1. Puerto Rico   4.69
2. Mexico   4.38
3. Denmark   4.24
4. Colombia   4.18
5. Ireland   4.16
6. Iceland   4.15
7. N. Ireland   4.01
8. Switzerland   3.88
9. Netherlands   3.86
10. Canada   3.86
11. United States 3.50

Source: World Values Survey

 **The Economics of Everyday Life**

◖Chapter Openers

Discussion Questions

▶ Complete the chart with your answers to the following questions. Share your ideas with a partner or a small group.

1. a. During a typical week, what part of your day do you spend doing the following activities?

   b. If you could do as you please, how much time would you spend on these activities?

   c. What is the difference between the two?

Activity	Time Spent	
	Actual	**Ideal**
Work or study		
Relaxing		
Interacting with family or friends		
Shopping		
Household chores		
Taking care of a family member		

2. a. Check (✔) the areas in our lives listed below that money can affect in a positive way.

_____ Good health	_____ Education
_____ Friendships	_____ Housing
_____ Job opportunities	_____ Family relationships
_____ Job satisfaction	_____ Values

   b. Can money have a negative effect on people's lives?

3. Can having money make people happy?

Exploring and Understanding Reading

What's Your Opinion?

▶ Circle *A* if you agree or *D* if you disagree with the following statements.

1. A   D   Having too much money leads to depression.

2. A   D   In today's economy, the only important currency is money.

3. A   D   Money tends to divide people rather than unite them.

4. A   D   People aren't satisfied with what they have for long.

5. A   D   People feel good about life only if they have something better to look forward to.

6. A   D   In today's economy, only the wealthy are really happy.

▶ Work with a partner or a small group. Explain the reasons for your opinions.

Surveying

▶ Read the introduction and the beginning sentences of every paragraph in the next reading. Notice the key words and write the main idea of the paragraph in the margin.

Chunking

> **Tip**

Subtitles can help you **identify** the **main idea**. Don't, however, make the mistake of thinking that subtitles always state that idea. Formulate the main idea in your own words.

▶ Analyze which paragraphs develop one general idea. Bracket the paragraphs that develop this idea and write it in the following table. The first one is done for you as an example.

Paragraphs	Main Idea
1–3	Introduction: The contradictions between having money and being happy Thesis:
13	Conclusion: The real key to happiness

◗ Share your ideas with a partner or a small group.

The Real Truth About Money

Americans, keen for their green, provide a warning for the rest of us about the money trap.

❶   If you made a graph of American life since the end of World War II, every line concerning money and the things that money can buy would soar upward, a statistical monument to materialism. Inflation-adjusted income per American has almost tripled. The size of the typical new house has more than doubled. A two-car garage was once a goal; now the United States is nearly a three-car nation. Designer everything, personal electronics, and other items that didn't even exist a half-century ago are now affordable. No matter how you chart the trends in earning and spending, everything is up, up, up. But if you made a chart of American happiness since the end of World War II, the lines would be as flat as a marble tabletop. In polls taken by the U.S. National Opinion Research Center in the 1950s, about one-third of Americans described themselves as "very happy." The center has conducted essentially the same poll periodically since then, and the percentage remains almost exactly the same today. (In a December *Time* poll on happiness that phrased the question differently, 17 percent of respondents said they were filled with happiness "just about all the time" and about 60 percent said they were frequently happy.)

❷   Yet if you charted the incidence of depression since 1950, the lines suggest a growing epidemic. Depending on what assumptions are used, clinical depression is three to ten times as common today as two generations ago. A recent study by Ronald Kessler of Harvard Medical School estimated that each year, one in fifteen Americans experience an episode of major depression—meaning not just a bad day but depression so debilitating that it's hard to get out of bed. Money jangles in wallets and purses as never before, but Americans are no happier for it, and for many, more money leads to depression. How can that be? And what can the rest of the world learn about a nation that prizes personal wealth—despite the fact that it often gives more social anxiety than satisfaction?

❸   The American generation that lived through the Depression and World War II said money can't buy happiness. Today's descendants don't act as though they listened. Millions spend more time and energy pursuing the things money can buy than engaging in activities that create real fulfillment in life, like cultivating friendships, helping others, and developing a spiritual sense. Today's Americans say they know that money can't buy happiness. In the *Time* poll, when people were asked about their major source of happiness, money ranked fourteenth. Still, they behave as though happiness is one wave of a credit card away. Too many view expensive purchases as "shortcuts to well-being," says Martin Seligman, a psychologist at the University of Pennsylvania. But people are poor predictors of where those shortcuts will take them.

4   To be sure, there is ample evidence that being poor causes unhappiness. Studies by Ruut Veenhoven, a sociologist at Erasmus University in Rotterdam, show that the poor—those in Europe earning less than about $10,000 a year—are made unhappy by the relentless frustration and stress of poverty. But everyone knows that.

Circumstances don't seem to have much effect on happiness

5   The surprise is that after a person's annual income exceeds $10,000 or so, Veenhoven found, money and happiness decouple and cease to have much to do with each other. The study has been replicated in the United States. Over the past two decades, in fact, an increasing body of social-science and psychological research has shown that there is no significant relationship between how much money a person earns and whether he or she feels good about life. *Time*'s poll found that happiness tended to increase as income rose to $50,000 a year. (The median annual U.S. household income is around $43,000.) After that, more income did not have a dramatic effect. Edward Diener, a psychologist at the University of Illinois, interviewed members of the Forbes 400, the richest Americans. He found the Forbes 400 were only a tiny bit happier than the public as a whole. Because those with wealth often continue to feel jealousy about the possessions or prestige of other wealthy people, even large sums of money may fail to confer well-being.

6   That seems true because of a phenomenon that sociologists call reference anxiety—or, more popularly, keeping up with the Joneses. According to that thinking, most people judge their possessions in comparison with others'. People tend not to ask themselves, "Does my house meet my needs?" Instead they ask, "Is my house nicer than my neighbor's?" If you own a two-bedroom house and everyone around you owns a two-bedroom house, your reference anxiety will be low, and your two-bedroom house may seem fine. But if your two-bedroom house is surrounded by three- and four-bedroom houses, with someone around the corner doing a tear-down to build a McMansion, your reference anxiety may rise. Suddenly that two-bedroom house—one that your grandparents might have considered quite nice, even luxurious—doesn't seem enough.

And so the money you spent on it stops providing you with a sense of well-being.

7   Americans' soaring reference anxiety is a product of the widening gap in income distribution. In other words, the rich are getting richer faster, and the rest of the population are none too happy about it. During much of U.S. history, the majority lived in small towns or urban areas where conditions for most people were approximately the same—hence, low reference anxiety. Also, most people knew relatively little about those who were living higher on the hog.

8   But in the past few decades, new economic forces have changed all that. Rapid growth in income for the top 5 percent of households has brought about a substantial cohort of people who live notably better than the middle class does, amplifying our reference anxiety. That wealthier minority is occupying ever-larger homes and spending more on each change of clothes than others spend on a month's rent. It all feeds middle-class anxiety, even when the middle is doing O.K. In nations with high levels of income equality like the Scandinavian countries, well-being tends to be higher than in nations with unequal wealth distribution such as the United States. Meanwhile, television and the Web make it easier to know how the very well off live. (Never mind whether they're happy.) Want a peek inside Donald Trump's gold-plated world? Just click on the TV, and he'll show you. Wonder what Bill Gates's 65,991-square-foot megamansion is like? Just download the floor plan from the Internet!

It's all relative

9   Paradoxically, it is the very increase in money—which creates the wealth so visible in today's society—that triggers dissatisfaction. As material expectations keep rising, more money may result in only more desires. "What people want in terms of material things and life experiences has increased almost exactly in lockstep with the postwar earnings curve," Diener notes. As men and women move up the economic ladder, most almost immediately stop feeling grateful for their elevated circumstances and focus on what they still don't have. Suppose you've lived in a two-bedroom house for years and have been dreaming of three bedrooms. You finally get that three-bedroom house. Will it bring you happiness? Not necessarily. Three bedrooms will become your new norm, and you'll begin to long for a four-bedroom abode. That money never satisfies is suggested by this telling fact: polls show that Americans believe that, whatever their income level, they need more to live well. Even those making large sums said still larger sums were required. People seem conditioned to think they do not have enough, even if objectively their lives are comfortable.

⑩   Then again, if they think their lot is improving, happiness follows. Carol Graham, an economist at the Brookings Institution in Washington, found that people's expectations about the future may have more influence on their sense of well-being than their current state does. People living modestly but anticipating better days to come, Graham thinks, are likely to be happier than people living well but not looking forward to improvements in their living standards. Consider two people: one earns $50,000 a year and foresees a 10 percent raise, and the other makes $150,000 but does not expect any salary increase. The second person is much better off in financial terms, but the first is more likely to feel good about life.

⑪   And guess what? The United States hasn't had a decent raise in two decades. Income growth has almost come to a halt for the middle class. In real terms, although median household income is higher than ever, median household income has increased only around 15 percent since 1984. That means most people have never had it better but do not expect any improvement in the near future. People tend to focus on the negative part and ignore the positive.

⑫   Living standards, education levels, and other basic measures of U.S. social well-being have improved so much so quickly in the postwar era that another big leap seems improbable. If the typical new house is more than 2,293 square feet, if more than half of high school graduates advance to university, if there are more cars and trucks in the United States than there are licensed drivers—all current statistics—then the country may need stability and equality more than it needs more money. But because Americans are all conditioned to think there's something wrong if they don't make more money each year, high standards of living in the United States may, paradoxically, have become an impediment to happiness. Fixated on always getting more, they fail to appreciate how much they have. Of course, in the grand scheme, it's better that there are large numbers of Americans who are materially comfortable, if a bit whiny about it, than who are destitute. One in eight Americans is poor. Poverty remains a stark reality amid American affluence.

⑬   Psychology and sociology aside, there is a final reason money can't buy happiness: the things that really matter in life are not sold in stores. Love, friendship, family, respect, a place in the community, the belief that one's life has purpose—those are the essentials of human fulfillment, and they cannot be purchased with cash. Everyone needs a certain amount of money, but chasing money rather than meaning is a formula for discontent. Too many people today have made materialism and the cycle of work-and-spend their principal goals. Then they wonder why they don't feel happy.

Scanning

▶ **A Supporting an Argument with Evidence** Scan the reading for the answers to these questions. Mark the question number in the margin of the page. Write your answers in note form.

1. a. What evidence is given about the relationship between American income and happiness?

   _____

   b. What conclusions can be drawn from this evidence?

   _____

2. What contradiction seems to exist between what people know about the relationship of money to happiness and the way people act?

   _____

3. What surprising information about income and happiness have studies shown?

   _____

4. a. What is reference anxiety?

   _____

   b. What example is given to show how it affects people?

   _____

   c. Why is it particularly problematic in the United States today?

   _____

5. What explains the fact that even wealthy people may be dissatisfied with their standard of living?

   _____

6. What facts about the future of the U.S. economy could actually be seen as an impediment to happiness?

   _____

7. What problem does the writer consider more important than the dissatisfaction of people who may have a comfortable standard of living?

   _____

8. According to the writer, what should people do and not do in order to be happy?

_____

▶ Work with a partner to ask and answer the questions. Use the information you marked in the margin to support your answers.

▶ **B** After completing the scanning exercise, work with your partner to highlight information that supports or disproves each of the agree/disagree statements on page 192.

Reacting to the Information

▶ **A Free Writing** Write your ideas about the link between money and happiness. Is money necessary to our well-being? Why or why not?

▶ **B Discussion** Share the ideas you wrote with a partner or with others in a small group and then give your opinion on the following questions. Circle *A* if you agree and *D* if you disagree. Explain the reasons for your opinions.

1. A   D   Only governments can issue money.

2. A   D   Only paid work is real work.

3. A   D   Strong communities are important to the economy.

Applying the Information

▶ **Exploring Alternatives** Can communities find innovative ways to find value in the work that people do? Skim the next article and, as you read, think about how the ideas presented in the next article compare with those presented in the previous one.

Skimming

▶ Quickly skim the article again and answer the following questions.

1. What institutions have become involved in today's money-based economy?

_____

2. What are some examples of how new kinds of money help to develop community?

_____

3. How can these new kinds of money be used?

_____

Is There Another Way to Pay?

❶   There was a time when only governments could create money, and as Mike Rowbotham explains in his excellent book, *The Grip of Death*, they have long since delegated 97 percent of that responsibility to the banks—which create it in the form of mortgages or interest-bearing loans.

❷   They are helped by the credit card companies, which give the power to customers to create their own debts—and create their own money at the same time—every time their card is swiped through a till. Credit card companies in the United States now market their products by sending unsolicited $5,000 checks through the mail. If you want the money, you can cash the check and the card and statement follows in the mail. "Like feeding lettuce to hungry rabbits," according to one American commentator. No wonder the average American family manages to accumulate savings of just $2,300 after fifty years of work.

❸   But now there are also supermarkets and airlines issuing their own money. Tesco, Safeway, and other businesses all issue their own points to encourage regular customers. A whole range of businesses deal in frequent-flier miles, which you can spend on an ever-increasing variety of goods and services, and which then disappear when you've spent them. In the United States, there are now a range of off-the-shelf "incentive cards" along the same lines for companies to offer their customers. There is even one card that acts as a combined loyalty and credit card. You can use it to buy things with "loyalty points" you haven't earned yet, but which then have to be repaid with increased customer loyalty.

❹   None of these innovations help us to improve either the shortage of money, the collapse of local communities, or the damage done by worldwide human greed. But they do open up new possibilities for experiments with new kinds of money which are kinder to the planet—and maybe even turning the base metal of human poverty into something closer to gold. As we know, with Local Exchange and Trading Systems (LETS) in the United Kingdom, people have been experimenting with this technology to invent their own new kinds of money. LETS money is available to anyone with time and skills, is less dependent on the increasingly bizarre fluctuations of the market, and does less damage to the planet by not charging ruinous interest.

❺   Similar ideas are suddenly popping up all over the world. There are now regional scrip systems such as australs in Argentina, SOCS in Scotland, or tlalocs in Mexico. There are computerized community barter systems like green dollars in Australia and New Zealand, banco del tempo in Italy, and

SEL systems in France. But in America, as befits the great money innovators, the field is even broader, with a range of local currencies all launched to achieve a different aspect of local sustainability. Time dollars, for example, are a way of providing non-medical services to older people, to keep them healthy and living at home and help offset the cuts in public spending. They are now operating in 200 U.S. and Japanese cities, and are being hailed as the elusive key to rebuilding "social capital."

❻   Time dollars were actually developed in the United Kingdom, at the London School of Economics in the early 1980s, the brainchild of the American civil rights lawyer Edgar Cahn, who imagined a non-market kind of money that recognizes the contribution people make to the places they live. Time dollars record, store, and find new ways of rewarding the human transactions where neighbors help neighbors, such as giving lifts to older people, taking them to the doctor, or tutoring local children. One hour is worth an hour, whether you are a rich lawyer or an elderly widow making supportive phone calls to neighbors. Issouf Coulibaly is a member of the Maine Time Dollar Network, a collection of nearly 300 people in Portland, Maine, from all walks of life—elders, doctors, single moms, engineers, personal trainers, welders, teachers, musicians, and refugees among them—along with organizations such as the ballet and the city's adult-education program. Coulibaly, a refugee from the Ivory Coast, lives in Portland and has a full-time job with decent pay, working the night shift as a machine operator in a rotor factory. By day, he can often be found helping out at the ballet, or baby-sitting, or assisting English speakers translate correspondence into French, or gardening, or wallpapering. For every hour that Coulibaly contributes to the ballet, for instance, he receives an hour of credit in the Time Dollar bank. For members of the network, it's an equal exchange—an hour for an hour, no matter how it's earned or how it's spent. An hour of baby-sitting for an hour of tax preparation. An hour of translation for an hour of haircutting. An hour of wallpapering for an hour of massage. All of the work is voluntary, yet none of it is volunteer work.

❼   Research shows that "paying" volunteers in Time dollars can boost the number of volunteers available, can make people healthier and—and here's the important bit—have a major impact on a range of social problems. "Market economics values what is scarce—not the real work of society, which is caring, loving, being a citizen, a neighbor, and a human being," said Cahn. "That work will, I hope, never be so scarce that the market value goes high. So we have to find a way of rewarding contributions to it." The Time dollar idea also helps us to see work differently, recognizing that caring work—which neighbors traditionally do for each other, and which we all rely on—is productive work. Governments may not define it as such, economists may balk at the whole idea, but it is. And the special insight of Time dollars is to recognize that crucial fact.

8   Then there are Hours, the innovative printed currency, which has revolutionized the local economy of Ithaca in upstate New York. If Time dollars are about building social capital by encouraging public goods, Hours are a way of building local economies by exchanging private goods. The idea of printing a local currency emerged after a successful local campaign to fight plans for an out-of-town Wal-Mart superstore. Now Ithaca is home to what is probably the biggest local currency in the world, the brainchild of self-styled community economist Paul Glover, who wanted to find a way of keeping money circulating locally. Like so many other small cities, Ithaca local business was threatened by large nationwide chains that took money away from local business and sent profits out of the area. The result was that local incomes were falling, economic self-determination—such as there was—was crumbling, and the city was increasingly dependent on expensive, packaged imports to the area, usually brought in from great distances by multinational traders.

9   Glover believed that a local currency, because it could only be spent within a 20-mile radius of Ithaca, could at least stem the flood. It could give an advantage to local businesses which accepted Hours, provide more income for people on the margins of the economy, substitute local products and services for those flooding in from outside, and make the local economy more sustainable, diverse, and able to survive recession. Hours notes are a "hard currency" designed by Glover and incorporating the slogan "In Ithaca We Trust" in parody of the dollar. They are accepted as being worth $10. By 1996, about 5,700 Hours ($57,000) were in circulation around Ithaca, and organizers believed they had been used to create about $1.5 million in trade among local business since 1991.

10   These experiments may be difficult to sustain, but they could potentially give people the means to provide themselves with the money they need—when it normally seeps away to the big cities and massive world capital flows. Taken together, they could mean an economic breakthrough for tackling poverty and social collapse and, given the implications of economic collapse in Russia or the Far East, an urgent one for the whole of humanity.

Adapted from Sue Halpern, *Mother Jones,* and David Boyle, *Funny Money: In Search of Alternative Cash*

Recapping the Information

▷ **A** Highlight the facts in the reading that relate to these main ideas.

1. Use of credit and debit cards in the United States
2. Experiments with new kinds of money in different parts of the world
3. Time dollars
4. Hours in Ithaca, New York
5. Other local currency experiments
6. The potential of new kinds of money

▷ **B** Working with a partner, compare what you highlighted. Discuss whether you highlighted too much or too little. Complete any additional highlighting needed.

▷ **C** Using *only* what you highlighted, write notes using a divided main ideas/details format. Take turns telling each other the important information in the article from your notes. Make sure you explain the information as completely as possible.

Reacting to the Information

▷ Based on the information in your notes, discuss these questions with your partner.

1. Why is saving money so difficult for Americans? Why is it important to do?
2. What is the purpose of experiments such as Time dollars and Hours notes?
3. What do these experiments tell us about community life in the United States?

Arguing a Point of View

▷ In the reading, "The Truth About Money," the author states, "There is no significant relationship between how much money a person earns and whether he or she feels good about life." And in "Is There Another Way to Pay?" we read, "The Time dollars idea also helps us to see work differently, recognizing that caring work—which neighbors traditionally do for each other, and which we all rely on—is productive work." How can we reconcile the different needs and demands on our time that we all face?

▷ **Debate Topic** Using the information from the readings, discussions, and ideas of your own, decide if you agree or disagree with this statement: "Money is necessary to our well-being." Find examples to support your point of view and prepare to argue it.
   To do this, follow these steps:

▷ **1.** Decide which argument you will make.

   2. List the points you think are important for your argument. Give examples for each point from the readings, research on the Internet, and from your own information or experience.

3. Compare your list with others.

4. Prepare a list of all the arguments and order them from strongest to weakest.

5. Practice explaining your arguments with a partner.

6. Form a small group with people who prepared a different argument and take turns explaining and defending your argument.

7. Prepare to present your conclusions to others in the class.

Vocabulary Building

Word Form ▶ **A** Study these five words and their forms. Then choose the correct form for each part of speech in the chart below. These words are commonly found in general and academic texts.

accumulate (v.)	anticipate (v.)	approximate (v.)	collapse (v.)	pursue (v.)
accumulation (n.)	anticipation	approximation	collapsing	pursuit
accumulating (adj.)	anticipatively	approximating	collapse	pursuer
accumulated (adj.)	anticipated	approximately	collapsible	pursued
	anticipating	approximate	collapsibility	

Verb	Noun	Adjective	Adverb
anticipate	1.	1.	1.
		2.	
approximate	1.	1.	1.
		2.	
collapse	1.	1.	
	2.	2.	
pursue	1.	1.	
	2.		

▶ Compare lists with a partner.

▶ **B** Write three sentences using words from the list.

▷ **C** In English, the form of the word can change when it is used as a different part of speech. Provide the correct form of the word in each of the following sets of sentences.

1. measure

   a. When economists _____ the productive capacity in terms of our work force, they exclude children, teenagers, the disabled, persons on public assistance, volunteers, and seniors.

   b. The productive contribution of home, family, community is not included in any of the economists' _____ of GDP.

   c. _____ the value of "public goods" is very difficult.

2. contribute

   a. Eighty percent of the labor that keeps seniors out of nursing homes is unpaid labor _____ by family.

   b. That amount doesn't include the unpaid _____ of children and adolescents who also volunteer.

   c. _____ to the public good is an important civic duty.

3. produce

   a. Rearing children amounts to the _____ of "public goods."

   b. _____ some public goods cannot be paid for with public funds.

   c. We think of public goods as being _____ by the government.

   d. Forty percent of the country's _____ work goes on outside of the market economy.

4. calculate

   a. If the same _____ were used to assign value to unpaid work in developing countries, the differences would be even greater.

   b. Studies have _____ the value of this work as between 48 and 65 percent of the national GDP.

   c. She hadn't expected that _____ the value of this work would be so difficult.

5. imply

 a. That assumption may be valid and, if so, then it has _____ for society as a whole.

 b. This type of understanding _____ that individuals who devote little time or energy to child-rearing owe a debt to society.

 c. I am unhappy with what you are _____ about me.

Antonyms

▶ **A** Refer to "The Truth About Money" to find these words in context. Match the words in Column A with words that have the opposite meaning in Column B.

Column A

_____ 1. frustration

_____ 2. substantial

_____ 3. visible

_____ 4. excluded

_____ 5. objective

_____ 6. modest

_____ 7. foresight

_____ 8. comfortable

_____ 9. principal

Column B

a. hidden

b. included

c. secondary

d. showy

e. hindsight

f. destitute

g. subjective

h. satisfaction

i. inconsequential

▶ **B** In English, we can transform some words into words with the opposite meaning by adding a prefix such as *il-, im-, non-, un-, in-,* and *dis-*. Scan the readings in this chapter and circle the words with negative prefixes. Check these with others in your class.

Expressions

▶ Match the phrases in Column A with a word or phrase that means the same in Column B.

Column A

_____ 1. keeping up with the Joneses

_____ 2. have a sense of well-being

_____ 3. take a peek

_____ 4. move in lockstep

_____ 5. be better off

_____ 6. come to a halt

_____ 7. in the grand scheme

Column B

a. do the same thing at the same time

b. have more money

c. feel satisfied

d. looking at the larger picture

e. stop

f. look quickly or secretly

g. match the lifestyle of others close to you

▶ Compare your answers with a partner. Look for other examples of expressions used in the chapter readings and circle any that you find.

Vocabulary in Context

▶ What is the meaning of the word in boldface in these sentences from "The Real Truth About Money"? Underline the words that help you guess the meaning.

1. The surprise is that after a person's annual income exceeds $10,000 or so, money and happiness **decouple** and cease to have much to do with each other.

2. Because those with wealth often continue to feel jealousy about the possessions or prestige of other wealthy people, even large sums of money may fail to **confer** well-being.

3. That seems true because of a phenomenon that sociologists call **reference anxiety**—or, more popularly, keeping up with the Joneses. According to that thinking, most people judge their possessions in comparison with others'.

4. As material expectations keep rising, more money may **engender** only more desires.

▶ Compare your answers with a partner.

Expanding Your Language

Reading

▶ The previous readings focused on alternatives to our money-based economy. This reading focuses on the ways in which debit cards have become an important part of the money-based economy and the effects that this is having on the spending habits of many Americans.

Read the following questions and, after reading the article, answer as many as you can based on the information in the text.

1. Why does Edward L. Farrell like to use his debit cards?
2. What kinds of purchases can people make using their debit cards?
3. How much has the use of debit cards grown in recent years?
4. What are the advantages of using a debit card for customers?
5. What are the advantages of using a debit card for businesses?
6. Why are companies interested in the market for recurring payments?
7. How do cash cards work?
8. How popular are cash cards becoming?
9. What other benefits do credit card companies offer their customers?
10. What is the advantage of using a credit card that doubles as a cash or debit card?

Just Swipe It

❶   Edward L. Farrell is a card-carrying American. The thirty-seven-year-old Montclair, New Jersey, resident and father of two maxes out merchant-reward programs using whatever plastic he can. A bank auditor, Farrell uses his ShopRite card to earn grocery discounts and rewards at Continental Airlines Inc. He reloads his Starbucks Corp. cash card with his Chase Manhattan Bank debit card—which deducts the expense from his bank account—to accumulate even more miles. His one problem: how to keep his coffee intake under control now that he can waltz into any Starbucks, "swipe, and leave," he says. "I'm trying to limit it to once a day."

❷   These days, just about any expense can be paid for with some type of card. Live in a $5,000-a-month luxury rental in Manhattan? Charge it automatically to your credit card each month. Stepping into a McDonald's for a Happy Meal? A swipe of your debit card covers the $1.99 charge. Slackening growth and fierce competition, especially for customers who carry big balances, have banks and credit-card companies scrambling into untapped markets for plastic. Visa, MasterCard, and American Express want customers to make regular bill payments—such as for rent, gym memberships, utilities, and day-care center fees—with a card instead of a check. And they want consumers to pull out their debit cards instead of small bills at convenience stores, gas stations, and theaters.

3   All eyes are on the debit card. Even though there are twice as many credit cards as debit cards, debit cards generated 16.5 billion transactions (excluding ATM withdrawals) in 2003, a 22 percent jump over 2002 and, for the first time, debit outpaced credit transactions. By 2007, debit-card purchases could top $1 trillion, forecasts *The Nilson Report*, a payments industry newsletter. And the amount spent on debit cards will increase 130 percent (vs. 49 percent for credit cards). Indeed, debit use is growing so fast at Visa, where it accounts for more than half the transactions, vs. 7 percent a decade ago, that it no longer calls itself a credit-card company but a "payments company."

Merchant's Choice

4   Why the fast growth in debit-card business? Consumers save time, feel more secure carrying fewer dollars, and track their spending better. Lost or stolen cards are quickly replaced by the bank. Merchants avoid credit risk and the costs of late payments, postage, employee theft, and check-clearing fees. More important, customers—who are costlier to acquire than to retain—are more loyal. In some markets, cable giant Cox Communications Inc. persuaded up to 20 percent of its 6.3 million subscribers to pay with plastic and found that renewals jumped. "There was no need for any other incentive programs," says Warren Jones, director of competitive strategy and customer retention at Cox.

5   The race is on to find new customers and markets to generate income. Fast food is fertile ground. McDonald's is using swipe-and-pay machines in cities such as Chicago and Dallas. Pizza Hut and KFC are also testing the system. In all, according to credit-card executives, the quick-service food market is valued at a lucrative $130 billion a year or more. Says Fred P. Gore, MasterCard senior vice-president: "We're pretty much talking to everyone in the top forty to fifty chains in the United States."

6   As for paying regular household bills, plastic is rapidly moving in to replace paper checks. There's no mystery why: The market for recurring payments, such as rent and insurance, is huge. For the first time, electronic payments will outnumber the roughly 40 billion checks written for such expenses this year, says the Federal Reserve, which forecasts a 9 percent decline in checks processed next year. Even American Express, traditionally focused on corporate travel and entertainment outlays, is targeting such everyday expenses: Last year, two-thirds of its charge volume was generated to pay dentists, cable, and other similar services—a reversal of the business that has been its standard since 1958.

❼ Cash cards that are loaded up with electronic dollars by banks or merchants are also flourishing. Already, some 6.2 million prepaid cards are in circulation, and that number is expected to grow to nearly 40 million by 2007, says the Pelorus Group. By year end, the prepaid market will hit $71.5 billion, according to *The Nilson Report*, up 31 percent since last year. By 2007, Americans will be walking around with $349 billion worth of cash cards in their pockets. That could be in the form of a Bloomingdale's or Toys "R" Us cash card, instead of a gift certificate. Employers are expected to hand out these cash cards as employee bonuses or even pay. All aspire to the success of Starbucks's reloadable cash cards: 20 million customers have signed up for one since 2001, and they now account for 20 percent of the Seattle company's sales.

The Frappuccino Dividend

❽ Convenience is nice, but instant rewards are a new lure for customers. There's no quicker way to earn a plane ticket to Hawaii than to collect a frequent-flier mile for each dollar of your rent. Visa is accepted at 1,000 rental properties nationwide and American Express has recruited landlords in San Francisco, New York, and Chicago. In July, Related Rentals, one of the nation's largest privately owned real estate companies, agreed to let New York City tenants in 4,500 units put the monthly rent on their American Express cards. Renters earn all kinds of goodies: free flights, golf lessons, or Broadway tickets. Landlords are sold, too. Says David Wine of Related, "Renewal rates will be higher and collections more efficient."

❾ In the brave new world of plastic, cash cards, credit cards, and debit cards are beginning to meld into one. Looks like with cash, you can finally leave home without it.

Adapted from Mara Der Hovanesian, *Business Week,* November 17, 2003. Copyright © 2003 by The McGraw-Hill Companies. Reprinted with permission.

Speaking

▶ **Three-Minute Taped Talk** Choose one of the following topics and prepare a three-minute talk based on the information in the readings in this chapter as well as any information of your own.

1. Compare and contrast the advantages that debit cards and local cash cards offer people.

2. Explain how Time dollars were developed and how they help people in communities such as Portland, Maine.

3. Describe the paradox of the high American standard of living and the sense of dissatisfaction in American society.

▶ To prepare your talk, complete the following steps.

▶ **1.** Decide on the main points you will explain for the topic you chose.

2. Decide on the important supporting points and make a short outline for each main point.

3. Choose the details you need to explain each point.

4. Use a divided page format to write an expanded outline including these details in note form.

5. Use the notes you prepared and practice your talk a few times before you record it.

6. Record your talk on tape or audio CD and give it to your teacher for feedback.

Writing

▶ **Topic Writing** Using the information you prepared for your taped talk, write a draft of this topic. Do this work in your journal notebook. Reread the draft and, if possible, show it to a partner for peer review. Make any changes in the essay, i.e., reorganizing or adding information, and editing for grammar and spelling. Then rewrite your essay and give the final draft to your teacher for feedback.

 ***Online Study Center*** For addtional activities, go to the *Reading Matters* Online Study Center at *college.hmco.com/pic/wholeyfour2e.*

10   The Business of Ethics

Chapter Openers

Discussion Questions

Think about these questions. Share your ideas with a partner or a small group.

1. What is your definition of the term "ethics"?
2. How do people decide if their behavior is ethical or not?
3. Why should people act ethically?
4. What causes people to act unethically?
5. Why is ethical behavior important in:
   - business?
   - school?
   - family?
6. Give three examples from the business world that could make someone think we live in a "wicked" world.
7. Look at the following graph and decide if you agree or disagree with the rankings. What bad business behavior bothers you most?

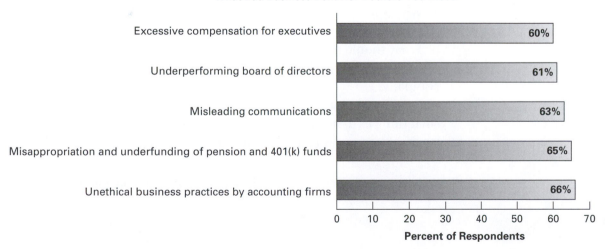

What Bad Business Behavior Bothers You Most?

Behavior	Percent
Excessive compensation for executives	60%
Underperforming board of directors	61%
Misleading communications	63%
Misappropriation and underfunding of pension and 401(k) funds	65%
Unethical business practices by accounting firms	66%

Percent of Respondents

Source: USA Today

Exploring and Understanding Reading

Previewing

▶ This article is taken from an interview. Before reading it, quickly read the questions used as subheadings (in boldface) to get an idea of the topics addressed in the article.

Scanning for Details

▶ Read the article quickly. Then, scan the reading and highlight the information that answers these questions. Prepare to answer them in your own words by writing your ideas in note form.

1. Who is Randy Cohen?

2. Why is ethical behavior in everyone's interest?

3. a. What example shows that people need structures to guide their actions?

   b. Why do these structures work?

4. Why does Cohen think it's hard to act ethically?

5. According to Cohen, how do people influence others to act ethically?

6. What kind of structures need to be created to regulate payment for CEOs?

7. According to Cohen, what should workers do in order to follow their moral principles?

8. a. Why is it difficult to refuse work at a company that violates a person's ethical standards?

   b. What should a person do?

9. Why does Cohen think it's impossible for anyone to work for a tobacco company?

10. What example does Cohen give to support his argument that there is no such thing as a "free market"?

11. What type of commercial system does Cohen suggest?

▶ Work with a partner to take turns asking and answering the questions.

How to Tell Right from Wrong

Randy Cohen knows right from wrong. As the author of *The New York Times Magazine*'s column "The Ethicist"—also syndicated in newspapers nationwide as "Everyday Ethics"—he receives an abundance of questions from people grappling with moral dilemmas. "I don't really tell people what to do," explains Cohen. "They often know what the right answer is. My job is to logically construct why it follows ethically that they behave a certain way."

Cohen, 53, recently compiled many of his columns into a book. Among the puzzles he addresses are workplace issues dealing with privacy, religion, hiring, firing, and CEO compensation. But does he always follow his own advice? "No, certainly not!" he exclaims. "I'm not an unusually virtuous person. But I am more acutely aware of the ways in which I'm not behaving the way I'd like to."

Cohen spoke to *Across the Board* assistant editor Vadim Liberman about *The Good, the Bad & the Difference: How to Tell Right from Wrong in Everyday Situations* (Doubleday).

Why should one act ethically?

Well, if you look at the world, the wicked do, indeed, prosper, and the virtuous don't necessarily, so there's no practical value to acting ethically in the short run. But I think that there are pragmatic reasons for being virtuous in the long run. It's only by building a just society that one can have a comfortable life. If everyone acted wickedly, then all windows would have bars on them. It's in everyone's interest to live in a society where people behave honestly and virtuously. That's what it means to be a decent human being. Although, in a wicked society, there's very little advantage to being the one virtuous person.

Do we live in a wicked society?

I certainly don't think we're in the most wicked period in history. A wide range of behavior was possible in every period of history. But there's been a certain moral progress due to the growth of democracy. It's a profoundly moral enterprise in that it gives you a chance to create structures within which people can be good. For example, in New York the streets used to be covered with dog droppings. It was awful. But five minutes after we had the law that said you have to pick up after your dog, nearly everyone did. It wasn't because they were afraid of the police; the police weren't going to do anything. But once a social structure was created, it was really encouraging how well everyone acted.

What, then, causes people to act unethically?

People tend to be as good or bad as their neighbors. Most people are not saintly, and neither are they great villains. It's very hard to be good when you look around and see your neighbors acting very badly. It's hard to drive at 65 mph when everyone else is driving at 100 mph.

But the police can catch you for speeding. Does the fear of getting caught encourage ethical behavior?

While the fear of getting formally caught by the judicial system of our society is a motive for people to act ethically, so is the fear of getting shamed by your neighbors. For example, right in front of Madison Square Garden, there's that stairway where people are getting out of a subway stop, exiting Penn Station, or spilling out of a game. There used to be a war for taxis; people would push each other out of the way. A couple of years ago, a yellow line was painted on the street, along with two words: "taxi line." Now people stand in line—because you gave them a structure that made it possible for everyone to behave equitably and civilly to one another. People still cheat, but most don't. It's extraordinarily inspiring. There's no fear of getting caught by the police. People do the right thing because they *want* to do the right thing and because they see those around them behaving ethically.

Do corporations generally behave ethically?

Some companies do things that I regard as repulsive but that are not unethical in the narrow sense of the word.

Many critics feel that corporations are unethical in overpaying CEOs. In your book, you present a hypothetical dilemma in which a CEO is paid $10 million annually but would happily do his job for $2 million. Is he ethically wrong to accept the $10 million the board wants to pay him?

If this CEO has it in him to reduce his salary, that's a lovely thing, but this is more of a case of civil rather than individual virtues. For an individual to do that is asking more than any human can do. Yet it's not too much to ask him to take some effort toward creating a system where that is not the case. Right now, people who sit on corporate boards tend to be senior executives of other corporations. They live in a very narrow culture of people who think you should get $10 million a year even if the company loses money. There is no rational defense for these kinds of pay disparities. The CEO and his fellow executives should recognize that paying him so much money does not benefit the company in any way, and they should start looking at long-term solutions. You have to institutionalize these solutions and create mechanisms that don't rely on individual rectitude.

It sounds as if there are differences between corporate and personal ethics.

Your moral principles should be the same whether you're in your underwear at home or a CEO at work. A lot of businesspeople justify what strikes me as dubious behavior by saying, "Well, we have a responsibility to the stockholders." That covers a lot of ground, because it lets them sincerely believe that they're acting selflessly. The other thing I've noticed, from the point of view of employees, is how easily they're willing to waive their civil rights at the workplace. They think, "It's the boss's company. If I don't like it here, I should work somewhere else." They seem surprisingly unwilling to demand rights that they would in ordinary civic society.

How should a worker balance his own ethics with those of his supervisor or his company?

I would hope that the employee's and the company's ethics would be consistent, but I realize it gets tricky. If the job violates your values, and the only thing keeping you there is your self-interest, like the desire to make a good salary, then you shouldn't be there. I recognize at the same time that you have to survive in the world, and if you hold out for the perfect job for perfectly virtuous people, you'll never live. Your ethical obligation is not to starve. For example, I used to work at the *Late Night with David Letterman* show, both pre- and post-acquisition by General Electric, a company that has done some things I personally don't like. But did that mean that I was now to quit?

Vast corporations control many different enterprises, and you yourself may be doing benign work for the company. You should ask yourself if you're directly helping to serve activities that you think are wicked—although there is no justification for anyone working for any tobacco company, ever. Tobacco is a toxic product that kills 400,000 people a year. No honorable person can work for any tobacco company in any capacity.

But take a tobacco company that has non-tobacco divisions. Are employees who don't directly work on the tobacco end also unethical?

The further you get from what you regard as the immoral practice of the company, the more ethical your activity. If you were a saintly person or had a family fortune, you could choose to have nothing to do with the parent company, but even then it's hard: Perhaps the company you're working at has a pension fund that's going to include the tobacco company. You can never live in isolation of practices that you find unwholesome. But you can try to minimize the harm that you yourself are doing by not taking a job you feel is unethical or promotes harmful products.

You speak about how the marketplace corrupts values. Is capitalism at odds with ethical behavior?

The thing about the marketplace is that the buyer's profit is the seller's loss. Their interests clash. Yet the essential nature of ethical thought is to consider the effect of your actions on others, look not to harm another person, and to improve the lot of one another—to see your interests as bound up together. Relentless marketplace values do not make for a humane society. The free market also seems essentially false. The most vigorous proponent of the fantasy they call the free market is offensive because it denies that our lives are obviously all bound up together. There are no autonomous individuals. We're civic creatures, and any approach to thinking about life and virtue has to acknowledge that. Anyone who has a lot of money is happy to think he got it through his own effort, as if he were suddenly transported to the surface of the moon and had to build something out of nothing. But, for example, the reason you're able to run your company is because all of your employees went to public school, and they drive to your company on roads paid for out of the public purse.

So if not capitalism, then what?

A more benign and human form of capitalism. The events of the marketplace need to be regulated well in all sorts of democracies. For instance, all over Western Europe there are laws that say that a factory that's been in a town for fifty years can't just pack up and move overnight. It has reciprocal obligations to its employees and to that town. Commerce is a wonderful thing.

Across the Board, The Conference Board

Reacting to Arguments

▶ **Finding Support for Opinions** The following opinion statements are taken from "How to Tell Right from Wrong." Analyze what argument is given for each, i.e., a positive or a negative example. Write your answers and comment on whether or not you think the example supports the argument.

1. I think there are pragmatic reasons for being virtuous in the long run.
2. There's a certain moral progress to the growth of democracy.
3. While the fear of getting formally caught by the judicial system of our society is a motive for people to act ethically, so is the fear of getting shamed by your neighbors.
4. Your moral principles should be the same whether you're in your underwear at home or a CEO at work.
5. There are no autonomous individuals. We're civic creatures, and any approach to thinking about life and virtue has to acknowledge that.

▶ Discuss your answers with a partner or a small group.

Personalizing   ▶ Think of an ethical issue you are interested in. One example could be copying music or movies illegally or downloading them from the Internet. Another could be putting false information on your resumé or job application. Prepare to explain the issue. You can look for news reports, find information on the Internet, or use examples of your own. Explain the issue and give your position: Is this behavior ethical or not?

▶ Paired Readings

▶ What happens when a company is led by a CEO whose ethical standards are high? Does the company prosper or suffer? Explore these issues in the following readings.
   Choose one of the readings. Work with someone who has chosen the *same* reading.

Personalizing   ▶ Read the following and check (✔) the ones that would be important in deciding if you would give a company your business or not. In the column at the right, rank those you chose in order of importance with "1" as the most important.

		Importance
_____	Paying its employees good wages	_____
_____	Manufacturing top quality products	_____
_____	Providing good benefits for its employees	_____
_____	Staying competitive in the market	_____
_____	Ethical leadership from the CEO	_____
_____	Doing good for the community	_____

▶ Discuss your list with a partner or a small group.

❶ The Rewards of Ethical Behavior

Skimming   ▶ Read the following article quickly and highlight the information that would help answer these questions.

1. What crucial decisions did Aaron Feuerstein make when fire destroyed Malden Mills?
2. What problems has the company experienced since 2001?
3. What kind of support has he received?
4. What is needed to make the company profitable?

Is Ethics Its Own Reward?

A Cautionary Tale

❶   After my first grandson, Evan, was born three years ago, a friend gave him a sage-green blanket made of Polartec fleece. The blanket was made by Malden Mills, the textile company in Lawrence, MA, that nearly burned to the ground on December 11, 1995. Some 3,000 people worked at the mill. Their fate was in the hands of the factory owner. I hadn't noticed the blanket's label until this past November, just after Malden Mills filed for Chapter 11 bankruptcy protection.

❷   As the fire was raging in 1995, Aaron M. Feuerstein, the chief executive, decided to keep paying all of his employees as he rebuilt the company, which was privately held. He decided that during the period of the reconstruction of the business, many of his employees who would be actively employed in doing the reconstruction as well as those who were not actively employed would be paid by the company for a period of 90 days. It was a few weeks before Christmas, and these people had no other income. For his actions, Mr. Feuerstein, now in his 80s, was heralded as a hero, someone whose commitment to his employees and community went beyond any ethical obligation.

❸   But by late 2001, the company had run short of cash. Its annual sales stagnated at $180 million, and its earnings dropped to nearly nothing from $35 million in 2000. Already on the hook for $140 million in loans, Mr. Feuerstein asked his creditors for an additional $20 million to keep the company operating. They agreed, but only if he first filed for bankruptcy protection so that the new loans would receive priority payment should the company not survive. "I begged them on my knees not to go into this chapter," he said. But he recognized that it was the only way he could get the funds.

❹   Given Mr. Feuerstein's magnanimous behavior in the past, are any of his constituents—employees, customers or the company's hometown—ethically obligated to help him now? So far, none of his customers—manufacturers such as L. L. Bean, Patagonia, and North Face that use Polartec in their high-end garments—have left him. His union workers have agreed to a salary freeze until 2003 and are giving up paid personal days this year. He estimated that those and other concessions would save Malden Mills around $2 million. He has also received letters of support, some including small donations.

❺   "It's one thing when you have a fire and you decide to rebuild," he said. But when a company is in Chapter 11, he added, "who would ever anticipate that you would have thousands of letters of encouragement from strangers?" Mr. Feuerstein said he never expected anything in return after keeping his employees on the payroll in 1995. "You're supposed to do what's right because it's right, not because there's a payoff," he said. "And so I don't expect anything of people." The question is: Should he?

6 As part of its "Polartec Promise" campaign started in December, the company is asking consumers to buy products made with Polartec fleece. Those generally cost more than those featuring fleece made in countries where labor costs are lower. "Any individual certainly can do that," said Jon P. Gunnemann, a social ethics professor at Emory University. "But there's no moral obligation to do it. At some point, if you decide to live in a market system, you can't function that way. The only thing that's going to fix his problem is a profitable business." ...

7 It's difficult not to want Malden Mills to succeed. As stories abound of corporate executives paying themselves fat bonuses before filing for bankruptcy while leaving the retirement funds of rank-and-file employees eviscerated, we are desperate for business heroes like Mr. Feuerstein. But did his lenders have an ethical obligation to grant him the new loan? Or his union employees to agree to concessions? Do we have an obligation to buy from Mr. Feuerstein simply because of his past good deeds?

8 Absolutely not, just as he had no obligation to keep paying his employees six years ago. For him, it was the right thing to do. Without obligation, his constituencies can now decide what's right, whether that means buying a North Face jacket lined with Polartec or a less expensive knockoff.

9 I, for one, have my eye on another blanket made of Polartec fleece for my new grandson, Lucas.

From "A Boss Saved Them. Should They Save Him?" by Jeffrey L. Seglin, *The New York Times*, January 20, 2002. Copyright © 2002 by The New York Times Co. Reprinted with permission.

Scanning for Specific Information

▶ Reread the article to find the answers to these questions. Note the number of the question in the margin for future reference. Write the answer in note form and in your own words as much as possible.

1. How would you describe Malden Mills?

_____

2. Why was Aaron Feuerstein considered a hero?

_____

3. Why did the company have to declare bankruptcy?

_____

4. How could you compare the expectation for concessions from customers and creditors with that of Feuerstein himself?

_____

5. In the writer's opinion, why should people buy a Malden Mills product?

_____

◗ Compare your answers with your partner. Try to agree on the answers. Refer to the article if you disagree.

Recapping the Information

◗ **A Note Taking** Identify the main ideas of the article. Highlight the information corresponding to each main idea.

◗ **B** Use what you highlighted to make notes on each main idea.

◗ **C** Working with your partner, compare the notes you made. Discuss whether they are too detailed or too brief. Add to or remove from your notes if necessary.

◗ **D** Using only your notes, take turns telling each other the important information in the article. Make sure you explain the information as clearly and completely as you can.

Reacting to the Information

◗ Discuss these questions with another person who read the *same* article. Explain your ideas as completely as possible.

1. How can you explain the fact that Feuerstein decided to rebuild Malden Mills?
2. Do you think that he should have paid workers while the rebuilding went on?
3. Is it important to buy products from Malden Mills even if there are cheaper products available?
4. Should more CEOs make ethically-based decisions of the kind presented in the story of Malden Mills?

②Mixing Business and Morals

Skimming

▶ Read the following article quickly and highlight the information that would help answer these questions.

1. Why is the story of Malden Mills considered a "morality tale"?
2. What action did Ed Shultz take to change the guns his company produced?
3. What was the result of his decision?
4. What is the lesson of this story?

Can Business and Morals Mix?

❶   Stories about courageous chief executives who, when faced with business pressures to do otherwise, choose to do the right thing invariably end up reading like morality tales. The message? Good ethics leads to good business results.

❷   The fire that devastated Malden Mills Industries just before Christmas 1995 was just such a story. Rather than collect the insurance money, lay employees off, and close the textile company, Aaron Feuerstein, the owner, promised to keep the employees on the payroll while he rebuilt. Mr. Feuerstein rescued the business, saved about 3,000 jobs, and kept the town of Lawrence, MA, where the company is based, from economic disaster. While stories like Mr. Feuerstein's are inspiring, they add to the myth that good ethics and good business always go hand in hand. That is simply not the case.

❸   "One could argue that responsible management and doing the right thing are often characterized by the same things," Jon P. Gunnemann, a professor of social ethics at Emory University, said. "But you can't infer that every decision about the right thing to do is necessarily going to be good for the company. Sometimes, doing the right thing can have tragic consequences."

❹   A prime example may involve Ed Shultz, the former chief executive of Smith & Wesson, the gun manufacturer based in Springfield, MA. ... In an attempt to defuse lawsuits the company was facing from at least twenty-nine municipalities that held handgun manufacturers responsible for violent crimes, Mr. Shultz entered into an agreement with the federal government. He said that Smith & Wesson would include locks on its handguns, research and implement "smart-gun" technology that would only allow the owner of a gun to operate it, and improve the way retailers sold its products. Much of this, said Mr. Shultz, was already being done. "It was a business decision," Ken Jorgensen, a company spokesman, said. Tomkins P.L.C., the British company that owns Smith & Wesson, wanted to sell the company. This goal was impossible as long as the lawsuits were pending. The company knew the reaction to the agreement with the federal government might be harsh. "There wasn't any question there was going to be a hit," Mr. Shultz said. "The question was how big the hit would be and for how long."

❺ As it turns out, the hit was huge. The company was vilified by its customers, retailers, and perhaps most vocally by the industry lobbying group, the National Rifle Association. Sales dropped off dramatically, and by October the company announced that it was laying off 125 of the 725 employees at its Springfield plant. Mr. Shultz left the company in September to run another company that had been sold by Tomkins.

❻ Why would a company very publicly decide to implement changes in its products that it knew would likely meet with disapproval among its core constituents? Up until this time, Mr. Shultz said, the company had done everything required by the government that it had to do in manufacturing guns—no more, no less. But the decision to do more, he said, "came because I couldn't answer the question, 'Was I doing everything I knew how to do to prevent accidents?'" When he asked himself, "Would I put locks on our guns if it might save one child? The answer was yes. ... I had to make those decisions based on the tradition of the company and my own beliefs of what's right," said Mr. Shultz, who still describes himself as "an enthusiastic gun owner." He said the formal agreement made sense because Smith & Wesson was already doing most of what the municipalities were asking for.

❼ In the short-term, Smith & Wesson is suffering consequences that from a business standpoint might be considered tragic. What adds to the tragedy is that no other manufacturers followed Smith & Wesson's lead and the deal ultimately unraveled. "Shultz may have done something that was in the best long-term interests of the company—making it seem like a corporate citizen and just doing the right thing—but because the law doesn't require others to do it, in the short run it may have hurt the company," said Joseph W. Singer, a law professor at Harvard and author of *The Edges of the Field* (Beacon, 2000).

❽ The thorny dilemma for company managers, then, is what to do when deciding between doing the right thing and doing what is best for the business. Ultimately, the ethical choice is clear: do the right thing regardless of whether you are rewarded for doing so. "If you take your morality seriously," Mr. Gunnemann said, "then what's most important to you is not the bottom line, it's whether you can sleep at night."

From "When Good Ethics Aren't Good Business," by Jeffrey L. Seglin, *The New York Times,* March 18, 2001. Copyright © 2001 by The New York Times Co. Reprinted with permission.

Scanning for Specific Information

▶ Reread the article to find the answers to these questions. Note the number of the question in the margin for future reference. Write the answer in note form and in your own words as much as possible.

1. What can happen to companies with bosses who try to "do the right thing"?

_____

2. a. What action did Ed Shultz, the former chief executive of Smith & Wesson, decide the company should take?

_____

   b. Why did he think this was a good thing to do?

_____

3. a. What was the reaction to the company's decision?

_____

   b. What was the effect on the employees?

_____

4. a. In the writer's opinion, what long- and short-term effects are predicted for the company?

_____

   b. What reasons are given for this prediction?

_____

5. In the writer's opinion, what should CEOs do when faced with making an ethical decision?

_____

▶ Compare your answers with your partner. Try to agree on the answers. Refer to the article if you disagree.

Recapping the Information

▶ **A** **Note Taking** Identify the main ideas of the article. Highlight the information corresponding to each main idea.

▶ **B** Use what you highlighted to make notes on each main idea.

▷ **C** Working with your partner, compare the notes you made. Discuss whether they are too detailed or too brief. Add to or remove from your notes if necessary.

▷ **D** Using only your notes, take turns telling each other the important information in the article. Make sure you explain the information as clearly and completely as you can.

Reacting to the Information

▷ Discuss these questions with another person who read the *same* article. Explain your ideas as completely as possible.

1. What are a CEO's most important priorities: keeping the company profitable, keeping workers employed, or holding true to moral principles?
2. Do you think that Ed Shultz made the right decision?
3. Do you think that the government should have improved the industry standard in this case?
4. Should more CEOs make ethically-based decisions of the kind presented in the story of Smith & Wesson?

Comparing the Readings

Discussing the Stories

▷ Work with a partner who prepared notes based on information from the other story. Use your notes to retell the information you read. Explain the ideas clearly in your own words. Encourage your partner to ask questions about the information or write some of the important facts you explain.

Vocabulary Building

Word Form

▷ **A** Study these five words and their forms. Then choose the correct form for each part of speech in the chart on the next page. These words are commonly found in general and academic texts.

compile (v.)	institutionalize (v.)	justify (v.)	structure (v.)	violate (v.)
compilation (n.)	institutional	justification	structured	violating
compiler (n.)	institution	justified	structure	violator
compiled (adj.)	institutionally	justifiable	structurally	violated
		justifiably	structural	violation

Verb	Noun	Adjective	Adverb
institutionalize	1.	1.	1.
justify	1.	1.	1.
		2.	
structure	1.	1.	1.
		2.	
violate	1.	1.	
	2.	2.	

▶ Compare lists with a partner.

▶ **B** Write three sentences using words from the list.

Antonyms

▶ **A** Refer to "How to Tell Right from Wrong" to find the words in context. Match the words in Column A with words that have the opposite meaning in Column B.

Column A

_____ 1. pragmatic

_____ 2. virtuous

_____ 3. saintly

_____ 4. shameful

_____ 5. equitable

_____ 6. repulsive

_____ 7. hypothetical

_____ 8. disparate

Column B

a. unfair

b. similar

c. proven

d. wicked

e. villainous

f. prideful

g. attractive

h. idealistic

▶ **B** In English, we can transform some words into words with the opposite meaning by adding a prefix such as *il-, im-, non-, un-, in-,* and *dis-*. Scan the readings in this chapter and circle the words with negative prefixes or those that can be changed by adding a negative prefix. Check these with others in your class.

Adverbs

▶ Adverbs are parts of speech that tell us about the how of things. Adverbs modify verbs, adjectives, or other adverbs. Many adverbs end in *-ly*.

Read each statement from the reading "How to Tell Right from Wrong." Circle the adverb. Write *V* if the adverb modifies a verb, *ADJ* if it modifies an adjective, or *ADV* if it modifies an adverb.

1. _____ So there's no practical value to acting ethically in the short run.

2. _____ If everyone acted wickedly, then all windows would have bars on them.

3. _____ It's a profoundly moral enterprise in that it gives you a chance to create structures within which people can be good.

4. _____ They live in a very narrow culture of people who think you should get $10 million a year even if the company loses money.

5. _____ The free market also seems essentially false.

▶ Check your answers with a partner. Together find other examples of adverb usage in the reading.

Vocabulary in Context

▶ **Jigsaw Sentences** Match each clause in Column A with the clause in Column B that makes the best sentence. Decide if part A should be placed *before* or *after* part B. Add the correct punctuation and capitalization to the final sentences.

Column A

_____ 1. So there's no practical value to acting ethically in the short run

_____ 2. But once a social structure was created

_____ 3. So is the fear of getting shamed by your neighbors

_____ 4. If this CEO has it in him to reduce his salary, that's a lovely thing

_____ 5. If the job violates your values, and the only thing keeping you there is your self-interest

Column B

a. While the fear of getting formally caught by the judicial system of our society is a motive for people to act ethically

b. If you look at the world, the wicked do, indeed, prosper, and the virtuous don't necessarily

c. Then you shouldn't be there

d. It was really encouraging how well everyone acted

e. But this is more of a case of civil rather than individual virtues

▶ Compare your combinations with a partner. Refer to the reading "How to Tell Right from Wrong" and find other examples of two-clause sentences in the readings.

Expanding Your Language

Speaking

A Oral Presentation Think of a company or a business person you are interested in. You may want to focus on a well-known CEO like Bill Gates or a company such as Wal-Mart. You may decide to focus on a person or company that you are familiar with. It may be a person or company that has experienced ethical problems or one that has not.

Prepare to talk about your subject by researching the following:

- Background or general information about your subject
- The qualities or aspects of the business or business person that you will focus on
- Difficulties and successes this person or business faced
- Reason(s) you admire this person or business

Using these points, prepare notes for a five-minute presentation. Practice your presentation and then give your talk to others in a small group. Prepare three questions for your audience to give them a focus for discussion after your presentation.

B Debate Work with a partner to set up a debate. To do so, follow these steps.

1. Read the scenario below.

A husband and wife both have high-paying executive positions with a large and seemingly successful corporation. They have a great life—two homes, one of them a vacation home in a desirable location, and two children aged seven and ten in private school. They are rising in the company and hope to enjoy many more years of successful employment in the future. Recently though, the company has acquired a number of plants in countries where people are paid very poorly and where they have heard charges that child labor is used in the manufacturing. They are worried that their jobs will require them to be involved with these operations. What arguments can you make for or against staying with the company?

2. Choose to be either in favor of or opposed to staying with the company.

3. Brainstorm a list of ideas in support of your position.

4. Work with a partner to add to the list. Think of as many reasons and examples as you can to defend your position.

5. Prepare to talk for one minute for each point you want to make.

6. Debate your position with two students who chose another position.

7. Take turns presenting your points.

8. Listen carefully to your partners and ask questions about the information. Share your conclusions with your classmates.

Writing

▶ A Reaction Writing Write your opinion about doing work that is in keeping with your ethical beliefs in today's business world. Include your own feelings about the future. Is it becoming easier or harder to find work with companies that espouse values that you support?

▶ B Topic Writing Choose a topic related to the discussions in the chapter readings or to the topic of your oral presentation. Try to write about the topic every day for a week. Use the mind-mapping technique in Chapter One on page 35 to help you develop and expand on your ideas.

Sample Outline

An Essay on the Importance of Ethics in the Workplace
　　Paragraph 1. The Reasons Why Businesses Act Unethically
　　Paragraph 2. The Explanations for Why People Agree to Unethical Behavior
　　Paragraph 3. The Importance of Ethical Standards in Business

Reading

▶ In the next reading, which is a short story, the author describes an incident that leaves an important impression on a young boy accused of a small crime. As you read, think about the type of relationship that exists between this father and son. How does the father react to his son's actions? What life lessons does the boy learn? Is this a story about ethics? Why or why not?

A Small Crime

By Jerry Wexler

When he was nine years old, he was brought to the door by a policeman who kept one hand on his arm as if to stop him from running away. He had been caught writing with a crayon on a wall of the subway station and his parents were expected to discipline him. The entire rest of the day he stayed in his room waiting for his father to come home from the shirt factory. A slap in the face, he thought, perhaps that's all I'll get. And maybe no allowance for the coming week. Still, he could not help but be apprehensive.

At five thirty he heard the front door open. His mother was talking to his father. They talked for a long time, much longer than he felt was necessary. Then the family ate supper. He was not invited and he felt that his punishment had already started.

This saddened him greatly because he enjoyed eating supper with his father and telling him about the day's adventure. He tried to pass the time by reading through his comic books, but he was anxious and could not follow through from beginning to end. At seven o'clock he heard the television come on as the family sat down in the living room. Every so often someone changed a channel. By eight thirty night had fallen and he felt more alone than he had ever been at any time in his life. He looked out into the garden behind his room. He could see the outline of the young tree his grandfather had planted a month before. It was beginning to sprout leaves and he tried to decide how many it would have that summer. He decided on fifteen. That knowledge made him feel better.

By nine o'clock he was feeling drowsy and had lain out on his bed.

Shortly afterwards his father came into the room and sat down on the bed. The boy sat up, putting his feet over the side of the bed. His father looked at him then turned away clasping his hands together. They were sitting side by side. The boy looked down at the floor the whole time.

"I remember when I left Romania," his father said. "I went to the train station in my town and had to sit in a special section for people who were emigrating from the country. There were many other people sitting there, and I remember how funny it was that we all looked the same with our best clothes and old suitcases almost bursting with clothes. But what I remember most of all were the walls. It seemed that every person who had ever sat in that part of the railway station had written on the wall his name, his home town, and the new place to which he was going. I spent a long time reading all the names on the wall. Many towns were represented and I even recognized the names of many people with whom I had once been friends. And do you know what I did? I took out my pen, found a clear space on the wall, and wrote my own name, my home town, and the date. But you see I did not write on the wall out of mischief, it was my own way of saying *this is who I am—now I am ending an old life and starting a new one*. Perhaps one day you will have the same reason. But as long as times are good and we are welcome here, there are other and better ways of letting the world know who you are."

He put his hand on the boy's shoulder as if to say, "don't worry, everything is all right." Then he rose slowly and said, "Be good to your mother and me and leave the walls alone." Then he left the room.

The boy lay back on his bed. Ordinarily it took him only two or three minutes to fall asleep. That night he lay awake for almost half an hour.

▶ React to the reading and discuss the following question: What lessons did you learn in your youth about ethical behavior?

▶Read On: Taking It Further

Reading for Pleasure

 Tip

Remember to write your reading journal and vocabulary log entries. ■

▶ Find some readings on the topics in this unit that you are interested in and that are at your level. Your teacher can help you prepare a list of some books, stories, or magazine articles to read for your pleasure. For example, you could choose a biography of a business leader, a book about a business scandal such as an account of what happened at Enron, or a book such as *The Seven Habits of Highly Effective People* by Steven Covey.

Discuss what you would like to read with others in a small group. Your group members could recommend something good for you to read. Try to work with a reading partner. Select a reading that your partner or partners will read as well. Make a schedule for the times when you plan to do your personal reading and a time when you would like to finish. Write your reactions to the reading in your reading journal. You can also include your reactions to readings presented by your fellow students.

 **Online Study Center**   For additional activities, go to the *Reading Matters* Online Study Center at *college.hmco.com/pic/wholeyfour2e*.

The World of Man and Animals

You have to be fast on your feet and adaptive or else a strategy is useless.

—*Charles de Gaulle*

Introducing the Topic

Studies into the lives of animals and the origins of human life have raised some very interesting questions about human nature. The chapters of this unit explore these topics and the questions they raise. Chapter 11 looks at the nature of chimpanzees and the questions that concern our understanding and treatment of animals. Chapter 12 contains readings on the topic of evolution. What are some of the processes by which humans evolved that influence our lives? What questions do we have about these processes?

Points of Interest

Giving Explanations

▶ Read the short explanation of evolution below, then discuss the questions with a partner or in a small group.

1. How does the theory of evolution link humans and animals?
2. How has the human body changed with evolution?
3. What kinds of changes have been the most important?
4. Are human beings still evolving? What changes could occur in the future?

What is Evolution?

The father of the modern idea of evolution is Charles Darwin, a British naturalist who in 1831 went on a two-year voyage around the world observing plants and animals. The idea of evolution was based mainly on his observations, especially those on the Galapagos Islands, which are about 559 miles off the West Coast of Ecuador. In simple terms, his theory supposes that all creation is linked and has grown more complex over great periods of time. Most famously, his theory supposes that humans evolved from their most closely related ape ancestor. His theory is based on two principles: gene mutation and natural selection. Gene mutation is a random process in which genes change or mutate due to natural or unnatural causes, e.g., radiation. Natural selection states that a species whose characteristics (which are determined by its genes) best allow it to adapt to its environment will survive and continue, whereas a species whose characteristics are not suited to the environment will die off and become extinct.

Analyzing Quotes

▶ **Free Writing** What do these quotes say about people and animals? Circle *A* if you agree with the idea and *D* if you disagree. Write any ideas you have about these questions. Discuss your ideas with others.

1. A D The greatness of a nation and its moral progress can be judged by the way its animals are treated. —*Mahatma Ghandi*

2. A D Time spent with animals is never wasted. —*Sigmund Freud*

3. A D Man is the only animal that blushes—or needs to. —*Mark Twain*

4. A D Man is an animal that makes bargains; no other animal does this. —*Adam Smith*

5. A D Every animal leaves traces of what it was; man alone leaves traces of what he created. —*Jacob Bronowski*

6. A D An animal's eyes have the power to speak a great language. —*Martin Buber*

7. A D How we humans came to be the way we are is far less important than how we should act now to get out of the mess we have made for ourselves. —*Jane Goodall*

11 The Lives of Chimps: The Treatment of Animals

Chapter Openers

Discussion Questions

▶ Before reading, share your ideas about these questions.

1. Have you ever seen a chimpanzee or other great ape?
2. How do you think chimpanzees behave?
3. Why are people interested in these animals?

Chimpanzees in Africa

❶   Chimpanzees live mainly in Central Western Africa as well as Western and Eastern Africa. They are also exported and imported from Africa to "customer countries." For example, chimpanzees in North America originated in Liberia and Sierra Leone. Chimpanzees in Europe originated in the Congo and the Democratic Republic of the Congo.

❷   The best estimates now are that there are approximately 2.85 chimps per square kilometer in those areas of Africa. Chimpanzee population is something that is very difficult to track, and almost as difficult to estimate. However, we know that the number of chimpanzees in the wild is rapidly decreasing. One cause of this is that a large number of chimps are being captured and taken out of the wild. They are then put into zoos or used for medical research. Another major cause of declining numbers is poaching. Chimpanzees are being illegally trapped for food and also sold on the black market. When this happens, the chimps are not properly cared for and will often die before they reach their destination.

❸   Many things are being done to increase the number of chimpanzees in the wild. For example, there are five field sites set up to study chimps. In these sites, scientists study behaviors of male and female chimpanzees. These sites are located in the Bossou, Gombe, Kibale, Mahale, and Tai areas of Africa. Scientists are also doing more controlled studies in captivity to learn more about them.

This map shows the distribution of chimpanzees. The dark gray areas are "known" areas where it is a fact that chimpanzees are currently located. The lighter gray areas are areas in which chimpanzees lived previously.

Examining Outlines

 Reading Tip

Outlines can contain **information** that is **specific** to the **topic**. Notice how the questions help you to focus on the key ideas in the information. ■

▶ Use the information below to answer the following questions.

1. When did apes first appear on earth?

2. Do people and chimps have very similar DNA?

3. Are chimpanzees classified in the same family as humans?

4. What do you think are the characteristics of primates? Explain as much as possible.

5. Based on the information you have, how similar to man would you consider chimps to be?

The Evolution of Chimpanzees

The earliest-known primates date from about 70 million years ago. The greater apes (family Pongidae, gorillas, chimpanzees, bonobos, and orangutans) split off from the lesser apes (family Hylobatidae, gibbons and siamangs) 20 million years ago. The chimpanzee is the animal that is closest to people genetically; people and chimps have very similar DNA (about 98 percent of human and chimpanzee DNA is identical). Genetic studies show that chimpanzees and humans share a common ancestor.

Classification

Chimpanzees belong to the:
- Kingdom **Animalia** (all animals)
- Phylum **Chordata**
- Subphylum **Vertebrata** (animals with backbones)
- Class **Mammalia** (warm-blooded animals with fur and mammary glands)
- Order **Primates** (which comprises eleven families, including lemurs, monkeys, marmosets, lesser apes, great apes, and humans)
- Family **Pongidae** (the great apes, including gorillas, chimpanzees, bonobos, and orangutans)
- Genus *Pan* (chimpanzees and bonobos)
  - Species *troglodytes*—the Chimpanzee
    - Subspecies *P. t. verus*—the western subspecies (found in Côte d'Ivoire, plus some small populations in Guinea, Sierra Leone, and Liberia)
    - Subspecies *P. t. troglodytes*—the central subspecies (found mostly in Gabon, also from eastern Nigeria to the Ubanghi River and south to the Zaire River)
    - Subspecies *P. t. schweinfurthi*—the eastern subspecies studied by Jane Goodall (found from southern Lake Tanganyika in Tanzania, and from there northwards to Burundi, Rwanda, Uganda and southern Sudan)
  - Species *paniscus*—the Bonobo or pygmy chimp, from the Democratic Republic of the Congo, along the Zaire River

Exploring and Understanding Reading

Discussing the News

> **Reading Tip**

Remember! **Newspaper articles** have very short paragraphs so surveying to get the main ideas is not very useful. The **best strategy** is to **skim**. ■

◉ Read the news article that follows and underline the facts about the following topics. Mark the number of each topic in the margin of the text.

1. Profile of Kanzi
2. Kanzi's Abilities
3. Profile of the Research Center
4. Research Procedure
5. Research Questions for the Future
6. Facts About Monkey's Abilities

Chimpanzees: Signs of Intelligence?

❶   London—A chimpanzee who has grown up among humans may have developed the ability to talk, challenging the widely held view that animals do not have language by making up its own words from scratch. A U.S. research team report says Kanzi, an adult bonobo (or pygmy chimpanzee) kept at Georgia State University, Atlanta, has come up with four distinct sounds for the things closest to his heart—banana, juice, grapes, and yes. Although the choice of words may be a little predictable, it is the first report of an ape making sounds that seem to have the same meaning across different situations. The findings, published in Britain's *New Scientist* magazine, have astonished ape experts, who believe Kanzi has come the closest to mastering a simple form of speech.

❷   Kanzi has grown up among people and is skilled at communicating with symbols. He understands some spoken English and can respond to simple phrases such as, "Do you want a banana?" the magazine reports. In the Atlanta Language Research Center, Kanzi has been taught to communicate with humans by pointing to printed symbols on a keyboard. In return, Kanzi understands scores of spoken English words and sentences. The chimp demonstrates "the rudimentary language skills of two-and-a-half-year-old children," said one of his trainers. For example, if Kanzi is told to "pour the milk in the juice," he responds properly and does not pour the juice in the milk.

❸   But his language trainers, Jared Taglialatela and Sue Savage-Rumbaugh, discovered that he also made distinct noises during their "conversations." The team studied 100 hours of videotapes of Kanzi. They were most interested in situations where the chimp's meaning was obvious, such as when he was pointing to the symbol for grapes or eating a banana. The researchers found four noises used by Kanzi in different contexts. "We haven't taught him this. He's doing it all on his own," Dr. Taglialatela said. Kanzi's "word" for yes stayed the same across a range of emotions, suggesting the noises were not simply the result of differences in the chimp's emotional state.

❹ Kanzi is the latest in a line of primates to challenge the conventional view that animals have no language. Language used to be defined as symbolic communication until another chimpanzee, Washoe, learned to communicate in American Sign Language. Since then, the definition has been refined to put more emphasis on syntax and less on symbols.

❺ The researchers are now trying to discover whether Kanzi is imitating human speech. But they will not consider the chimp to be communicating until other chimps respond to the sounds. Primatologist John Mitani of the University of Michigan in Ann Arbor said, "Despite the fact that we have had glimmerings of this in the monkey world, few instances of anything like this have been documented among our closest living relatives, chimps and bonobos. There have to be evolutionary precursors to what we do. We are beginning to find them in the primate world."

❻ Here are some further examples of the surprising mental capacities researchers have discovered in animals:

- *Problem Solving* Harvard psychologist Marc Hauser tested a monkey's ability to solve the problem of getting food that was out of reach outside its cage. In one experiment, the food was located on a piece of cloth that the monkey could pull toward itself, while another morsel was placed off the cloth. In a second test, the monkey had to choose between food placed on a single cloth or on one of two pieces of cloth separated by a gap. In both cases, the monkey pulled the right cloth, thereby solving the problem, usually on the first try, Hauser reported. These experiments show monkeys can see the connection between an action on one object and its effect on another. "This comprehension is at the root of all tool use," Hauser said.

- *Tool Use* To crack nuts, chimpanzees put a shell on a flat rock and hammer it open with a stone. They may store a favorite hammer under

Chimpanzee using a stick to eat termites.

a familiar tree so they can use it over and over again. In the presence of their infants, mother chimps use their hammers slowly to show how the job is done. Sometimes, mothers correct their pupils' mistakes.

- *Self-Awareness* Researcher Gordon Gallup, a psychologist at the State University of New York in Albany, has demonstrated that apes, unlike most animals, can be trained to recognize themselves in a mirror. Gallup anesthetized chimpanzees and, while they were unconscious, put dabs of color on their faces. When the chimps woke up and looked in the mirror, they spontaneously touched the marks.

    Penny Patterson, an animal psychologist at Santa Clara University in Santa Clara, California, has trained Koko, a female gorilla, to use sign language to express her wishes, feelings and thoughts. When a trainer put a mirror in front of Koko and asked her what she saw, the 300-pound gorilla made the signs for "Me, Koko."

- *Communication* Con Slobodchikoff, an expert on animal cognition at Northern Arizona University in Flagstaff, said … when a vervet monkey, an African species, emits the call for eagle, his fellow monkeys look up to the sky. When the call is for leopard, they climb a tree. When it's for a snake, they stand up and look around for the danger.

Adapted from David Derbyshire, *National Post,* and Robert S. Boyd, *The Gazette*

Paired Readings

▶ The next two readings are newspaper articles dealing with two different points of view about animal rights. Choose one of the readings. Work with a partner who is reading the *same* article.

Free Writing

▶ **Debating Animal Rights** Write about any ideas you have on these questions. Write as much as possible. Share your ideas with a partner or a small group.

1. How should we treat animals with signs of intelligence such as monkeys?
2. What rights should these animals have?

❶The Animal in Our World: The Case in Favor

Skimming   ▶ Read the article quickly and answer the following questions.

1. Which animals does Professor Steven Wise argue we should recognize the rights of?
2. What kind of animal abuse are the students discussing?
3. What motivates Steven Wise to argue in favor of animal rights?
4. What puzzles law professor Richard Epstein?
5. What comparison does Wise make between a chimpanzee and his children?

▶ Compare your information with your partner. Refer to the reading to support your answers.

The Animal Rights Revolution

❶   The students and their professor talk heatedly of slaves and property, of children, torture, slaughter and common decency. This could be a class in human-rights law or history, a discussion about former Chilean dictator Augusto Pinochet's return home, the American Civil War, or the holocaust in Rwanda. But it's not.

     The talk today revolves around Rocky, an unfortunate tortoise from San Diego, and the location is a small lecture hall at Harvard University's law school, where Professor Steven Wise is conducting its first course in animal-rights law.

Arguing for the Defendant

❷   Listen closely and you will hear the rumblings of a revolution beginning to gain credibility in North America. This is a revolution that is happening on campuses across the United States over an issue some still consider as radical as the nineteenth-century contention that black slaves were people, not pieces of property to be dealt with as one would a cow or a horse. "This is one of the most difficult social revolutions we have ever had," says Wise, a fiery, likable animal-rights lawyer and author whose recently published book, *Rattling the Cage—Toward Legal Rights for Animals*, has earned lots of attention, both good and bad. In *Rattling the Cage*, Wise makes the case for legal rights only for chimpanzees and their relatives, bonobos. His is a cautious approach, with victories counted in terms of increments.

Thus, the Rocky Problem

❸   With Wise, who has also taught at the University of Vermont and the Tufts School of Veterinary Medicine, as their referee, the thirty-five students argue the case. They talk about the condition Rocky was in when he was seized from a San Diego petting zoo, about his shell that was split down the middle, about his worn toenails from all that pacing and his bad case of diarrhea. They talk of how the California courts could do no more than treat him as a piece of property, chained by existing laws. "Can Rocky feel pain?" Wise asks the class. "Does it matter?"

❹   One student says it was as if Rocky was a sofa that had been abused by its malicious maker. Another notes that one of the judges in the appeals court made a weak joke about there being a "Rocky II." The talk goes off in many directions, touching on the kosher slaughter of animals, the transport of chickens, the right of lobsters to swim free, and the sign language of chimpanzees. They make arguments for first one side, then the other.

❺   Wise is as curious and as much in the dark as his students. He is working his way through a perplexing number of issues that are inevitable when one is in the middle of a revolution to change how people have thought for a long, long time—some say ever since the Bible first told us we were made in God's image or when Aristotle posited that everything in the world is here only to serve man. Wise, who works in a cluttered office in the basement of his home near Boston, says his mantra is the excerpt taped on the wall over his computer, from Winston Churchill's speech about the World War II retreat from Flanders: "We shall fight on the beaches, landing grounds, in fields, in streets, and on the hills. We shall never surrender."

Remembering Jerom

❻   He dedicates *Rattling the Cage* to a chimpanzee named Jerom, whom he calls "a person, not a thing." Jerom died ten days short of his fourteenth birthday in a small, windowless, concrete cell. Over the course of his sad life, he had been infected with three strains of the HIV virus, two of which eventually combined to kill him. He had not been outside for eleven years.

From the Other Side

❼   Critics such as Richard Epstein, a law professor at the University of Chicago who is against animal rights being written into law because they are not humans, are at a loss to explain how the issue has caught the public fancy. He doesn't know why courses have recently proliferated at schools from Harvard and Georgetown University in Washington, DC, to the more conservative University of Florida in Gainesville. "I'm stunned at the level of interest this topic has generated," he said from his office. "The courses are in danger of becoming a propaganda effort because there is a bias in the field—everybody who teaches them is for 'the cause.' But as far as I know, a chimpanzee has never yet made a case for itself before a court."

Arguing for Animals

8   That may change soon. Recent court cases include a federal appeals-court decision in 1998 that granted legal standing to a human zoo visitor to sue on behalf of lonely chimpanzees. Wise and his wife and law partner, Debi Slater-Wise, both have cases working their way through the Massachusetts legal system in which they petition for animals to stop being identified as "things." In one that is currently before the Appeals Court, Wise represents a couple who were bereft after losing seven beloved sheep to marauding dogs. "These were companion animals. They'd have muffins baked especially for them. Their birthdays would be celebrated with balloons and they'd go on outings to Dunkin' Donuts," Wise said. "One should be able to sue for emotional loss, but the lower court would not admit evidence to that effect because one does not do that when talking about property." He objected. "How can we go around arguing that we, as human beings, deserve fundamental rights when we are drawing arbitrary lines?" he asked. "What's the difference between my two-year-old twins and a chimpanzee who speaks with a repertoire of 1,000 signs?"

Adapted from Lisa Fitterman, *The Gazette*

Scanning

◐ Highlight the answers to the following questions.

The Case for Rocky

1. Explain the case of Rocky. Where does the discussion of this case take place?
2. Who is Steven Wise?
3. What argument does he make and for which animals?
4. What aspects of this case do the students discuss?

The Question of Rights: Pro

5. What are some of the long-established ideas of human rights?
6. What quote inspired Steven Wise?
7. What case inspired Wise's book?

The Question of Rights: Against

8. Who is Richard Epstein?
9. What is his position?
10. What surprises him?

Conclusion

11. What arguments are the Wises making on behalf of animals?
12. How does Wise feel about the rulings from the lower court?

Recapping the Information

▶ Working with a partner, compare what you highlighted. Remove any unnecessary highlighting. Complete any additional highlighting needed. Using *only* what you highlighted, take turns telling each other about the important information in the article. Explain the information as completely as possible.

Reacting to the Information

▶ Discuss these questions with your partner.

1. What rights do you think animals should have?
2. Should animals be considered property in the eyes of the law? What evidence is given?
3. Do you agree with the position of Richard Epstein when he says, "I'm stunned at the level of interest this topic has generated. The courses are in danger of becoming a propaganda effort because there is a bias in the field—everybody who teaches them is for 'the cause.' But as far as I know, a chimpanzee has never yet made a case for itself before a court."
4. Do you agree with the position of Steven Wise when he says, "How can we go around arguing that we, as human beings, deserve fundamental rights when we are drawing arbitrary lines? What's the difference between my two-year-old twins and a chimpanzee who speaks with a repertoire of 1,000 signs?"

2 The Animal in His World: Where Do Rights Lead?

Skimming

▶ Read the article quickly and answer the following questions.

1. What is Dr. Goodall's position on legal human rights for great apes?
2. What example does the writer use to question Dr. Goodall's position?
3. What kind of support does Dr. Goodall have?
4. What reactions have people had to the murder?
5. What is Frodo like?
6. What facts are given that raise questions about the differences between chimps and humans?

▶ Compare your information with your partner. Refer to the reading to support your answers.

Me Frodo, You Jane?

❶   Dr. Jane Goodall, the chimpanzee expert, wants legal human rights to be extended to great apes because she claims that they are so similar to us. Why, then, has Frodo, the alpha male of her chimp study group in Gombe Stream National Park in Tanzania, just gotten away with the horrible murder of a human child?

❷   The story begins on a morning in May. The wife and toddler son of Moshi Sadiqi, a park attendant, were collecting firewood in Gombe, on the shores of Lake Tanganyika. Like many staff families, they lived inside the park. The pair ventured into the rain forest. Frodo struck without warning. He swung out of the jungle, snatched up the boy and, as the distraught mother looked on, retreated into the trees. Here, Frodo flung his prey against the branches repeatedly, until the boy was as limp as a rag doll. The mother ran for help and park rangers rushed to the scene. Frodo had by this time disemboweled the boy and eaten part of his head.

❸   Goodall, who arrived to study Gombe's chimps in 1960, departed from scientific convention by christening her apes with human names rather than with serial numbers. She conferred on them all the characteristics of people, creating in her films and books the world's longest-running animal soap opera. With her trademark gray ponytail, she ascended to become a queen among animal-rights activists. She calls for "some kind of fundamental rights within the legal system" for chimps, based on the common heritage with *Homo sapiens* of 98 percent of their genes, together with chimp cognition, emotions, and game-playing. "The line between humans and the rest of the animal kingdom, once thought to be so clear, has become blurred," she says.

4 Her position is widely supported, though not in Africa, where leaders have been too busy exterminating their human populations to ponder animal rights. Rather, her support comes from fans in the rich world and the United Nations. Jane Goodall, CBE, has won the Mahatma Gandhi/Martin Luther King Award for Non-Violence, at UN headquarters. The United Nations also appointed her a "peace ambassador," praising her for "fostering human rights and the liberation of the human spirit." On her travels, Goodall carries a soft toy "peace" chimp holding a banana, which she claims two million people have touched.

5 If chimps deserve basic legal rights, then I assumed that, by the same argument, Frodo should face justice for murdering Moshi Sadiqi's son. I asked the Jane Goodall Institute (JGI) what action was being taken. Would he face some sort of chimpanzee trial? "The Tanzanian authorities have decided not to punish Frodo for behaving like a chimp in his own territory," replied Dilys MacKinnon, executive director of JGI in Britain. "The child's family has said that they do not blame Frodo … Government officials came to talk to those involved and to express condolences. It appears that all concerned have been very understanding."

6 Even if Frodo were merely a wild animal in his own territory, one might expect him to be put to sleep like a dangerous dog. In Tanzania, if elephants plunder peasants' crops, the state game department responds by shooting the offending herd's ringleaders. This is despite the wide acceptance that pachyderms are, together with chimps and whales, the most aware of creatures after humans.

7 But Frodo is no mere animal; he's a global celebrity. If *Hello!* had a beast edition, Frodo would feature on the cover in a tuxedo. He's a star of the silver screen with a filmography dating back to the 1970s. His latest billing is in Jane Goodall's *Wild Chimpanzees*, an Imax movie premiering around the globe this year. The JGI's website publicizes the film, but not Frodo's recent behavior. Born in 1976 to mother Fifi, Frodo grew up to become Gombe's heavyweight at 120 lbs. He seized power as alpha male of his Kasekela clan in 1998 after his elder brother and former don, Freud, contracted mange, a fatal disease. Frodo rules as a dictator, assisted by his vizier, the dastardly Goblin. He chews his upper lip when psyching himself up for violence. He rolls boulders down hills. He throws stones with deadly accuracy. The visitors he's beaten up include the Far Side cartoonist Gary Larson. He once pummeled Jane's head so hard that he nearly broke her neck.

❽   … Chimps are hard-core. They hunt and eat primate meat. They practice cannibalism. Killing excites them. They mutilate prey. … Bloodletting between clans can be so systematic that one feud was called the Four Years' War. What is more, the murder of Moshi Sadiqi's son was not unique in terms of attacks on human children. "Two incidents involving children occurred quite a few years before research in the park started in 1960," MacKinnon told me. "A baby was taken for food [and] a seven-year-old boy was wounded when he rescued his infant sister." Goodall's own son, Grub, was terrorized by a chimp named Flint in the 1970s. Grub spent much of his childhood in a cage for protection and grew up loathing chimps so much that today he's a shark fisherman. There are scientists who reject Goodall's idea of our consanguinity with chimps. In his recent book, *What It Means to be 98% Human*, the molecular anthropologist Jonathan Marks reveals that we share 40 percent of our genes with fish and 25 percent with dandelions. Should rights be extended to goldfish? Marks argues that the 2 percent that divides us from chimps is what makes all the difference. …

❾   To me, the moral is that Frodo is wild, and he should be given the space to be wild. He's no human. If he were, he'd be sent to Broadmoor. Instead, this ape's on his way to Broadway.

Adapted from Aidan Hartley, *The Spectator*

Scanning

▶ Highlight the answers to the following questions.

Dr. Goodall's Attitude Toward and Work with Chimps

1. Why does Dr. Goodall believe in granting legal rights to apes?
2. What case proves this position may be problematic?
3. What are the details of the murder?
4. What is unorthodox in Goodall's study of chimps?

Reaction to Dr. Goodall's Position

5. Where is Dr. Goodall's position on legal rights for apes supported?
6. Where is her position not supported?

How Should Frodo be Treated?

7. What reaction does the author have to the murder?
8. What is the response from people at the Jane Goodall Institute?
9. What surprises the writer?
10. How does the writer describe Frodo's nature?

Conclusion

11. What evidence does the writer offer to support the idea that chimps can be dangerous?
12. How do some scientists react to Dr. Goodall's ideas about apes?
13. What is the writer's opinion about what should happen to Frodo?

Recapping the Information

▶ Working with a partner, compare what you highlighted. Remove any unnecessary highlighting. Complete any additional highlighting needed. Using *only* what you highlighted, take turns telling each other about the important information in the article. Explain the information as completely as possible.

Reacting to the Information

▶ Discuss these questions with your partner.

1. What rights do you think animals should have?
2. What do you think should be done in the case of Frodo?
3. Should animals be considered dangerous in the eyes of the law?
4. Do you agree with Jane Goodall's position that "the line between humans and the rest of the animal kingdom, once thought to be so clear, has become blurred"?
5. Do you agree with Aidan Hartley's argument that "Even if Frodo were merely a wild animal in his own territory, one might expect him to be put to sleep like a dangerous dog"?

Comparing the Readings

Discussing the Stories

▶ Work with a partner who read and highlighted information from the other story. Use your highlighting to retell the information. Explain the ideas clearly in your own words. Encourage your partner to ask questions about the information or write some of the important facts you explain. Then, discuss the questions in the "Reacting to the Information" sections on page 242 and page 246.

Reacting in Writing

▶ **Essay Writing** Write your opinion about giving animals legal standing. Are you in favor of the position held by Steven Wise, Jane Goodall, and others that animals should be given legal rights? Or do you agree with Aidan Hartley and others who argue that animals are wild and essentially unlike humans?

▶ To do this, follow these steps:

▶ **1.** Outline your position and the arguments in support of this position. For each argument (i.e., biological, legal, humanitarian), give clear supporting points. For each supporting idea, give an explanation or an example to express the idea in detail.

2. Use your outline to write three or four complete paragraphs. Try to do the writing within an hour.

❯Vocabulary Building

Word Form

▶ **A** Study these five words and their forms. Then choose the correct form for each part of speech in the chart below. These words are commonly found in general and academic texts.

confer (v.)	randomize (v.)	refine (v.)	revolutionize (v.)	trace (v.)
conference (n.)	random	refined	revolutionizing	trace
conferee (n.)	randomness	refinement	revolutionary	traceable
conferring (adj.)	randomly	refining	revolution	tracing
conferrable (adj.)		refinery	revolutionary	

Verb	Noun	Adjective	Adverb
randomize	1.	1.	1.
refine	1.	1.	
	2.	2.	
revolutionize	1.	1.	
	2.	2.	
trace	1.	1.	
		2.	

▶ Compare lists with a partner.

▶ **B** Write three sentences using words from the list.

Vocabulary in Context

> **Reading Tip**

An **important** part of reading is **explaining** the ideas. After reading you may find that you want to explain orally or in writing. If you want to do this without quoting the writing, you can do it by **paraphrasing**, i.e., explaining the idea in your own words. ■

▶ **Verb Phrases** Refer to "Chimpanzees: Signs of Intelligence?" to find the boldface words in context. Match the words in Column A with words that have the same meaning in Column B.

Column A   **Column B**

_____ 1. **making up** its own words   a. curious about

_____ 2. **growing up** among people   b. select among

_____ 3. **interested in** situations   c. inventing

_____ 4. **pull toward** itself   d. search or investigate

_____ 5. **choose between** one and another   e. bring close to

_____ 6. **look around** for the danger   f. being raised

▶ Find other phrases in the reading and express the ideas in your own words. Discuss with a partner.

The Language of Research

▶ Researchers often use certain words to explain their work. Some of the most common words include the following verbs: *state, report, find, discover, raise, consider, show, study, suggest, test, witness, observe, involve,* and *describe.* In cases where the meaning is the same, writers can choose to use a different verb to express an idea. In choosing, read carefully. It is important that the verb convey the statement's meaning accurately. For example, the words *state, express,* and *explain* can all be used to convey the same or similar meanings in research.

▶ **A** Circle the verb that best completes each of the following sentences.

1. The language trainers **discovered / tested** that Kanzi made distinct noises during their "conversations."

2. Hauser **reported / studied** that in both cases the monkeys pulled the right cloth.

3. A critical test **involved / found** asking Kanzi to respond to an instruction such as, "Pour the milk in the juice."

4. Investigators have also **reported / claimed** to discern grammatical structure in Kanzi's own keyboard strokes.

5. In the field sites, scientists **study / suggest** behaviors of male and female chimpanzees.

6. Harvard psychologist Marc Hauser **tested / involved** a monkey's ability to solve the problem of getting food that was out of reach outside its cage.

▶ **B** Find the sentences in "Chimpanzees in Africa" and "Chimpanzees: Signs of Intelligence?" to check your answers. Look for other examples of explanations and notice the verbs that are used.

Recognizing Descriptive Language

▶ In essays, writers often use descriptive language that helps the reader understand an idea in an emotional way. This makes the ideas more convincing to the reader. In the following sentences, choose a word or words with the same meaning for the descriptive language in boldface. Use a dictionary *only* as a last resort.

1. Listen closely and you will hear **the rumblings** of a revolution beginning to gain credibility in North America.

   _____

2. His is a cautious approach, with victories counted in terms of **increments**.

   _____

3. Wise represents a couple who were **bereft** after losing seven beloved sheep to marauding dogs.

   _____

4. Goodall departed from scientific convention by **christening** her apes with human names rather than with serial numbers.

   _____

5. He once **pummeled** Jane's head so hard that he nearly broke her neck.

   _____

▶ Look for these and other examples of descriptive language in either "The Animal Rights Revolution" or "Me Frodo, You Jane?" Check your answers with a partner and with your teacher.

⟨Expanding Your Language

Reading   ▷ This article presents a short news report on research that continues to look at the parallels in human/monkey behavior. Read the report and prepare to discuss the following questions.

1. What are the details of how this research was carried out?
2. What is the purpose of the research and who is carrying it out?
3. What conclusions can we draw from this research?
4. What is your reaction to this research?

What's Fair is Fair, Even to a Monkey

Do children learn morality from their parents and teachers, or is ethical behavior wired into their genes? Researchers at Emory University in Atlanta reported in September that capuchin monkeys, which are found in South America, display at least some sense of fairness, a key criterion for judging right from wrong. They trained the monkeys to trade pebbles for food. If a monkey saw a researcher giving her neighbor a grape in return for a pebble, but she herself received only a cucumber slice, she would signal displeasure by slamming down the pebble or refusing to eat the cucumber. The study suggests that monkeys have a sense of fair treatment and protest when their expectations are violated. The research is part of an effort by evolutionary biologists to prove a genetic basis for social behavior. If a sense of fairness exists in these monkeys, it probably developed early in primates, and the genes that promote it are likely present in people too.

Nicholas Wade, *New York Times Upfront*

Speaking   ▷ **Debate** One of the important debates linked to animal rights is over the use of animals in medical research. There are those who argue that it saves lives, but there are those who say it is unnecessary and cruel. Prepare to debate this statement:

We should use animals such as chimpanzees for medical testing.

To carry out this activity, complete the following steps.

▷ **1.** Choose to be either in favor of or opposed to using animals such as chimpanzees for medical testing.

2. Brainstorm a list of ideas in support of your position.

3. Research the issue on your own. You can find articles and other reading material on the Internet, in the library, or from your teacher. Highlight the information you find that provides facts to support your position.

4. Work with a partner who is arguing the same position to add to the list of ideas.

5. Choose 3–4 important points, with as many reasons and examples as you can find, to defend your position.

6. Prepare to talk for one minute for each point you want to make.

7. With your partner, debate your position with two students who chose the opposite position.

8. Take turns presenting your points. Take careful notes of your opponents' points.

9. Prepare to answer your opponents' position and defend your own.

10. Share your conclusions with your classmates.

Writing

▶ **Topic Writing** Choose a topic related to the discussions in the chapter readings or to the topic of your debate. Try to write about the topic every day for a week.

Sample Outline

An Essay on the Importance of Ethical Treatment of Chimpanzees
   Paragraph 1. Why People are Interested in Chimpanzees
   Paragraph 2. Why People Should or Should Not Extend Legal Rights to Chimps
   Paragraph 3. The Ethical Treatment of Chimpanzees

 *Online Study Center*   For additional activities, go to the *Reading Matters* Online Study Center at *college.hmco.com/pic/wholeyfour2e.*

12 The Sole of €volution

▶ Chapter Openers

Discussion Questions

▶ Think about these questions. Share your ideas with a partner or a small group.

1. Why are our feet so important to our identity as humans?
2. How did the evolution of the human foot and the ability to walk upright change human existence?
3. What are the advantages and disadvantages of walking barefoot?
4. How common is it to walk barefoot today in comparison to the past?
5. How would you compare how fast you usually walk to that of most people?
6. How do you choose the kind of footwear you like to wear for different occasions?
7. How do shoes affect the shape and health of the human foot?

▶ €xploring and Understanding Reading

Previewing

▶ Read the title, subtitle, and headings and look at the graphics in the reading. Note three to four ideas that you think will be discussed in the article.

1. _____

2. _____

3. _____

4. _____

▶ Discuss your ideas with a partner or a small group.

Surveying

One **main idea** can cover more than one paragraph. ■

▷ Read until you think you have reached the end of the introduction—that is, when you have identified the thesis statement. (See page 66 for the elements of an introduction). Read the first sentence of every paragraph after that and the last paragraph. Note the main ideas in the margin. Verify or modify the ideas you listed above.

The Foot: Mother of Humanity

Mankind owes homage to our uniquely human feet, without which it could not have evolved to its present state.

❶   The human foot. It occupies the lowest rung of the human anatomy. It is ridiculed, taunted, and cursed. It is forced to live constantly in dark, cramped quarters, covered by soil and bacteria, stifled by heat, punished by constant pressure and friction, blanketed by sweat, choked by offensive odors.

❷   Yet it is this same humble, socially ostracized foot that is the mother of all humanity. It will come as a shocking reality to almost everyone, but we are human only because of our distinctive human foot. That unique foot is responsible for everything that distinguishes us from all other creatures: our physical body form, our remarkable brain and intelligence, our speech and language, our arts and creative talents, our sciences and technologies, our laws and governments. And civilization itself.

❸   Were it not for the human foot developing as it has over evolutionary time, there would have been no civilization, not even a human species. We would still be swinging from branches in the jungle. Incredible? A gross exaggeration? No, a factual, demonstrable scientific truth.

❹   Here is a tiny sampling of views from distinguished scientific authorities:

Donald C. Johanson, anthropologist, Institute of Human Origins: "Human bipedalism, made notable by the distinctive human foot, is what originally made us human."

John Napier, eminent anatomist: "The assumption of the upright posture, resting on the unique structure of the human foot, was the primary adaptation that led to the emergence of the human stock. All of man's characteristics—his culture, his ability to speak and use language, his technology, and his large brain—is the consequence of his standing and walking upright on his own two unique feet."

C. Owen Lovejoy, anthropologist, Kent State University: "Bipedal locomotion, emerging from a new design of foot, enabled us to become human and became the prime catalyst that launched us into humanhood."

Stephen Jay Gould, Harvard University paleobiologist: "The anatomical transition to upright posture and gait on two feet was the most profound change in our evolution from apelike creatures. It was the prime trigger of human evolution, resulting in a complete restructuring of our anatomy and the emergence of the huge human brain that propelled us upward…. When God praised Job as 'an upright man' he caught the very essence of man's image."

❺   So deeply established is the link between the foot, erect bipedal walking, and humanhood, that it's bred into the culture. Take for example what many fathers say to their sons, "You'll become a man when you can stand on your own two feet." But how can this be—one small remote part of the human anatomy responsible for so much? Let's see how it happened.

From the Bottom Up

❻   The oldest human fossil is a hominid (early human) unearthed in Ethiopia in 1994 and labeled *Ardipithecus ramidus-ramidus*. It dates back 5.6 million years as confirmed by a modern technique known as argon-argon dating. But perhaps the most famous, because it the most complete hominid skeleton to date, is the one found in 1974 by anthropologist Donald Johanson and labeled *Australopithecus afarensis* or "Lucy," dating back 3.7 million years.

❼   How do we know for certain that those fossils were actually human? By the design of the leg and pelvic bones, which clearly revealed that they were erect, bipedal walkers—the single most distinctive feature of humans that distinguishes us from all other creatures. In the three-billion-year history of life on this planet, no other creature has walked in this manner. And upright, two-legged walking began with the unique structure of the foot that made such a distinctive posture and gait possible. States Columbia University anatomist and orthopedist Dudley J. Morton, "The human foot is the only specialized organ that belongs strictly to the locomotor function .... Not only is it a remarkable example of Nature's engineering principles in the design of locomotion structures, but it is also in itself a combination of progressive landmarks recording the whole history of human evolution."

8 That's a powerful tribute to one small part of our anatomy. That hominid foot was constantly exposed to the most rugged terrain: jagged rocks, gravel, briars and thorns, unlevel surfaces, etc. And always barefoot. Like a car's axles and springs, it had to be split-second adaptable to escape fractures or sprains that could have left the hominid easy prey for predators. The foot, therefore, was the vital and primary element in the survival of the emerging human species. A modern example of the required ruggedness of the foot is the rickshaw men of nineteenth-century China. A century ago, Shanghai alone had over 10,000 rickshaw men at work. Each averaged over twenty-five miles of trotting each day, seven days a week, running barefoot over cobblestone streets and gravel roads. Even a slight injury could threaten their livelihood. Despite the rugged terrain, the feet remained strong and mostly trouble-free. The feet of the early hominids had the same rugged nature.

9 At this point it might be asked, "What's so important about being a biped? Other bipeds exist. Fowl and birds and penguins, for example. Bears and apes can stand and take a few steps on two legs." But none comes close to being a full-fledged biped with full-scale walking ability. Examples: the bear can stand and take a few steps on its very short hind legs, then must drop on all fours. The penguin stands a lot on its two tiny legs and even steps (waddles) a short distance, then must stand again. Fowl and birds have bodies on a horizontal plane over two legs. They can run a few steps and then must resort to winged flight. The squirrel can run on hind legs and even use its "hands" but cannot step on two legs. Apes are not bipeds, but are knuckle walkers requiring four limbs.

Striding

10 Furthermore, none of these creatures can stride. They are not physically designed to support and balance a vertical body balanced on two long lower limbs, propelled forward by a foot engineered exclusively for body support and forward propulsion and to do so with a stride at high-speed locomotion.

While other bipeds walk in a similar fashion, human walk is unique. Bipedalism by itself offers no comparison with the distinctive human gait form. And, significantly, no other biped can actually cover more than a tiny fraction of the walking distance that can be sustained by humans.

⓫   Striding requires a special design of hip, knee, and ankle joints, plus an arched foot, plus long lower-limb bones. These "finishing touches" demanded extended evolutionary time. Striding provided numerous advantages over the simple stepping gait. For example, the ability to cover twice the distance with the same number of steps is a definite survival advantage. It also added much speed to running, more height in jumping.

⓬   None of this would have been possible without, first, a foot equipped to support and balance an erect body and to produce the leverage necessary to propel the body forward in locomotion. The ape foot was not suited for this. A new kind of foot was essential if those hominids were to become full-scale bipeds. Indeed a pair of human feet has one-fourth of all the body's 206 bones and 244 joints. Why this extraordinary number of bones and joints concentrated in such a small part of the body? Because of the intricate network of the many different parts required not only for supporting and balancing a heavy superstructure but to enable the multiple motions and actions, hundreds or thousands of times daily. No other part of the body comes even close to the amount and degree of stresses imposed on it.

⓭   The human foot had to go through an extensive evolutionary development in which it underwent enormous design changes in cohesing its 28 bones, 37 joints, 107 ligaments, and 32 muscles and tendons to adapt to the body weight and numerous torsions. In fact, it probably wasn't until only about 400,000 years ago that early humans were fully striding, the final touch of human gait. Orthopedist Philip J. Mayer writes in the *Orthopedic Review*: "The development of a true stride on an orthopedic foot was the most crucial of all the steps of human evolution." Nature had perhaps never undertaken an anatomical engineering project of such complexity.

A New Body Emerges

⓮   Why did it take more than five million years for us to become skilled erect walkers? The answer is because human locomotion is one of the body's most complex functions. To begin with, the "simple" act of walking involves half of all the body's 650 muscles and tendons. For us to become efficient upright walkers required hundreds of "adaptations" throughout the body bottom to top. The body had to comply with that prime law of nature: form follows function. Our radical new gait form required repositioning of everything in the body. And that would take several million years of evolution to accomplish.

⑮   The arms, no longer needed for branch swinging, became shorter, the legs longer, the pelvis wider, the shoulders narrower, the neck longer and more slender, the spine changed from C-shape to S-shape. Major changes were required in the hip, knee, and ankle joints. Hundreds of muscles, tendons, ligaments, and joints gradually shifted in position, size, and function. And of course, the new posture and gait required important changes in the size and position of all the organs of the chest and abdomen.

⑯   Some of these adaptive changes were biomechanically of Olympian proportions. The blood circulation system, for example. With four-legged animals, the body moves mostly on a horizontal plane. But with the erect human it means defiance of the laws of gravity. It requires some 74,000 quarts of blood to move daily through 100,000 miles of blood vessels upward from the feet and legs to the brain and back again every 24 hours. The brain itself was to grow to such size and neural density as to require 25 percent of the body's total blood supply. Even with the heart pumping 44,000 beats a day, this defiance of gravity to sustain a steady flow of blood from foot to head was a stupendous challenge of body engineering.

⑰   While our brain mass comprises only 2 percent of all adult body weight, it consumes 20 percent of our total body energy. This may help to explain why, in moments of anger or emotional turmoil, we get acute or severe headaches, followed by a sudden need to "walk it off" and "cool it." The rhythm and cadence of walking helps to release the massive buildup of explosive energy and accelerated blood flow pressure to become its own kind of built-in tranquilizer.

Walk Like a Man

⑱   An important question arises. If upright walking on two legs required so many changes in anatomical design throughout the body, why did those early hominids take on such a high-risk venture in the first place? Why did they abandon knuckle walking, which had served the apes so well for millions of years, to adopt walking with its many difficulties and risks?

⑲   Nature never makes an anatomical change in a species unless there is some survival advantage to be gained. The scientists are still pondering and debating the "why" of the upright gait. Several plausible theories have been advanced. One popular (though not scientific) version is that we shifted to upright walking to free the hands for manual tasks. Not so. The freed hands were not a prime motive but an adaptive consequence.

⑳   Anthropologist Henry McHenry, of the University of California, Davis, has a different theory. He champions the idea that climate variation was part of the picture. When Africa dried out, say McHenry and his colleague Peter Rodman, the change left patches of forest widely spaced between open savanna. The first hominids lived mostly in these forest refuges but couldn't find enough food in any one place. Learning to walk on two legs helped them travel long distances over ground to the next woodsy patch, and thus to more food.

㉑   Meave Leakey, head of paleontology at the National Museums of Kenya and a member of the world's most famous fossil-hunting family, suspects the change in climate rewarded bipedalism for a different reason. Yes, the dryer climate made for more grassland, but our early ancestors, she argues, spent much of their time not in dense forest or on the savanna but in an environment with some trees, dense shrubbery, and a bit of grass. "And if you're moving into more open country with grasslands and bushes and things like this, and eating a lot of fruits and berries coming off low bushes, there is a hell of an advantage to be able to reach higher. That's why the gerenuk [a type of antelope] evolved its long neck and stands on its hind legs, and why the giraffe evolved its long neck. There's strong pressure to be able to reach a wider range of levels."

㉒   Perhaps a more plausible motive was that the erect gait consumed much less energy and added substantially to stamina and the ability to move over long distances, a vital survival asset. It requires less energy to move a well-balanced vertical column on two supporting legs than to move a horizontal body on four legs. Four moving legs consume twice the energy as two. Further, on two legs, with the body tilted slightly forward there is the added propulsive force of gravity.

㉓   Many ordinary humans today can run a 26-mile marathon nonstop and do so under 2.5 or 3 hours. Even animals with high locomotor stamina (horse, wolf, and husky dogs as examples) cannot sustain such nonstop distances. The record for nonstop walking by a male in 24 hours is 142.4 miles. Women have also demonstrated some remarkable examples of stamina walking. The women's record for nonstop walking is 72 miles. Dr. Barbara Moore, an Englishwoman, walked the 3,387 miles from New York City to San Francisco in 85 days. Another Englishwoman, Gertrude Benham, spent 30 years walking around the world. During that extended span she climbed more than 300 peaks of 10,000 feet or more. She did the world walking "tour" seven times, each time a different route.

㉔   Kent State's Lovejoy has a very different theory. For him the real answer is sex. Males who were best at walking upright would get more of it, leading to more offspring who were good on two legs, who in turn got more sex. His reasoning, first proposed nearly two decades ago, goes like this: like many modern Americans, monkeys and apes of both genders work outside the home—in the latter case, searching for food. Early humans, though, discovered the "Leave It to Beaver" strategy: if males handled the breadwinning, females could stay closer to home and devote more time to rearing the children, thus giving them a better shot at growing up strong and healthy.

㉕   And if you're going to bring home the bacon, or the Miocene equivalent, it helps to have your hands free to carry it. Over time, female apes would choose to mate only with those males who brought them food—presumably the ones who were best adapted for upright walking. Is that the way it actually happened? Maybe, but we may never know for sure. Leakey, for one, is unconvinced. "There are all sorts of hypotheses," she says, "and they are all fairy tales really because you can't prove anything."

Evolution in a Nutshell

㉖   But whichever way it happened, one thing is for sure. There were several stages before man started walking as we know it today. If you want a simple and amazingly compressed view of the course of human evolution right before your eyes, study the physical development of a baby from fetal stage to first steps. Millions of years of evolution are condensed into about sixteen months. The "walking genes" become active as early as the eighth week with the "kicking" of the fetus in the womb. At the end of the eighth week the fetus has a visible, rudimentary tail—a humble reminder of our very early origins. Throughout most of the fetal stage the big toe is positioned thumb-like, the same as the ape foot, and the feet are inverted, again anthropoid-like. The toenails are claw-like rather than flat. And the toes are long and shaped for grasping, also an anthropoid trait.

㉗   But our pre-human ancestry really becomes visible at about the eighth month after birth when the infant begins to crawl on all fours (animal quadruped). By the tenth or eleventh month, it is pulling itself up on two legs by gripping a chair or table leg to stand upright—a common anthropoid tactic. A few weeks later, it has taken its first experimental steps—legs and arms spread out for balance, much the same as an adult chimp walker. The steps are jerky, the body equilibrium insecure, again a rough replica of simian gait (and perhaps similar to the early hominids). The whole process is a replica of human locomotion from anthropoid to hominid to modern human.

Adapted from William A. Rossi, *Podiatry Management*

Analyzing the Introduction

▶ Read the introduction again and answer the following questions.

1. What impression does the writer give about the foot in the first paragraph?
2. What type of information does the writer give in the second paragraph?
3. a. In what way is the language in the second paragraph different from the first?

   b. Why do you think the writer uses such different language?
4. a. Why does the writer quote a number of authorities in the fourth paragraph?

   b. What does the writer hope to prove?
5. After reading the introduction, what information do you expect to find in the body of the text? Restate the writer's position in your own words.

▶ Discuss your answers with a partner or a small group.

Scanning

Throughout this series, you have used several important critical reading strategies. As you find ideas in different parts of "The Foot: Mother of Humanity," notice how well you can **scan**, **skim**, **take notes**, and **analyze introductions and conclusions** to get information from a text. ▪

▶ Quickly read the sections "From the Bottom Up" and "Striding" from the above article to find the answers to these questions. Mark the question number in the margin of the page and underline the relevant information. Write your answers in note form.

1. a. Give two examples of early human fossils.

   _____

   b. What one characteristic identifies these fossils as human?

   _____

2. What is unique about the human foot?

   _____

3. Why was it vital to the survival of early humans?

   _____

4. In what way is bipedalism among animals different from that of man?

   _____

5. a. What are the requirements for striding?

   _____

   b. What are the advantages?

   _____

6. What evidence is there of the complexity of the human foot?

_____

◗ Compare your answers with a partner or a small group.

Note Taking

◗ **A** Read the sections "A New Body Emerges" and "Walk Like a Man" and underline the information for each of the following ideas:

- Changes necessary to allow efficient walking
- Theories/hypotheses explaining why man began to walk

◗ Using the divided page format (see page 31), make notes on each of the above ideas. Use your own words as much as possible. Use your notes to take turns explaining the information to a partner.

◗ **B Making a Time Line** Restate the main idea of the section "Evolution in a Nutshell" in your own words. Read the section and underline the important information.

◗ Complete the following time line with the stages in the development of upright walking in a human child.

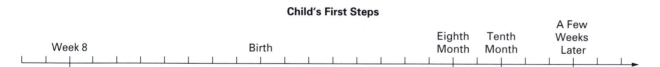

Child's First Steps

| Week 8 | | Birth | | Eighth Month | Tenth Month | A Few Weeks Later | |

Analyzing the Conclusion

▶ **A Predicting** Read the following statements and predict whether they are true or false. Circle *T* for True and *F* for False.

1. T F   Most people have normal feet.

    _____

2. T F   Very few people in the world today have never worn shoes.

    _____

3. T F   Shoes are mainly worn for non-functional purposes.

    _____

4. T F   Fashion footwear will become less dangerous in the future.

    _____

5. T F   The foot is expected to remain basically the same two centuries from now.

    _____

6. T F   The foot is expected to remain basically the same 40,000 years from now.

    _____

▶ **B Skimming** Quickly read "End of Foot Evolution?" (the conclusion of "The Foot: Mother of Humanity") to verify or change your predictions. Write the supporting information for each statement in note form on the lines above. Compare your answers with a partner.

End of Foot Evolution?

㉘   Has the human foot ceased evolving? Probably not. Podiatrists, orthopedists, and related professionals habitually refer to the "normal." But in any shoe-wearing society there is no normal foot. All shoe-wearing feet have, to varying degrees, become deformed anatomically and deficient functionally. Repeat: all comparisons between the pristine feet of native peoples who have never worn shoes (nearly a billion such people) and those of habitual shoe wearers (about 5.5 billion) are dramatic in contrasts. The shod foot—shod since infancy—has become shaped more like a shoe and functions at below-natural levels. And because we rarely see a natural foot but only the shoe-shaped, deformed foot, we assume that the unnatural is natural, the abnormal normal.

㉙   Since the beginning of shoe wearing some 8,000 years ago, the large majority of footwear has been worn for aesthetic, ornamental, sexual, and status purposes. This is very unlikely to change in the foreseeable future. Just as man does not live by bread alone, so does he not live by common sense alone. So all the alarms about the "health hazards" of fashion footwear are wasted words into the wind. But won't the advancing technology of the future bring remedial change—biomechanically compatible footwear without sacrifice of fashion? It is highly improbable. The podiatrists, orthopedists, and footwear industry have remained motionless on this for centuries. It is very unlikely that they will change in any significant way in the generations ahead.

㉚   Evolution moves slowly, but perhaps 30,000 or 40,000 years into the future, we can expect, as a result of the influences cited, the following adaptive foot changes:

a. The fifth toe will have been squeezed out of existence, made functionally useless, as it is today, by constant shoe pressures. The third and fourth digits will continue to atrophy due to much diminished functional use. The first and second digits, carrying almost all the workload, will enlarge. Some 50,000 years from now we shall have become essentially two-toed creatures, much as the horse and deer, once three-toed, have now become one-toed.

b. The toenails will have disappeared, their original clawing function having long become obsolete.

c. The Achilles tendon will have become permanently shortened by as much as an inch or more as a result of the lifelong wearing of heeled (low to high) shoes.

㉛   In another couple of centuries there will be no more shoeless people with natural, pristine feet. With advanced living standards, they will have joined the shod people of the "advanced" cultures. But despite the foot's loss of virginal purity, and despite our becoming an almost totally wheeled and winged civilization, the foot will remain essentially the same because of its vital and primary role in supporting, balancing, and moving an erect body column above. We will still have to walk to keep the blood flowing.

Reacting to the Information

▶ **Free Writing** Write any ideas you have on these questions. Write as much as possible. Share your ideas with a partner or in a small group.

1. What surprises you most when you consider the type of structural physical changes the body has undergone over time?
2. What is your reaction to the writer's suggestion that the human foot could continue to change in the future?

Applying the Information

▶ Scan the following statistics and comment on the extent to which these statistics support this quote from "The Foot: Mother of Humanity":

Just as man does not live by bread alone, so does he not live by common sense alone. So all the alarms about the "health hazards" of fashion footwear are wasted words into the wind.

▶ Who should be concerned about these statistics? How should these people respond?

My Aching Feet	
The Costs of Sore Feet	**The Extent of the Problem**
$28 billion a year is spent on American foot health care.	Two-thirds of American people have foot problems. Investigation reveals that problems are caused by shoes.
$5.4 billion is spent on medical services, doctors, hospitals, Medicare, and Medicaid. $1.3 billion is spent on over-the-counter and mail-order foot aids.	Foot ills affect approximately 3 percent of shoeless people vs. 70 percent of shoe wearers in the United States.
$2.7 billion is spent due to absenteeism, medical insurance, and low productivity annually.	A recent Gallup Survey shows that 73 percent of Americans say feet hurt occasionally. 62 percent consider it normal for feet to hurt.

Compiled from the Rogers Corporation: *PORON® Insider,* June 1992, and *The New York Times.*

Vocabulary Building

Word Form

▶ **A** Study these five words and their forms. Then choose the correct form for each part of speech in the chart below. These words are commonly found in general and academic texts.

alter (v.)	emerge (v.)	impose (v.)	initiate (v.)	reveal (v.)
alteration (n.)	emergence	imposingly	initiation	revelation
altered (adj.)	emerging	imposing	initially	revealingly
altering (adj.)	emerged	imposition	initiated	revealed
		imposed	initial	revelatory
			initiator	revealing

Verb	Noun	Adjective	Adverb
emerge	1.	1. 2.	
impose	1.	1. 2.	1.
initiate	1. 2.	1. 2.	1.
reveal	1.	1. 2. 3.	1.

▶ Compare lists with a partner.

▶ **B** Write three sentences using words from the list.

▶ **C** In English, the form of the word can change when it is used as a different part of speech. For example, a suffix (ending) can be added to change the adjective *good* to the noun *goodness*. Some common noun suffixes are *-ent, -ence, -ness, -ive, -tion, -ment, -ate, -or, -y, -al, -ity*, and *-on*.

▶ Read each sentence and circle the correct word to use in the sentence. Write *N* if the word is a noun or *ADJ* if the word is an adjective. Refer to "The Foot: Mother of Humanity" to check your answers.

1. _____ The foot is **responsible / responsibility** for everything that distinguishes us from all other creatures.

2. _____ The human foot is the only **specialized / specialization** organ that belongs strictly to the locomotor function.

3. _____ The unique structure of the foot made such a **distinctive / distinction** posture possible.

4. _____ The human foot had to go through an extensive evolutionary **developed / development**.

5. _____ Nature never makes an **anatomical / anatomy** change in a species unless there is some survival advantage to be gained.

6. _____ The ability to move over long distances is a vital **survival / surviving** asset.

7. _____ You should study the physical **developed / development** of a baby from fetal stage to first steps.

8. _____ A few weeks later it has taken its first **experimental / experiment** steps.

9. _____ All **comparing / comparisons** between the pristine feet of native peoples and shoe wearers are dramatic in contrasts.

10. _____ We can expect the following **adaptive / adaptations** will take place.

Synonyms

▶ Refer to the reading "The Foot: Mother of Humanity" to find these words in context. Match the words in Column A with words that have the same meaning in Column B.

Column A

_____ 1. ridicule

_____ 2. distinguish

_____ 3. assume

_____ 4. confirm

_____ 5. resort

_____ 6. stride

_____ 7. propose

_____ 8. sustain

_____ 9. propel

_____ 10. condense

Column B

a. to suppose or believe something

b. to walk at a quick pace

c. to make fun of

d. to go for help

e. to squeeze or concentrate something

f. to detect or see a difference

g. to verify or tell something is true

h. to put forward or suggest an idea

i. to uphold or keep something up

j. to push something forward

Paraphrasing and Quoting

The author of "The Foot: Mother of Humanity" incorporates the opinions of several "experts." To do this, he uses either a:

- **Direct quote**

Example: Orthopedist Philip J. Mayer writes in the *Orthopedic Review*: "The development of a true stride on an orthopedic foot was the most crucial of all the steps of human evolution." (paragraph 13)

- **Paraphrase**

Example: When Africa dried out, say McHenry and his colleague Peter Rodman, the change left patches of forest widely spaced between open savanna. The first hominids lived mostly in these forest refuges but couldn't find enough food in any one place. Learning to walk on two legs helped them travel long distances over ground to the next woodsy patch, and thus to more food. (paragraph 20)

Quotes are easy to identify because of quotation marks. Certain words, however, are needed to indicate a paraphrase. In the example above, the author used the word *say*. This is a neutral word. It carries no "hidden" meaning. Other words however, e.g., *claim*, do carry a meaning. *Claim* indicates that the author does not really believe the opinion being paraphrased.

▶ Find two more examples of quotes and two more examples of paraphrasing. Highlight them and discuss why the author decided to use one or the other. Underline the word(s) used to indicate the beginning of the paraphrases. Discuss whether these words are neutral or if they carry a "hidden" meaning.

Paraphrasing

 Tip

A **paraphrase** should be approximately the **same length** and carry the **same meaning** as the original. However, it should be **different** in terms of **vocabulary** and **grammatical structure**. ▪

▶ Paraphrase the following quotations.

1. "The human foot is the only specialized organ that belongs strictly to the locomotor function .... Not only is it a remarkable example of Nature's engineering principles in the design of locomotion structures, but it is also in itself a combination of progressive landmarks recording the whole history of human evolution." (paragraph 7)

   _____

   _____

2. "And if you're moving into more open country with grasslands and bushes and things like this, and eating a lot of fruits and berries coming off low bushes, there is a hell of an advantage to be able to reach higher. That's why the gerenuk [a type of antelope] evolved its long neck and stands on its hind legs, and why the giraffe evolved its long neck. There's strong pressure to be able to reach a wider range of levels." (paragraph 21)

   _____

   _____

▶ Compare your paraphrase with that of your partner. Make any changes you think are necessary. Check with your teacher.

Expanding Your Language

Speaking

▷ **Analyzing Quotes** Discuss the meaning of the following quotes. Use information in the reading as well as your own ideas to explain your reaction to each.

1. A man's feet should be planted in his country, but his eyes should survey the world. —*George Santayana*
2. It is better to die on your feet than to live on your knees. —*Emiliano Zapata*
3. Keep your eyes on the stars, and your feet on the ground.
   —*Theodore Roosevelt*
4. A shoe that is too large is apt to trip one, and when too small to pinch the feet. So it is with those whose fortune does not suit them. —*Horace*
5. One who has imagination without learning has wings without feet.
   —*Joseph Joubert*

Writing

▷ **A Journal Entry** Write in your journal about one or more of the quotes you discussed. Over the next few weeks, look for newspaper, magazine, or Internet articles on the topic of evolution or how people are influenced by their environment and write your reaction to them.

▷ **B Summary Writing** Use the information from the Note Taking (page 262) and Making a Time Line (page 262) activities to make an outline that includes the following information. Refer to the tips on summarizing on pages 114–115.

- The important physical changes that resulted from walking upright
- The survival potential of walking upright
- The stages of development for upright walking

▷ Use your outline to write a short summary of about 100–150 words on separate pages of your own. Give your summary to a partner. As you read each other's writing, check for the following:

- Highlight the ideas from the reading that are included in the summary.
- Ask yourself whether or not all the important ideas are included.
- Ask yourself whether these ideas are paraphrased.
- Are any ideas left out?
- Are any unnecessary details included?
- How would you rate this summary? (Use a scale where 5 = excellent, 4 = very good, 3 = good, 2 = incomplete, and 1 = very incomplete.)

▷ Use the feedback from your partner to rewrite your summary. Give the summary to your teacher for feedback.

ⓑ Read On: Taking It Further

Reading

🔵 **Information in the News** Have you or anyone you know had a pair of shoes that were important to them? Parents often keep their children's first shoes. In the past, some parents had their children's first shoes bronzed to preserve them. In this article, we discover that shoes can tell many different stories.

🔵 Read the story and prepare to discuss the following questions.

1. Why are shoes important in our daily lives?
2. What can shoes tell us about the past?
3. Why does Alexandra try so hard to repair her shoes?

A Look at Heels

Vancouver—Ah, shoes. … What is it about shoes? We fawn over them, blow our paychecks on them, keep some long past their wearable expiration date, and mourn the ones we tossed out. More than any other accessory or item of clothing (other than a wedding dress, perhaps), shoes inspire serious passion.

Sonja Bata, founding chairwoman of Toronto's Bata Shoe Museum, has said it's because footwear tells the whole human story. Bata's museum is the only one of its kind in North America and attracts more than 100,000 visitors a year. Tomorrow, it will celebrate its tenth anniversary with a huge street festival featuring cake, clowns, and sole readings. It all sounds like great fun, but if you wander through the museum's permanent collection, which includes woven funerary shoes from a royal tomb in ancient Thebes and Inuit boots made of eider skin, you'll quickly realize that footwear is anything but frivolous. It is actually an extremely insightful anthropological tool. "We don't think of shoes as being important," says curator Elizabeth Semmelhack, who has just finished redesigning the museum's permanent exhibit, All About Shoes, with a new family-oriented activity area and artifacts from Imperial China. "We just kick them off at the end of the day. But the fact is, we hem and haw about shoe purchases and what to wear for certain occasions. They're very much part of our uniform and the way we present ourselves to the world. There are many unconscious things we reveal about ourselves by the way we wear them and the choices we make. They tell a lot about the individual and the culture we live in."

Or the way we once lived. In 1991, when hikers in the Italian Alps discovered the intact skeleton of a 5,300-year-old hunter now known as the Iceman, Bata personally commissioned a scholar to examine his grass-stuffed leather shoes. What the researcher discovered—that the Stone Age leather had come from a far-off valley—debunked initial theories about the body being that of a local shepherd. He was more likely a political refugee fleeing violence. "Shoes really do offer us a different avenue of inquiry into different cultures, our own culture, and different time periods," says Semmelhack. "And it's a backdoor method. If we only approach these questions in the expected way, we only get one answer. But with shoes, they pique new questions and answers that are really worth investigating."

So what does the history of shoes tell us about Gold Diggers, the glittery slippers in Soles Exposed that were once used to deliberately capture the eye of a wealthy young suitor? That shoes are still the same symbol of wealth and rank they were in ancient Egypt or the Yoruba culture of Nigeria, where royal status was indicated by the quantity of beads on boots. And the mother who sent her guilt-stricken daughter a pair of old, scratched-up rubber boots in the mail, but no note of explanation? Perhaps that mother was connecting on some unconscious level with one of the many forgotten rituals once attached to footwear. According to one ancient Jewish custom, for example, an unwed brother-in-law of a childless widow was obliged to marry her. But if that widow untied and removed his shoes in public, she could release him from this duty.

As for me, it was an expensive pair of high heels. I certainly wasn't trying to be Cinderella when I bought them, but you might say I was playing out a drama in the style of fifth century, BC, Greek theater, when the dramatist Aeschylus required his actors to wear thick, cork-soled platforms so his tragic heroes would loom larger than life. And the moral of this story? I'll never pay that much money for a pair of shoes again. They are the most expensive shoes I've ever purchased. They cost about $600, are made by Prada, and were once perfect. With their long, pointy toes and thin, sculpted heels, I thought they were a classic pair that I could keep wearing forever.

I bought them after discovering that my lover had been cheating. I found out by snooping on his computer and I couldn't tell him what I knew without incriminating myself. So I bought these shoes, knowing it would drive him crazy when he found out how much I spent. We were on our way to Las Vegas for a wedding. By the time we got to the chapel, my feet were covered in painful blisters. Later that night, I popped my secret. The break-up was long and messy. When I finally walked away, I was still wearing these shoes. The leather eventually softened and they became the most comfortable shoes I'd ever owned.

About a year later, I was back in Vegas. One evening, on the way home from a club where I had danced on a table, my right heel snapped in half. I had it repaired the next day, but that same night the left heel broke and couldn't be fixed. Back at home, the manager of the local Prada boutique told me their products were only guaranteed for six months. I took them to every shoemaker in town. They scoured their inventories, called their suppliers, and searched at auctions, but no one could find me a pair of heels that came close to the exquisite originals. I gave up and succumbed to these clunky replacements. I hardly ever wear these any more. I'm still single. And my heart remains covered in calluses.

Adapted from Alexandra Gill, *The Globe and Mail*

Writing

> Write your reactions to this story or write a shoe story of your own in your reading journal.

> **Reading Tip**

View your reading journal and vocabulary log entries. Review your use of reading skills and strategies. Write a response to the following question: How has your reading improved? ▪

Online Study Center   For additional activities, go to the ***Reading Matters*** Online Study Center at *college.hmco.com/pic/wholeyfour2e.*

Exercise Pages

UNIT 3   **The Environment**

Chapter ❻ Urban Growth and Water Supply

Ranking   Check your answers to the ranking exercise on page 117 with the table below.

City	1950 Population (millions)	Rank in in 1950	City	2003 Population (millions)	Rank in in 2003
New York, USA	12.3	1	Tokyo, Japan	26.7	1
London, England	8.7	2	Sao Paolo, Brazil	18.9	2
Tokyo, Japan	6.9	3	Mexico City, Mexico	18.6	3
Paris, France	5.4	4	New York, USA	17.4	4
Moscow, USSR	5.4	5	Bombay, India	17.0	5
Shanghai, China	5.3	6	Los Angeles, USA	14.4	6
Essen, Germany	5.3	7	Calcutta, India	14.1	7
Buenos Aires, Argentina	5.0	8	Dhaka, Bangladesh	13.8	8
Chicago, USA	4.9	9	Delhi, India	13.5	9
Calcutta, India	4.4	10	Shanghai, China	13.0	10

Sources: March Ang and Amy Gluckman, *Dollars and Sense,* and *United Nations Report 2003.*

Text Credits

pp. 3–6: "The Science of Jokes," from "Why Canadians Aren't In On the Joke: Want to Know the World's Funniest Joke...," by Jeremy Sandler, *The Vancouver Sun*, December 20, 2001. Reprinted with permission.

pp. 9–14: "The Science of Laughter." Reprinted with permission from "The Science of Laughter," by Robert R. Provine, *Psychology Today Magazine*, November/December 2000. Copyright © 2000 Sussex Publishers, Inc.

p. 19: "How Laughter Works," as found on www.howstuffworks.com.

pp. 24–28, 30, 32–33: "The Creative Brain," from "Key to Creative Living: Reclaiming Our Passion," by Ned Herrmann, from *The Creative Brain*, © 1993. Reprinted with permission from Ned Herrmann. Copyright © 1993 Brain Books, Lake Line, NC.

pp. 35–36: "Mental Breakout," by Tawn Nhan. Reprinted with permission from *The Charlotte Observer*. Copyright owned by the Charlotte Observer.

p. 47: "The Ongoing Longevity Gap" (graph), National Center for Health Statistics.

pp. 53–56: "Second Thoughts on Extending Life Spans," by Donald B. Louria. Originally published in the January–February 2002 issue of *The Futurist*. Used with permission from the World Future Society, http://www.wfs.org.

pp. 61–62: "Science Values Grandmothers," from "Science Values Grandmothers," editorial by Barbara Peters Smith, *Sarasota Herald Tribune*, November 9, 2002. Reprinted with permission of the author.

p. 64: "How We Became So Sedentary" (graph), as seen in "Why Are We So Fat," *National Geographic*, August 2004.

p. 65: "Overweight: A Widening Problem," Cathy Newman/National Geographic Image Collection.

p. 65: "U.S. Health Club Membership" (graph) and "Weight Watchers Annual U. S. Attendance" (graph), as seen in "Why Are We So Fat," *National Geographic*, August 2004.

p. 65: "Estimated Number of Bariatric Surgeries in the United States" (graph), from American Society for Bariatric Surgery, Gainesville, FL.

pp. 67–71: "How We Grew So Big: Diet and Lack of Exercise Are Immediate Causes," by Michael D. Lemonick, *Time*, June 7, 2004. Copyright © 2004 Time, Inc. Reprinted by permission.

pp. 73–75: "The Gorge-Yourself Environment," from "The Gorge-Yourself Environment," by Erica Goode, *The New York Times*, July 22, 2003, p. F1. Copyright © 2003 by The New York Times Co. Reprinted with permission.

pp. 76–78: "Journey to Better Fitness Starts With 10,000 Steps," from "Journey to Better Fitness Starts With 10,000 Steps," by Nancy Heilmich, *USA Today*, June 29, 1999, a division of Gannett Co., Inc. Reprinted with permission.

pp. 80–81: "Short Intensive Workouts are Just as Effective as Long Sessions," from "Six Minutes of Exercise a Week Is As Good As Six Hours," by Peter Zimonjic, *The Sunday Telegraph*, June 5, 2005. Reprinted with permission.